CRYENGINE Game Development Blueprints

Perfect the art of creating CRYENGINE games through exciting, hands-on game development projects

Richard Gerard Marcoux III

Chris Goodswen

Riham Toulan

Sam Howels

PUBLISHING

BIRMINGHAM - MUMBAI

CRYENGINE Game Development Blueprints

First published: August 2015

Production reference: 1250815

Published by Packt Publishing Ltd.
Livery Place
35 Livery Street
Birmingham B3 2PB, UK.

ISBN 978-1-78439-987-0

www.packtpub.com

Credits

Authors
Richard Gerard Marcoux III
Chris Goodswen
Riham Toulan
Sam Howels

Reviewers
Anthony Barranco
Keith Homola
Guillaume Puyal

Commissioning Editor
Usha Iyer

Acquisition Editors
Indrajit A. Das
Rebecca Youé

Content Development Editor
Mamata Walkar

Technical Editor
Taabish Khan

Copy Editor
Roshni Banerjee

Project Coordinator
Shipra Chawhan

Proofreader
Safis Editing

Indexer
Priya Sane

Graphics
Abhinash Sahu

Production Coordinator
Nitesh Thakur

Cover Work
Nitesh Thakur

About the Authors

Richard Gerard Marcoux III is a very hardworking and intelligent software engineer with a passion for teaching and helping others. He has captured the attention of over 600,000 people through his YouTube channel with his efforts to educate beginners in the field of game development using the CRYENGINE technology. He also has an extensive IT background, working in the computer / software diagnosis / repair field for the past 7 years. Lately, he has been heavily involved in C++ games and middleware development, where he plans to create compelling 2D and 3D video games for all ages in genres ranging from platform games all the way to RPGs.

Chris Goodswen is a 3D character artist currently working at Crytek with 4 years of experience working with CRYENGINE. He has also worked on *Ryse: Son of Rome* for Xbox One as well as *Warface* and *Hunt*.

Chris is responsible for modeling and texturing characters as well as developing technical systems for characters; alongside this, he also works with universities, mentoring students and giving lectures on 3D character art and video game development.

Riham Toulan is a senior technical artist/animator working at Dice EA, who specializes in character rigging. She has more than 4 years of experience working with CRYENGINE. She worked on the highly cinematic Xbox One launch game *Ryse: Son of Rome* at Crytek, where she was responsible for developing rigging pipelines and tools in Maya, helping the R&D team develop new CRYENGINE technologies, and consulting the CRYENGINE licensees.

Sam Howels is a senior designer at the Nottingham-based Deep Silver Dambuster Studios. He is currently working on the upcoming sequel to the 2011 game *Homefront*, titled *Homefront: The Revolution*. He was recruited at the age of 18 after his dedicated contribution to the modding scene. He has a strong passion for technical problem solving as well as creating engaging and diverse gameplay experiences. Before joining Deep Silver, he worked on multiple AAA titles at both Crytek Frankfurt and Crytek UK, and he has over 8 years of experience in developing content with the CRYENGINE toolset.

Firstly, I would like to thank Crytek for creating such a powerful toolset for designers like me to use and abuse. The versatility and ease of use that it offered when I discovered it in 2007 is still present today, and it has enabled numerous absurd prototypes as well as facilitated the creation of the final shipped content of each title I've worked on. I'd also like to thank the team at Packt for their continued support and feedback during the writing process. It has been a fulfilling experience being able to put pen to paper and share my knowledge of setting up the content with the engine SDK. Finally, I'd like to thank everyone I've worked with at both Crytek and Deep Silver. The teams that build the technology and games are comprised of incredibly special and talented people, and working with this game engine each day would not be nearly as rewarding as it is without sitting next to a hundred other people who pour their hearts and souls into the work they create.

About the Reviewers

Anthony Barranco is a software developer who has worked at several AAA game studios, such as Ubisoft, after receiving a degree from Marist College in Poughkeepsie, New York. He is an avid gamer and programmer; whether it's Unity, Unreal Engine, CRYENGINE, Source, or Construct 2, he has tried and loved them all. He encourages new and veteran software developers to try any of these engines and help contribute to make more great games. If there is one thing he believes in, it's that game development should be accessible to anyone and everyone.

> I want to thank Packt Publishing for the opportunity, the authors for writing this book, and Crytek for making CRYENGINE. Books such as this helped me achieve my dream career, and I hope this book helps someone do the same.

Keith Homola is an independent game developer who dreams of working in a large studio one day. With dedication, he has learned the many different trades of game development, including programming, 3D and 2D art tools, and both the CRYENGINE and Unreal Engine 4 game engines. His experience comes from self-learning, and he puts it to use to make games and theory.

Keith has no formal employer in the game development field. All the experience that he has acquired is through his independent work, and he hopes to use his skills at a professional studio one day.

> I would like to thank my friends and family for the support over the years, the online development communities for helping me and other people to explore game development, and Packt Publishing for giving me this opportunity.

Guillaume Puyal lives in France and can be described as an enthusiastic polymath. After completing his degree in electronics, he began working on an ambitious but commercially unsuccessful web technology.

Thereafter, his passion for video games led him to lean toward game development with the CRYENGINE technology. Here, his curiosity pushed him to learn everything from modeling to the UI, and he now specializes in the lighting and materials areas.

When he isn't experimenting and implementing his ideas in CRYENGINE or trying to improve his programming skills, he works on his new software project, which he hopes to introduce to the world soon.

You can learn more about him and his work, including a CRYENGINE specific tool and documents, at http://www.guillaume-puyal.com.

I would like to thank the authors and the team at Packt Publishing for giving me the unique opportunity to review this book.

www.PacktPub.com

Support files, eBooks, discount offers, and more

For support files and downloads related to your book, please visit www.PacktPub.com.

Did you know that Packt offers eBook versions of every book published, with PDF and ePub files available? You can upgrade to the eBook version at www.PacktPub.com and as a print book customer, you are entitled to a discount on the eBook copy. Get in touch with us at service@packtpub.com for more details.

At www.PacktPub.com, you can also read a collection of free technical articles, sign up for a range of free newsletters and receive exclusive discounts and offers on Packt books and eBooks.

https://www2.packtpub.com/books/subscription/packtlib

Do you need instant solutions to your IT questions? PacktLib is Packt's online digital book library. Here, you can search, access, and read Packt's entire library of books.

Why subscribe?

- Fully searchable across every book published by Packt
- Copy and paste, print, and bookmark content
- On demand and accessible via a web browser

Free access for Packt account holders

If you have an account with Packt at www.PacktPub.com, you can use this to access PacktLib today and view 9 entirely free books. Simply use your login credentials for immediate access.

Table of Contents

Preface

This book is authored by Richard Marcoux, Chris Goodswen, Riham Toulan, and Samuel Howels; they will be your instructors and friends throughout this book. You are about to embark on a journey of discovery and find out what you can achieve in CRYENGINE, learn some tricks of the trade, the game programming techniques, the new aspects of the CRYENGINE code, and most importantly, how to create full working games. If there is one thing that we want you to take away after reading this book is that it's not the game we will be making, but instead the techniques and the problem solving that went into making it. The goal is to arm you with the knowledge and out-of-the-box thinking that is required to create a CRYENGINE game.

What this book covers

Chapter 1, *Getting Started*, shows you the CRYENGINE "Blank" Game Starter-Kit that was specifically designed to teach developers how to create a CRYENGINE game from scratch, and provide a blank slate for them to start with. You will install and compile this kit.

Chapter 2, *Creating a Playable Character*, shows you how to create a completely playable character from scratch and control its movement with the keyboard.

Chapter 3, *Implementing Weapons and Ammo*, shows you how to implement a weapon and ammo system, as the player will need a way to defeat bad guys.

Chapter 4, *Creating an Enemy AI*, shows you how to create an enemy AI and give it some basic intelligence.

Chapter 5, *Creating User Interfaces*, shows you how to create a complete start and end game menu by using Scaleform, Flash, and C++.

Chapter 6, The Modeling Workflow for Game Characters and Tools, gives an overview of the character art workflow principles, terminologies, and how to prepare for the tasks ahead.

Chapter 7, Highpoly Modeling, discusses why we need to create a highpoly model and its uses in the game in current and next-gen game development. In this chapter, we will be working with some of the principles of highpoly modeling and going through a basic workflow to create the highpoly model in Zbrush.

Chapter 8, Lowpoly Modeling, covers the lowpoly generation and some of the most important areas to remember, such as efficient topology, areas to remember for deformation, other important topics, such as an efficient UV mapping, and how to generate LODs from the original lowpoly.

Chapter 9, Texturing and Materials, explores the techniques required to create and bake textures. In this chapter, we will take a look at the tools, such as Photoshop and Zbrush, used for creating texture maps, how to bake the highpoly information to the lowpoly model by using xNormal, and also see how these baked maps can be used in the creation of textures.

Chapter 10, Building the Character Rig, shows you how to build an animator friendly rig for the character in Maya. We will also discuss the folder structure for the character files and explore the already made deformation skeleton on the character, and how to create a simple and efficient rig using that skeleton.

Chapter 11, Exporting the Character to CRYEngine, shows you how to export a character to CRYENGINE step-by-step and explains the animation pipeline and how to use Character Editor to debug and add extra secondary animations to your characters with CRYENGINE physics.

Chapter 12, Initial Level Blockout and Setup, covers the good working practices and tips used for quickly jumping into making a new level in the SDK, giving us a good base to start adding more complex scripted content later on.

Chapter 13, The Flow Graph Workflow, introduces you to the concept of Game Tokens to communicate with the Flow Graphs. We'll also cover how to set up the level logic to modularly accommodate the various scripted elements that go into making a single player level in CRYENGINE.

Chapter 14, Scripting Gameplay Content, dives deep into creating all the elements that make up a Crysis style action bubble, as we now have a solid grounding in how to efficiently and cleanly produce content for a level in CRYENGINE.

Chapter 15, Maintaining Our Work, covers testing the content or fixing the bugs that take place in the last few minutes of a half hour level, which can be a repetitive and time-wasting process.

What you need for this book

In this book, we would be using the following software:

- CRYENGINE (Version 3.8.1)
- The CRYENGINE "Blank" Game Starter-Kit (Version 2.1.0)
- Visual Studio 2013 (any version)
- 7-Zip or any 7-Zip LZMA2 compatible file archiver (any version)
- Autodesk Maya
- CRYENGINE3 Sandbox Editor

Who this book is for

This book is intended for CRYENGINE game developers wanting to develop their skills with the help of industry experts. You need to have a good knowledge level and understanding of CRYENGINE in order to allow the efficient programming of core elements and applications.

Conventions

In this book, you will find a number of text styles that distinguish between different kinds of information. Here are some examples of these styles and an explanation of their meaning.

Code words in text, database table names, folder names, filenames, file extensions, pathnames, dummy URLs, user input, and Twitter handles are shown as follows: "Create a new header file called CGameUIListener.h."

A block of code is set as follows:

```
if ( m_pGameUIListener )
  delete m_pGameUIListener;
m_pGameUIListener = nullptr;
```

When we wish to draw your attention to a particular part of a code block, the relevant lines or items are set in bold:

```
import cryEngine_BP as CE
```

Any command-line input or output is written as follows:

```
Task Completed: Compression of 'Animations/Animations/Boris/boris_
walkCycle01.caf'
```

New terms and **important words** are shown in bold. Words that you see on the screen, for example, in menus or dialog boxes, appear in the text like this: "Click on the **Create** button."

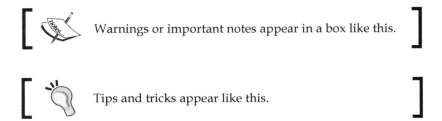

> Warnings or important notes appear in a box like this.

> Tips and tricks appear like this.

Reader feedback

Feedback from our readers is always welcome. Let us know what you think about this book—what you liked or disliked. Reader feedback is important for us as it helps us develop titles that you will really get the most out of.

To send us general feedback, simply e-mail feedback@packtpub.com, and mention the book's title in the subject of your message.

If there is a topic that you have expertise in and you are interested in either writing or contributing to a book, see our author guide at www.packtpub.com/authors.

Customer support

Now that you are the proud owner of a Packt book, we have a number of things to help you to get the most from your purchase.

Downloading the example code

You can download the example code files from your account at http://www.packtpub.com for all the Packt Publishing books you have purchased. If you purchased this book elsewhere, you can visit http://www.packtpub.com/support and register to have the files e-mailed directly to you.

Downloading the color images of this book

We also provide you with a PDF file that has color images of the screenshots/diagrams used in this book. The color images will help you better understand the changes in the output. You can download this file from https://www.packtpub.com/sites/default/files/downloads/B03477_Graphics.pdf.

Errata

Although we have taken every care to ensure the accuracy of our content, mistakes do happen. If you find a mistake in one of our books—maybe a mistake in the text or the code—we would be grateful if you could report this to us. By doing so, you can save other readers from frustration and help us improve subsequent versions of this book. If you find any errata, please report them by visiting http://www.packtpub.com/submit-errata, selecting your book, clicking on the **Errata Submission Form** link, and entering the details of your errata. Once your errata are verified, your submission will be accepted and the errata will be uploaded to our website or added to any list of existing errata under the Errata section of that title.

To view the previously submitted errata, go to https://www.packtpub.com/books/content/support and enter the name of the book in the search field. The required information will appear under the **Errata** section.

Piracy

Piracy of copyrighted material on the Internet is an ongoing problem across all media. At Packt, we take the protection of our copyright and licenses very seriously. If you come across any illegal copies of our works in any form on the Internet, please provide us with the location address or website name immediately so that we can pursue a remedy.

Please contact us at copyright@packtpub.com with a link to the suspected pirated material.

We appreciate your help in protecting our authors and our ability to bring you valuable content.

Questions

If you have a problem with any aspect of this book, you can contact us at questions@packtpub.com, and we will do our best to address the problem.

1
Getting Started

In this chapter, we will discuss the following topics:

- How to download the CRYENGINE "Blank" Game Starter-Kit
- How to install the starter-kit
- Important classes of the starter-kit and the roles they play
- How to compile a game project

Downloading the starter-kit

In order to create any CRYENGINE game, there is a need to have a clear place to start. For us, this comes as a blank slate using my very own starter-kit. By using it, we rid ourselves of overcomplications and gain several advantages:

- All code written is ours, so we have a clear and precise understanding of what the code does.
- All code written is specifically for our game, so we don't have unnecessary code bloat.
- Since all of our code is exactly and only what we need, our code will run faster.
- All starter-kit code is written cleanly and is heavily documented. This allows us to have a better understanding of how to use CRYENGINE's interfaces.

Now that we know why we will be using my starter-kit, let's see how to download it:

1. Navigate to the download page at `http://www.cryengine.com/community/viewtopic.php?f=355&t=124265`. It should look like this:

CRYENGINE Game Starter-Kits

33

◻ by Richmar1 » June 14th, 2014, 4:26 pm

CRYENGINE Game Starter-Kits

About:

Hello everyone! I'm here today to announce something very special: CRYENGINE Game Starter-Kits. The idea is to provide complete game starter-kits for many genres so that anyone can jump in and start making something amazing from the get go. In order to achieve this vision, some key important things have to take place:

- The kit, as a whole, MUST be free of major, project-stopping bugs.
- The included code base NEEDS to be simple, clean, and stick to a specific genre.
- The ENTIRE code base needs to be well documented. This means EVERY interface, class, function, and member variable needs to have well thought out comments that describe EXACTLY what it does and what it is used for.
- ALL art content such as models and textures MUST be of AAA quality, pertain to a specific genre, and pass harsh inspections by our dedicated team here at Hawk Eye Games LLC.
- Community feedback and criticisms MUST NOT be taken lightly and play a MAJOR role in the development process.

If all of the above conditions are not met, than this initiative's purpose cannot be fulfilled.
Over time, you will notice more and more starter-kits being released in this very post as they are completed. So without further ado, here is the first of many starter-kits to come.

Blank

Description:

A complete "Blank" CRYENGINE game starter-kit. If you are looking for a blank-slate to create an entire game from scratch, or just want to learn how a typical CRYENGINE game is started and implemented, than this is the starter-kit for you.

Features:

V1.0:
- COMPLETE source code implementing ALL needed interfaces to make a COMPLETE CRYENGINE game from scratch.
- NO sample default FPS Gamedll code.
- EVERY interface, class, method, and member variable is COMPLETELY documented and has per-parameter method documentation and Intellisense.
- FULLY featured Visual Studio project template and wizard.
- NO-FUSS installer that sets EVERYTHING up for you with no effort.
- VERY liberal license that allows you to do WHATEVER you like with the ENTIRE game template, even sell it.

2. Scroll down the page to the **Download** section and download Version 2.1.0 by clicking on its link.

For the sake of clarity and consistency, even if there is a newer version of the starter-kit available, it is *strongly* recommended that you stick with Version 2.1.0. Version 2.1.0 of the starter-kit is fully compatible with CRYENGINE Version 3.8.1 and, as such, it is *strongly* recommended that you use that version for the remainder of this book.

Installing the starter-kit

Before the starter-kit can be used, it must be installed. Installing the starter-kit is very easy and it is responsible for adding a project wizard to Visual Studio and setting up the needed CRYENGINE environment variables. So let's get started.

Part 1

Now that we have downloaded the starter-kit, it's time to install it:

1. Unzip the downloaded archive using **7-Zip** (http://www.7-zip.org/) or any other file archiver that supports the 7z file format with LZMA2 compression.

2. You should now see an application (.exe) called CRYENGINE Game Starter-Kit - Blank Installer V2.0.8.exe; launch it. It should look like this:

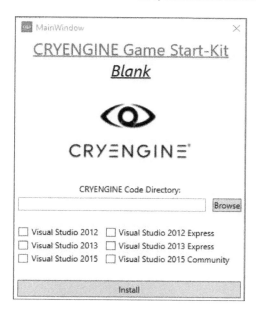

3. Click on the **Browse** button to search for the path to CRYENGINE's `Code` folder. It should look like this:

 It is important to note that CRYENGINE's `Code` folder is the one that contains all of CRYENGINE's code. It contains the `CryENGINE`, `GameSDK`, and `SDKs` subfolders. In the event that you do not have a `Code` folder at all, you will need to extract `CRYENGINE_GameCode_xxxxx` or a similar zip archive located in CRYENGINE's root folder. It is very important that the `Code` folder is in the right location. There should be exactly 2 subdirectories in CRYENGINE's root folder, like this: `CRYENGINE_ROOT/CRYENGINE_pc_eaascode/Code`.

4. Check all of the **Visual Studio** versions you want to install the starter-kit to, shown here:

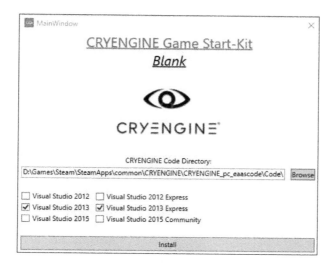

5. Lastly, click on the **Install** button to actually install the starter-kit. After the installation completes, you will get the following message:

Part 2

Now that we have successfully installed the **CRYENGINE "Blank" Game Starter-Kit** into Visual Studio, we can create our CRYENGINE game project:

1. Launch your preferred and supported Visual Studio IDE.

For this book, I will be using **Visual Studio 2013 Ultimate**. You are free to use any supported version you wish. However, you may notice some slight differences. Current supported versions of Visual Studio include any edition of 2012, 2013, and 2015.

2. Now that we have launched Visual Studio, we can create our game project by using the CRYENGINE "Blank" Game Starter-Kit we installed earlier. To do this, go to **File | New | Project**. You will see the following menu options:

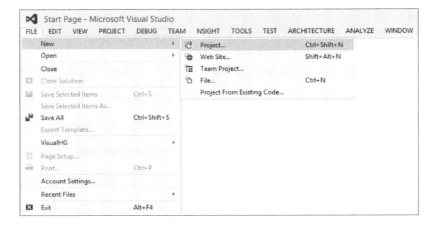

3. Go to **Templates | Visual C++ | CRYENGINE**. Select **CRYENGINE Game Starter-Kit - Blank** and fill in your project information.

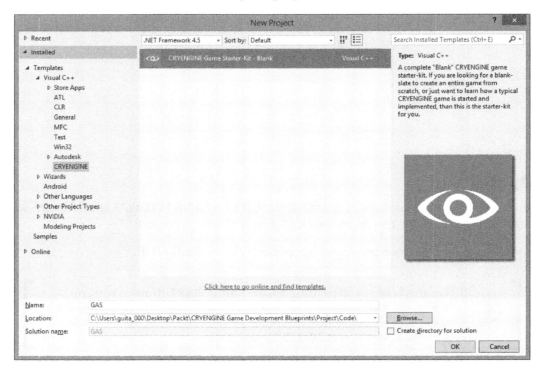

You are free to choose whatever name and location you wish. However, I *strongly* recommend you choose a location outside your CRYENGINE install directory. Throughout this book, we will be calling our game project *GAS*, which stands for *Great Action Side-Scroller*. Make sure to uncheck **Create directory for solution**.

4. Click the **OK** button. This will launch the CRYENGINE game starter-kit **Project Creation Wizard**. It should look like this:

5. Fill in all of the information for your game project, as shown here:

Since we have chosen to call our game *GAS*, it is recommended to set **Project Name** as *GAS* too. Also, it is *strongly* advised that you check the **Include PluginSDK** and **Set As Active Game** options. Including the PluginSDK developed by Hendrik Polinski allows users to add plugins to their game without modifying any actual game code. The advantage is that everything is modularized and features can be bundled up and shared between many projects. If you would like to get in contact with Hendrik, you can do so at https://github.com/hendrikp. Setting our game as active allows CRYENGINE to detect and use our game by modifying the system.cfg file in CRYENGINE's root folder. Although this is all advised, you are free to fill in the data however you wish.

6. Click on the **Create** button. After the project has been created, you will get the following screen:

Important classes within the starter-kit

As we have concluded the setting up of the starter-kit, it is probably a good time to bring up a few disclaimers:

- While starter-kits in general are extremely helpful, they are technically not a true blank slate.

- There are a few interfaces and classes that will need to be explained before writing code.

- Since there is absolutely no gameplay-specific or genre-specific code or classes, the gameplay mechanics and many other things must be implemented from scratch. Although I consider this to be a good thing, some may not.

To address the previous concerns, let's take a closer look at some of the more important classes within the starter-kit that we will be using on a regular basis, keeping in mind that the names of these classes will be different for you as they are based on the project's name:

- CEditorGASGame: This class implements CRYENGINE's IEditorGame interface. It is used to create, update, and shut down your game while you are running it inside the **CRYENGINE Sandbox Editor**. You often need your game to behave differently while testing inside the editor; this class allows us to do just that. It acts as a proxy for our game, giving us the ability to add or remove functionality that should only exist while playing your game in the editor. For now, we simply forward most calls to the actual Game class so that our game behaves similarly in the editor and in the **Launcher**.

- CGASGame: This class implements CRYENGINE's IGame interface. It is used to update your game and the rest of CRYENGINE's systems. It acts as a hub that manages every system that your game will use, controls communication between them, and facilitates all of the core mechanics of your game. You can view this class as your game's manager—something that orchestrates all of the little moving parts of your game. For now, we simply update the **Game Framework**, which, in turn, updates the rest of CRYENGINE's systems such as the **Renderer**, **Input Manager**, and **Physics System**.

- CGASGameRules: This class implements CRYENGINE's IGameRules interface. It is used to carry out your game's rules and works hand-in-hand with your Game class. It is a class that does and should receive notifications about any gameplay-specific events so that it may decide how best to handle them in accordance with your game's rules. It is also common for this class to dispatch gameplay-specific events to your Game class. For now, this class simply creates the player when asked to do so.

- `CGASModule`: This class is a completely custom class in that it doesn't derive from any CRYENGINE interface. I created this class to help you; by definition, it is a helper class. Its sole purpose is to provide project-wide access to all of your game's systems and instantiate them only when needed. It does so by exposing itself as a global pointer called `g_pCGASModule`, which can be used inside any scope, inside any class, and inside any file to retrieve/create any of your game's systems.

 It is *strongly* advised that if you create a custom system for your game, you should add and implement a singleton `get` method, as shown in the other `get` methods in this class.

- `CGASStartup`: This class implements CRYENGINE's `IGameStartup` interface. It is used to create and initialize all of CRYENGINE's systems and your `Game` class. This class is instantiated automatically from outside your **Game DLL** by the Launcher, and is expected to create and initialize all of CRYENGINE's modules and ultimately create and run your game. For now, we load `CryGameFramework.dll`, retrieve its exported factory method, and call it to instantiate an instance of the `IGameFramework` interface. We then proceed to initialize it, which, in turn, loads, creates, and initializes all of CRYENGINE's modules.

- `CPlayer`: This class implements CRYENGINE's `IActor` interface. Every CRYENGINE game needs to have a player implementation. This is the place to implement the logic that concerns the player, such as moving around the world and interacting with objects.

- `CSmoothCamera`: This class implements CRYENGINE's `IGameObjectExtension` and `IGameObjectView` interfaces. It's used to provide a *view* for our player so that we may see the world. The `CSmoothCamera` class implements `IGameObjectView` so that it may control a CRYENGINE `IView` instance. It implements `IGameObjectExtension` so that they may be added to a **game object** that's in the game's world. This class is slightly advanced and it would be better to read the in-code documentation to get a clearer understanding of how this class works.

- `IWindowEventSystem`: This interface is a completely custom interface in that it doesn't derive from any CRYENGINE interface. I created this interface to help you; by definition, it is a helper interface. Its sole purpose is to provide a mechanism for which to dispatch and handle various window events, such as window activation, closing, and various mouse/keyboard events.

- **CScriptBind_Game**: This class implements CRYENGINE's `CScriptableBase` class. It's used to expose your game's functionality to **Lua**. Although not required, any game-specific functionality you want to be exposed to Lua should be added here. For now, only the ability to set the game's current spawnpoint has been exposed.

By now, you should have a good understanding of what each of the classes do and what they are used for. For a more thorough understanding, you may want to take a look at the in-code documentation.

Compiling our game

Now that we have all of the setup ready and have a clear understanding of what all of the important classes in our game do, let's compile our project. Get ready to venture into the world of game programming and create the *Great Action Side-Scroller*.

Right-click on your game project in the **Solution Explorer** and click on **Build**, as shown here:

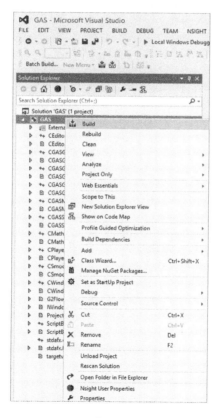

Summary

This concludes the chapter. If you come across any issues while compiling the game project, I suggest that you take a look at the starter-kit Crydev forum thread at `http://www.cryengine.com/community/viewtopic.php?f=355&t=124265`. In this chapter, you learned how to download and install my CRYENGINE "Blank" Game Starter-Kit, what all of the important classes in the kit do, and how to compile a CRYENGINE game project. The future is very bright as we move forward with the rest of the book. Good job!

2
Creating a Playable Character

In any game, the user will be interacting with and experience the world in which they inhabit. In order to achieve this, we need some way for us to interact with the game world. Like other games, **CRYENGINE** games also use something called a **player** to accomplish this. It acts as a sort of proxy or interface for the user to interact with and experience the world. In this chapter, you will learn how to create such a player. Here are the topics we will discuss:

- Implementing player lives
- Implementing player movement and rotation
- Making a camera follow the player

Implementing player lives

In games, there is often a need to have a mechanism that allows the user multiple attempts to accomplish a certain task. This concept is called **lives**, and our *Great Action Side-Scroller*, or *GAS*, game will use this mechanism. When we talk about player lives, we cannot avoid talking about player health, the mechanism for determining when a player's life has been exhausted. When health reaches zero, we die and another life will be consumed. Together, these two concepts form all that's needed to implement player lives. In this section, we will learn how to implement player lives. This is a two-step process which includes two subsections. Let's get started.

Part 1 – the player code

In this subsection, we will implement all the player-side code needed to implement the player lives gameplay-mechanic. Going forward, any class that is referenced can be assumed to be located in a file of the same name, for example, the CPlayer class **declaration** would be located in the CPlayer.h **header** file, and its **definition** would be inside the CPlayer.cpp **source** file. All the code used in this book should completely replace any default starter-kit code, unless otherwise instructed. So, let's dive in without further ado:

1. Add an m_fHealth private member variable of type float to the CPlayer class to store and keep track of the current player health. It should look like this:

```
private:
    float m_fHealth;
```

2. Add an m_iLives private member variable of type int to the CPlayer class to store and keep track of the amount of *lives* the player has left. It should look like this:

```
private:
    int m_iLives;
```

3. Add and implement public getter methods to the CPlayer class so that we can allow the rest of CRYENGINE to query our player's current health and lives. This is important as our class doesn't operate in a vacuum; more specifically, our **Game Rules** class should be able to query the player status in order to make gameplay decisions on what to do when we run out of health or exceed our maximum lives limit. We will not add/implement setter methods because we don't want to allow external code to set our health and lives variables. Instead, we want to exclusively use our damage/revive mechanism (ApplyDamage() or Revive()). It should look like this:

```
float CPlayer::GetHealth()const
{
  return m_fHealth;
}

float CPlayer::GetMaxHealth()const
{
  return 100;
}

unsigned int CPlayer::GetLives()const
{
  return m_iLives;
}
```

4. Add and implement a public `ApplyDamage()` method in the `CPlayer` class so that our player can take damage and dispatch when its health has been depleted. It should look like this:

```
void CPlayer::ApplyDamage( float fDamage )
{
  //Apply Damage
  m_fHealth -= fDamage;

  //If Health Is Less Than Or Equal To 0 Then Dispatch That
    Our Health Has Been Depleted.  Also Prevent Health From
    Being Negative.
  if( m_fHealth <= 0.0f )
  {
    //Avoid A Negative Health Value.
    m_fHealth = 0.0f;

    //Notify About Depleted Health.
    OnHealthDepleted();
  }
}
```

5. Add and implement a private `OnHealthDepleted()` method in the `CPlayer` class to handle player death. The method will be private so that it can only be called within the class. It should look like this:

```
void CPlayer::OnHealthDepleted()
{
  //Get Our Implementation Of The IGameRules Interface To
    Notify About The Player's Health Being Depleted. The
    Game's Rules Should Handle What Happens When The
    Player's Health Is Depleted.
  auto pGameRules = static_cast< CGASGameRules* > ( gEnv->
    pGame->GetIGameFramework()->GetIGameRulesSystem()->
    GetCurrentGameRules() );

  //Actually Notify The Game's Rules About Our Player's
    Health Being Depleted.
  pGameRules->OnPlayerHealthDepleted( this );
}
```

6. Add and implement a public `Revive()` method in the `CPlayer` class so that our player can be revived when it has died. It should look like this:

```
bool CPlayer::Revive()
{
  //If We Have Some Lives Left, Then Revive.
  if( m_iLives )
  {
    //Set Our Health Back To Maximum.
    m_fHealth = GetMaxHealth();

    //We Were Able To Revive.
    return true;
  }
  else
    return false; //We Have No More Lives Left So We Can't
      Revive.
}
```

7. Add and implement a public `Kill()` method in the `CPlayer` class so that the player can be killed. It should look like this:

```
void CPlayer::Kill()
{
  //Subtract 1 Life, And Prevent Lives From Being Negative.
  if( --m_iLives <= 0 )
    m_iLives = 0;

  //Get Our Implementation Of The IGameRules Interface To
    Notify About The Player Losing A Life. The Game's
    Rules Should Handle What Happens When The Player Dies.
  auto pGameRules = static_cast< CGASGameRules* > ( gEnv->
    pGame->GetIGameFramework()->GetIGameRulesSystem()->
    GetCurrentGameRules() );

  //Actually Notify The Game's Rules About Our Player's
    Life Being Lost.
  pGameRules->OnPlayerDied( this );
}
```

Congratulations, we have just implemented all of the player code necessary in order to use the player lives gameplay-mechanic. Now, we will move on to the **GameRules** side of the code.

Part 2 – the GameRules code

In this subsection, we will implement all the GameRules code needed to implement the player lives gameplay-mechanic. The steps are as follows:

1. Add and implement a public `OnPlayerHealthDepleted()` method in the `CGASGameRules` class so that we can handle the gameplay logic for what happens when the player's health reaches 0. It should look like this:

```
void CGASGameRules::OnPlayerHealthDepleted( IActor*const pPlayer )
{
  //Get Our Implementation Of The IActor Interface.
  auto pCPlayer = static_cast< CPlayer*const >( pPlayer );

  //If Pointer Is Valid, Kill Our Player.
  if( pCPlayer )
    pCPlayer->Kill();
}
```

2. Add and implement a public `OnPlayerDied()` method in the `CGASGameRules` class so that we can handle the gameplay logic for what happens when the player dies. It should look like this:

```
void CGASGameRules::OnPlayerDied( IActor*const pPlayer )
{
  //Get Our Implementation Of The IActor Interface.
  auto pCPlayer = static_cast< CPlayer*const >( pPlayer );

  //If Pointer Is Valid, Try To Revive Our Player.
  if( pCPlayer )
    if( !pCPlayer->Revive() ) //Try To Revive Our Player
      OnAllPlayerLivesLost( pPlayer ); //Failed To Revive
        Our Player. Notify About The Player Having No More
        Lives.
}
```

3. Add and implement a private `OnAllPlayerLivesLost()` method in the `CGASGameRules` class so that we can handle the gameplay logic for what happens when the player has lost all of its lives. This method is private to avoid other classes from calling this method. It should look like this:

```
void CGASGameRules::OnAllPlayerLivesLost( IActor*const
  pPlayer )
{
  //Should Probably Trigger End Of Game UI Menu.
}
```

Congratulations, we have just implemented all of the GameRules code necessary to use the player lives gameplay-mechanic.

The big picture

Let's look at the big picture so that we can get a clear view of the full flow and geography of the code. Externally (external from the `CPlayer` class), we will only be calling a couple of `CPlayer` methods, such as `ApplyDamage()`, `Kill()`, and `Revive()`. When the `ApplyDamage()` method is called, the player takes damage and checks if its health is depleted. If the player's health is depleted, we notify our GameRules implementation that the player has no more health by calling the GameRules' `OnPlayerHealthDepleted()` method. The GameRules then kills the player by calling the player's `Kill()` method, which subtracts one life and dispatches back to the GameRules that the player has died by calling the GameRules' `OnPlayerDied()` method. The GameRules then tries to revive the player by calling the player's `Revive()` method. If reviving the player fails, the GameRules will call its own `OnAllPlayerLivesLost()` method, which handles the *game over* gameplay logic. To help visualize this, I have created a simple flowchart explaining the system:

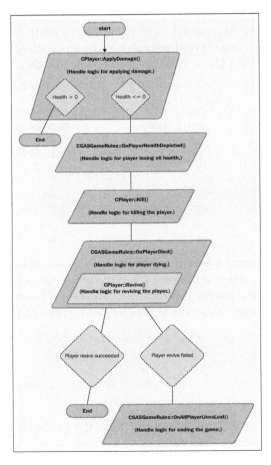

It may seem odd at first that we are seemingly and needlessly going back and forth between the CPlayer and CGASGameRules classes. Surely we could do without the communication and just implement the kill and revive logic right inside the CPlayer class? Yes, you could do that, but doing it the way we have offers one clear advantage: **modularity**. In game development (or in programming in general), it is very important to keep systems separate and modular, in order to have distinct roles between classes. The CPlayer class handles the player logic and the CGASGameRules class handles the game's rules. No direct communication exists between the two classes/systems. Instead, they communicate through notifications or events. This clear separation of logic allows us to have clean, modular code that can be changed in a vacuum without causing a cascading effect. We are free to change the logic of how the player should die for instance (CPlayer::Kill()). Maybe we want to add in a death animation and other death/kill effects. Using this event-based approach, we are free to add such code and the game would still know how to end the game on death or kill the player because the GameRules code is separate and untouched. This concludes the section on *implementing player lives*.

Implementing player movement and rotation

So what now? We created a character, but how do we interact with it? This is where player possession comes into play. In game development, the act of controlling an object (typically a *character*) is commonly known as player possession. This is the concept of taking input from the user to control how the player or object behaves in the game world. CRYENGINE has an extremely powerful mechanism for handling input called **Action Maps**, which maps input from devices to game actions. This allows your game to listen for these actions instead of raw input from devices, taking the pain out of handling multiple devices. Using Action Maps has another advantage: there can be multiple inputs mapping to the same action, for example, let's say you wanted your character to jump around and at the same time work for both gamepads and keyboards. You would simply define each input device's buttons/keys to an action named Jump. Then, our game could listen for the Jump action, completely removing the need to worry about low-level device input. Since *GAS* is a very small game, we do not need such a system and we will detect input manually. In this section, you will learn how to accept input from the keyboard and transform that data into the movement of the player.

Since *GAS* is a side-scroller game, this movement will only be on the *x* and *z* axis (left/right and up/down, respectively). Let's get started:

1. Implement the private `ProcessMovement()` method in the `CPlayer` class so that we can handle movement logic in every frame. It should look like this:

```
void CPlayer::ProcessMovement( float DeltaTime )
{
  //If Input System Doesn't Exists Then Don't Process
    Movement.
  if( !gEnv->pInput )
    return;

  //Get This Instance's Entity.
  auto pEntity = GetEntity();

  //Don't Process Movement If This Instance's Entity
    Doesn't Exist.
  if( !pEntity )
    return;

  //Get This Instance's Physical Entity.
  auto pPhysEnt = pEntity->GetPhysics();

  //Don't Process Movement If This Instance's Physical
    Entity Doesn't Exist.
  if( !pPhysEnt )
    return;

  //We Don't Know Whether We Should Move Or Not Yet So Set
    This To False.
  bool bMove = false;

  //Gets The Current Physics Status/State Of This Entity.
  pe_status_living StatusLiving;
  pPhysEnt->GetStatus( &StatusLiving );

  //Setup A "Move" Command.
  pe_action_move Move;

  //This Movement Should Add To the Current Velocity.
  Move.iJump = 2;
```

```
//We Don't Know Which Direction To Move In Yet.
Move.dir = Vec3( 0, 0, 0 );

//Specify A Default Run Speed Modifier.
float fRunModifier = 1.0f;

//If We Are Holding The Left Shift Key.  Set The Run
  Modifier To 2.
if( gEnv->pInput->InputState( "lshift", eIS_Down ) )
  fRunModifier = 2.0f;

//If We Are Not In The Air Then Go Ahead And Process
  Movement Commands.
if( !StatusLiving.bFlying )
{
  //We Should Move Left
  if( gEnv->pInput->InputState( "a", eIS_Down ) )
  {
    //We Should Move In The Negative X Direction.
    Move.dir = Vec3( -50, 0, 0 ) * fRunModifier;

    //Indicates That We Should In Fact Move This
      Instance.
    bMove = true;
  }


  //We Should Move Right.
  if( gEnv->pInput->InputState( "d", eIS_Down ) )
  {
    //We Should Move In The Positive X Direction.
    Move.dir = Vec3( 50, 0, 0 ) * fRunModifier;

    //Indicates That We Should In Fact Move This
      Instance.
    bMove = true;
  }

  //We Should Jump
  if( gEnv->pInput->InputState( "space", eIS_Down ) )
  {
    //We Should Move In The Positive Z Direction. We Add
      To The Current Move Command (+=) Because We Want To
      Combine Both Velocities (L/R U/D).
    Move.dir += Vec3( 0, 0, 600 );
```

```
            //Indicates That We Should In Fact Move This
              Instance.
            bMove = true;
          }

          //If We Should Move, Then Apply The "Move" Command.
          if( bMove )
          {
            //Calculate Final Movement By Factoring In The Delta
              Time.
            Move.dir = Move.dir * DeltaTime;
            pPhysEnt->Action( &Move );
          }
        }
      }
```

2. Implement the private `ProcessRotation()` method in the `CPlayer` class so that we can handle rotation logic in every frame. It should look like this:

```
void CPlayer::ProcessRotation( float DeltaTime )
{
  //Get This Instance's Entity.
  auto pEntity = GetEntity();

  //Don't Process Rotation If This Instance's Entity
    Doesn't Exist.
  if( !pEntity )
    return;

  //Get This Instance's Physical Entity.
  auto pPhysEnt = pEntity->GetPhysics();

  //Don't Process Rotation If This Instance's Physical
    Entity Doesn't Exist.
  if( !pPhysEnt )
    return;

  //Gets The Current Physics Status/State Of This Entity.
  pe_status_dynamics StatusDyn;
  pPhysEnt->GetStatus( &StatusDyn );

  //We Are Moving Left (In The Negative X) Direction. Let's
    Face This Instance In That Direction.
  if( StatusDyn.v.x < -0.1 )
```

```
    //Sets This Instance's Rotation Such That It Faces This
       Instance's Movement Direction On The X Axis.
    pEntity->SetRotation( Quat::CreateRotationVDir( Vec3(
       0, 1, 0 ) ), ENTITY_XFORM_ROT );

  //We Are Moving Right (In The Positive X) Direction.
     Let's Face This Instance In That Direction.
  else if( StatusDyn.v.x > 0.1 )
     //Sets This Instance's Rotation Such That It Faces This
        Instance's Movement Direction On The X Axis.
     pEntity->SetRotation( Quat::CreateRotationVDir( Vec3(
        0, -1, 0 ) ), ENTITY_XFORM_ROT );
}
```

The big picture

Let's look at the big picture so that we can get a clear view of the full flow and geography of the code. In every frame where the CPlayer class is updated by its Update() method, it makes calls to its ProcessMovement() and ProcessRotation() methods to handle movement and rotation. Inside ProcessMovement(), we get the current keyboard key that is pressed to decide which direction the player should move in. We then tell our player's physics to move us in that direction, making sure not to allow movement when we are in the air. After movement, rotation is processed. Inside ProcessRotation(), we get the player's current movement direction and then set its rotation so that it faces the direction it's moving in. To help visualize this, I have created a simple flowchart explaining the system:

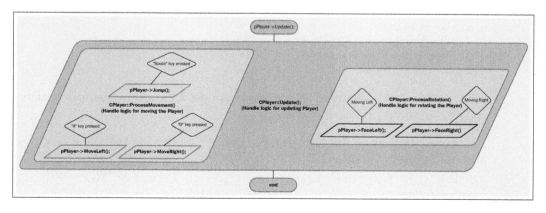

This concludes the section on *implementing player movement and rotation.*

Making a camera follow the player

At this point, I advise you to test our game in the editor. You can do this by right-clicking the solution in Visual Studio and clicking on **Build**. Once our game is compiled, you can launch the CRYENGINE editor as usual, and it will automatically load our game. It's wonderful. So far, we have a completely playable character, but what happens when our player moves out of the camera's view? As you can see, we need a way for the player to move around but always stay in view. We can easily accomplish this by creating a following camera. The steps are as follows:

1. The CPlayer class has camera code that we will not be using, so we need to remove such code. To do this, modify the PostInit() method in the CPlayer class so that all the camera-related code is removed. It should look like this:

    ```
    void CPlayer::PostInit( IGameObject * pGameObject )
    {
      //Allow This Instance To Be Updated Every Frame.
      pGameObject->EnableUpdateSlot( this, 0 );

      //Allow This Instance To Be Post-Updated Every Frame.
      pGameObject->EnablePostUpdates( this );

      //Register For Game Object Events.
      RegisterForGOEvents();

      //If We Are The Client Actor Than Notify The Game Of Us
        Being Spawned.
      if( m_bClient )
        ( ( CGASGame* )gEnv->pGame )->OnClientActorSpawned(
          this );
    }
    ```

    Now that we have removed all the camera code, let's add in the appropriate code to simulate a following camera.

2. At the very bottom of the ProcessMovement() method in the CPlayer class, add the following code:

    ```
    //Makes Sure That The Camera's Position Is Always At The
      Same X Position As The Player But Offset In The Y And Z
      Axis.
    m_pCamera->SetPos( pEntity->GetPos() + Vec3( 0, -10, 2 ) );
    ```

```
//Make Sure To Always Look At The Player.
m_pCamera->SetRot( Vec3( RAD2DEG( Ang3( Quat::
    CreateRotationVDir( pEntity->GetPos() - m_pCamera->
    GetPos() ) ) ) ) );
```

3. The default starter-kit code has the camera following the player pretty quickly. In *GAS*, we want the camera to follow the player more slowly, which adds a nice cinematic effect. To have a more lazy camera, let's modify the following function calls in the `Init()` method of the `CPlayer` class.

    We will change the following snippet:

    ```
    //Sets The Movement Speed Of The Player Camera.
    m_pCamera->SetMovementSpeed( 10.0f );

    //Sets The Rotation Speed Of The Player Camera.
    m_pCamera->SetRotationSpeed( 10.0f );
    ```

    Let's replace the previous snippet with this:

    ```
    //Sets The Movement Speed Of The Player Camera.
    m_pCamera->SetMovementSpeed( 2.5f );

    //Sets The Rotation Speed Of The Player Camera.
    m_pCamera->SetRotationSpeed( 2.5f );
    ```

The big picture

Let's look at the big picture so that we can get a clear view of the full flow and geography of the code. In every frame, the player's movement is updated. In order to keep the player in view, we tell the camera to follow the player's *x* position, while maintaining a constant offset in the *y* and *z* axis. To keep the player at the center of the screen, we instruct the camera to always look at the player. This concludes the section on *making a camera follow the player*.

Summary

At this point, you know how to implement the player lives gameplay-mechanic, how to accept keyboard input, how to turn that into player movement and rotation, and how to make a camera follow and look at the player.

In the next chapter, you will learn how to create a weapon and ammo class so that you and your enemies have a way of fighting. The future is very bright as we move forward with the rest of the book.

3
Implementing Weapons and Ammo

Any good side-scroller game wouldn't be fun if you didn't have cool weapons of great destruction. One thing to pay attention to is that CRYENGINE includes full support for weapons and ammo, right out of the box. However, my goal here is to show you how much you can do on your own. Many people struggle over figuring out how to add extensive new code while maintaining great integration with the rest of CRYENGINE. I want you to learn that anything you can think of is possible, and implementing a custom weapon and ammo system is no exception. In this chapter, you will learn how to create a complete weapon and ammo system and link them to events and other systems such as the **Game Rules**. Here is what you will learn:

- How to create a weapon class
- How to create an ammo class
- How to create ammo events

Creating a weapon class

We could create a simple weapon class and be done with it. However, I want to create a weapon system with the ability to create many weapons and pass them around the code using a simple **interface**. This interface approach is powerful, as it hides code and removes the requirement that every system must know about your exact weapon class. For example, wouldn't it be nice if we could give any weapon to a player and the player wouldn't need to know anything about it to use it? Using this interface approach, it is entirely possible. Interfaces are extremely powerful and add so much to a library or application in general that it is highly recommended to read a good book about it. It is a pattern that lends itself to well-written **Object-oriented programming (OOP)** code.

Creating the IWeapon interface

Since we need our game to support many weapons and we want to write clean, modular, OOP C++ code, it is essential that we create a weapon interface. Let's call this interface `IWeapon`. Since CRYEGNINE has its own interface called `IWeapon`, we will add ours to a custom namespace to avoid any name conflict. Let's do this:

1. Create a new file called `IWeapon.h`. Since this will hold an interface, there will not be a corresponding `IWeapon.cpp` file. Add only those methods to the interface that you would like all weapons to support and that are not weapon-specific; keep it general. It should look like this:

```
#ifndef __IWEAPON_HEADER__
#define __IWEAPON_HEADER__


namespace PACKT
{
  namespace GAS
  {
    namespace GAME
    {
      struct IWeapon
      {
        virtual ~IWeapon() {}

        ///////////////////////////////////////////////
        /// <summary>
        /// Shoots This Instance, Ammo Must Be Present. See
            This Instance's AddAmmo() Method.
        /// </summary>
        /// <returns> True If This Instance Was Shot
            Successfully, False Otherwise. </returns>
        ///////////////////////////////////////////////
        virtual bool Shoot()const = 0;

        ///////////////////////////////////////////////
        /// <summary> Gets Whether This Instance Can Shoot
            Or Not. </summary>
        /// <returns> True If This Instance Can Shoot,
            False Otherwise. </returns>
        ///////////////////////////////////////////////
        virtual bool CanShoot()const = 0;
```

```
///////////////////////////////////////////////
/// <summary> Adds The Specified Amount Of
    Ammunition To This Instance. </summary>
 /// <param name="iNumAmmo"> The Amount Of Ammo To
    Add To This Instance. </param>
///////////////////////////////////////////////
virtual void AddAmmo( std::size_t iNumAmmo ) = 0;


///////////////////////////////////////////////
/// <summary> Removes The Specified Amount Of
    Ammunition From This Instance. </summary>
/// <param name="iNumAmmo">
/// The Amount Of Ammo To Remove From This Instance
    (-1 Removes All Ammo).
/// </param>
///////////////////////////////////////////////
virtual void RemoveAmmo( std::size_t iNumAmmo ) =
  0;


///////////////////////////////////////////////
/// <summary> Gets This Instance's Ammo Count.
    </summary>
/// <returns> This Instance's Ammo Count.
    </returns>
///////////////////////////////////////////////
virtual std::size_t GetAmmoCount()const = 0;


///////////////////////////////////////////////
/// <summary>
/// Gets This Instance's Ammo Class. That Is, The
    Type Of Ammo That This Instance Is Compatible
/// With.
/// </summary>
/// <returns> This Instance's Ammo Class.
    </returns>
///////////////////////////////////////////////
virtual const string& GetAmmoClass()const = 0;

    };
   }
  }
}


#endif // !__IWEAPON_HEADER__
```

2. Notice how simple this interface is. Only methods that are generic enough to be used by all imaginable weapon types are added to this interface, as our game will need to know how to use the weapon without knowing about what underlying implementation it uses. Any method that is weapon-specific doesn't belong here.

Creating the AWeapon abstract base class

Now that our interface is complete, let's go ahead and create an abstract base class. We do this so that we can implement simple methods in the `IWeapon` interface that most likely won't need to be overridden with custom logic. Doing this significantly reduces code redundancy and allows us to only focus on the key methods that are important. Could you imagine having to implement every method of this interface every time you created a new weapon? We will create an abstract class that will implement most of the methods that will likely not need to be changed for each weapon class, and leave the other methods unimplemented so that specific weapon classes can define them.

1. Create a new file called `AWeapon.h` that will hold our abstract weapon class's declaration. Since all weapons will be an object that you can actually place into the world, we will derive this from the `IGameObjectExtension` interface. The `IGameObjectExtension` interface simply represents an extension to a game object. It is a class that allows adding extra code and functionality to game objects modularly without having to touch the actual game object code. Game objects are any objects that can exist in a CRYENGINE world/game and usually represent some specific, unique, game logic. The code should look like this:

```
#ifndef __AWEAPON_HEADER__
#define __AWEAPON_HEADER__


#include "IWeapon.h"
#include "IGameObject.h"



//////////////////////////////////////////////////////////////
/// <summary>
/// The AWeapon Abstract Class.  Implements All Of The
    Trivial IGameObjectExtension And IWeapon
/// Stuff, As To Serve As A Great Base Class For All
    Weapons.
```

```
/// </summary>
/// <seealso cref="T:IWeapon"/>
/// <seealso cref="T:CGameObjectExtensionHelper<AWeapon,
    IGameObjectExtension>"/>
///////////////////////////////////////////////////////
class AWeapon : public PACKT::GAS::GAME::IWeapon, public
  CGameObjectExtensionHelper < AWeapon,
  IGameObjectExtension >
{
public:

  AWeapon();
  virtual ~AWeapon();


  ////////////////IGameObjectExtension//////////////////

  virtual void GetMemoryUsage( ICrySizer *pSizer ) const
    override;
  virtual bool Init( IGameObject * pGameObject )override;
  virtual void PostInit( IGameObject * pGameObject )
    override;
  virtual void InitClient( int channelId )override;
  virtual void PostInitClient( int channelId )override;
  virtual bool ReloadExtension( IGameObject * pGameObject,
    const SEntitySpawnParams &params )override;
  virtual void PostReloadExtension( IGameObject *
    pGameObject, const SEntitySpawnParams &params )
    override;
  virtual bool GetEntityPoolSignature( TSerialize signature
    )override;
  virtual void Release()override;
  virtual void FullSerialize( TSerialize ser )override;
  virtual bool NetSerialize( TSerialize ser, EEntityAspects
    aspect, uint8 profile, int pflags )override;
  virtual void PostSerialize()override;
  virtual void SerializeSpawnInfo( TSerialize ser )
    override;
  virtual ISerializableInfoPtr GetSpawnInfo()override;
  virtual void Update( SEntityUpdateContext& ctx, int
    updateSlot )override;
  virtual void HandleEvent( const SGameObjectEvent& event )
    override;
  virtual void ProcessEvent( SEntityEvent& event )override;
  virtual void SetChannelId( uint16 id )override;
  virtual void SetAuthority( bool auth )override;
```

```
virtual void PostUpdate( float frameTime )override;
virtual void PostRemoteSpawn()override;


///////////////////IWeapon//////////////////


virtual bool CanShoot()const override;
virtual void AddAmmo( std::size_t iNumAmmo )override;
virtual void RemoveAmmo( std::size_t iNumAmmo )override;
virtual std::size_t GetAmmoCount()const override;
virtual const string& GetAmmoClass()const override;

protected:

    /// <summary> The Amount Of Ammo This Instance Has.
        </summary>
    std::size_t m_iAmmoCount;


    //////////////////////////////////////////////////////
    /// <summary>
    /// The Ammo Class That This Weapon Is Compatible With.
        (The Ammo Class That This Instance Can
    /// Use).
    /// </summary>
    //////////////////////////////////////////////////////
    string m_strAmmoClass;

};



#endif // !__AWEAPON_HEADER__
```

Notice how we leave the Shoot() method undefined. This is because most weapons will need to define custom logic to carry out that task.

2. Next, create a new file called AWeapon.cpp that will hold our simple implementation of the IGameObjectExtension and IWeapon interfaces. We can see why a nice abstract base class comes in handy, as we now have more than 25 methods for our weapon class. The implementation should look like this:

```
#include "stdafx.h"
#include "AWeapon.h"


AWeapon::AWeapon():
```

```
m_iAmmoCount(25)
{

}




AWeapon::~AWeapon()
{

}




////////////////AWeapon::IGameObjectExtension///////////////////


void AWeapon::GetMemoryUsage( ICrySizer *pSizer ) const
{
  pSizer->Add( *this ); /*Add This Instance's Size To The
    CRYENGINE Performance Monitor.*/
}




bool AWeapon::Init( IGameObject * pGameObject )
{
  SetGameObject( pGameObject ); /*Ensure This Instance
    Knows About Its Owning Game Object. IMPORTANT*/ return
    true;
}




void AWeapon::PostInit( IGameObject * pGameObject )
{

}
```

```
void AWeapon::InitClient( int channelId )
{
}




void AWeapon::PostInitClient( int channelId )
{
}




bool AWeapon::ReloadExtension( IGameObject * pGameObject, const
SEntitySpawnParams &params )
{
  ResetGameObject(); /*Ensure This Instance Knows About
    Its Owning Game Object. IMPORTANT*/
  return true;//This Extension Should Be Kept.
}




void AWeapon::PostReloadExtension( IGameObject * pGameObject,
const SEntitySpawnParams &params )
{
}




bool AWeapon::GetEntityPoolSignature( TSerialize signature )
{
  return true; //Our Signature Is Ok.
}




void AWeapon::Release()
{
```

```
    delete this; //Delete This Instance As Our Owning Game
       Object Has Been Deleted.
}




void AWeapon::FullSerialize( TSerialize ser )
{
}




bool AWeapon::NetSerialize( TSerialize ser, EEntityAspects
   aspect, uint8 profile, int pflags )
{
   return true;//Our Serialization State Is Up To Date An
       Valid.
}




void AWeapon::PostSerialize()
{
}




void AWeapon::SerializeSpawnInfo( TSerialize ser )
{
}




ISerializableInfoPtr AWeapon::GetSpawnInfo()
{
   return nullptr;//No Need For Spawn Information.
```

```
}


void AWeapon::Update( SEntityUpdateContext& ctx, int updateSlot )
{
}


void AWeapon::HandleEvent( const SGameObjectEvent& event )
{
}


void AWeapon::ProcessEvent( SEntityEvent& event )
{

}


void AWeapon::SetChannelId( uint16 id )
{
}


void AWeapon::SetAuthority( bool auth )
{
}
```

```cpp
void AWeapon::PostUpdate( float frameTime )
{
}



void AWeapon::PostRemoteSpawn()
{
}


////////////////IWeapon////////////////////


bool AWeapon::CanShoot()const
{
  return m_iAmmoCount;
}



void AWeapon::AddAmmo( std::size_t iNumAmmo )
{
  m_iAmmoCount += iNumAmmo;
}



void AWeapon::RemoveAmmo( std::size_t iNumAmmo )
{
  ( iNumAmmo == -1 ) ? ( m_iAmmoCount = 0 ) : (m_iAmmoCount
    -= iNumAmmo);
}



std::size_t AWeapon::GetAmmoCount()const
{
```

```
    return m_iAmmoCount;
}




const string& AWeapon::GetAmmoClass()const
{
  return m_strAmmoClass;
}
```

3. Notice how simple it was to implement; there would absolutely be no need to keep implementing these methods for each and every weapon class. Of course, we can override any of them if needed.

Creating the CBlaster weapon class

We created a nice `IWeapon` interface and an `AWeapon` abstract base class, now what? Well, since all the ground work is complete, it's time to actually create our weapon class:

1. Create a new file called `CBlaster.h`. This will hold our weapon's declaration. Make a note of how many methods need to be implemented in order to create a new weapon. The code should look like this:

```
#ifndef __CBLASTER_HEADER__
#define __CBLASTER_HEADER__


#include "AWeapon.h"


//////////////////////////////////////////////////////////
/// <summary> The CBlaster Class. A Ranged Weapon That
///     Shoots Fire Balls. </summary>
/// <seealso cref="T:AWeapon"/>
//////////////////////////////////////////////////////////
class CBlaster : public AWeapon
{
public:

  CBlaster();
  virtual ~CBlaster();
```

```
////////////////CBlaster////////////////

virtual bool Shoot()const override;

private:

};



#endif
```

Simple, and fast right?

2. Create a new file called `CBlaster.cpp` that will hold the implementation of the `CBlaster` weapon class. Ok, now let's implement the `Shoot()` method:

```
#include "stdafx.h"
#include "CBlaster.h"
#include "CGASGame.h"
#include "CGASGameRules.h"
#include "CFireBallAmmo.h"


////////////////CBlaster////////////////


CBlaster::CBlaster()
{
  //Set The Ammo Class That This Instance Is Compatible
    With.
  m_strAmmoClass = AMMO_CLASS_FIREBALL;
}




CBlaster::~CBlaster()
{
}
```

```
bool CBlaster::Shoot()const
{
  //Check If We Can Shoot.
  if( !CanShoot() )
    return false;

  //Get This Instance's Entity.
  auto pEnt = GetEntity();
  if( !pEnt )
    return false;

  //Get This Instance's Geometry.
  auto pStatObj = pEnt->GetStatObj( 0 );
  if( !pStatObj )
    return false;

  //Spawn The CFireBallAmmo Class.
  SEntitySpawnParams SpawnParams;
  SpawnParams.nFlags = ENTITY_FLAG_CASTSHADOW |
    ENTITY_FLAG_CALC_PHYSICS;
  SpawnParams.pClass = gEnv->pEntitySystem->
    GetClassRegistry()->FindClass( "FireBallAmmo" ); //The
    Name Used In REGISTER_GAME_OBJECT.
  SpawnParams.qRotation = IDENTITY;
  SpawnParams.vPosition = pStatObj->GetHelperPos(
    "BulletExit" );//Spawn At The Correct Position On The
    Weapon. (Weapon Model Must Have A Child Helper Named
    "BulletExit" ).
  SpawnParams.vScale = Vec3( 1, 1, 1 );

  //Actually Spawn The Entity.
  auto pAmmoEnt = gEnv->pEntitySystem->SpawnEntity(
    SpawnParams );
  if( !pAmmoEnt )
    return false;

  //Get It's Game Object.
  auto pAmmoGO = gEnv->pGame->GetIGameFramework()->
    GetGameObject( pAmmoEnt->GetId() );
  if( !pAmmoGO )
  {
    gEnv->pEntitySystem->RemoveEntity( pAmmoEnt->GetId(),
      true );
```

```
    return false;
  }

  //Get Our CFireBallAmmo Extension From It.
  auto pAmmoExt = pAmmoGO->QueryExtension( "FireBallAmmo"
    );
  if( !pAmmoExt )
  {
    gEnv->pEntitySystem->RemoveEntity( pAmmoEnt->GetId(),
      true );
    return false;
  }

  //Launch The Ammo.
  static_cast< CFireBallAmmo* >( pAmmoExt )->Launch(
    SpawnParams.vPosition, pEnt->GetForwardDir() );

  return true;
}
```

Congratulations, we created a complete weapon system. In the next section, you will do the same for ammunition. Get ready for some more fun.

Creating an ammo class

Now that we have created our weapon system, it is time for us to create an ammunition system. Ammunition is what our weapons use to cause damage. It can be anything from a bullet to a magic spell, anything that results in damage caused by firing some weapon. Since we wish to achieve a modular and extensible design, we will accomplish this using interfaces once again.

Creating the IAmmo class

Since we need our game to support many ammunition types and we want to write clean, modular, OOP C++ code, it is essential that we create an ammo interface which we will call IAmmo. Let's do it:

1. Create a new file called IAmmo.h that will hold our IAmmo interface declaration. It should look like this:

```
#ifndef __IAMMO_HEADER__
#define __IAMMO_HEADER__
```

```cpp
#include <CryString.h>
#include <Cry_Math.h>




/// <summary> The IAmmo Interface. Used To Represent Any Type Of
Ammunition/Projectile. </summary>
struct IAmmo
{
  virtual ~IAmmo() {}

  //////////////////////////////////////////////////////
  /// <summary> Launches This Instance In The Specified
      Direction. </summary>
  /// <param name="Pos"> The WorldSpace Position To Start
      The Launch From. </param>
  /// <param name="Dir">
  /// The Direction (And Velocity) To Launch This Instance
      (Not Normalized). The Magnitude Is
  /// Interpreted As the Velocity.
  /// </param>
  //////////////////////////////////////////////////////
  virtual void Launch( const Vec3& Pos, const Vec3& Dir ) =
    0;

  //////////////////////////////////////////////////////
  /// <summary> Gets Whether This Instance Is Launched. </summary>
  /// <returns> Whether This Instance Is Launched. </returns>
  //////////////////////////////////////////////////////
  virtual bool IsLaunched()const = 0;

  //////////////////////////////////////////////////////
  /// <summary> Gets This Instance's Launch Direction And
      Velocity. </summary>
  /// <returns> This Instance's Launch Direction And
      Velocity. </returns>
  //////////////////////////////////////////////////////
  virtual const Vec3& GetLaunchDir()const = 0;

  //////////////////////////////////////////////////////
  /// <summary> Gets The Amount Of Damage This Instance
      Causes. </summary>
  /// <returns> The Amount Of Damage This Instance Causes.
      </returns>
```

```
//////////////////////////////////////////////////////////
virtual float GetPower()const = 0;


//////////////////////////////////////////////////////////
/// <summary> Gets This Instance's Ammo Class. Used To Identify
This Type Of Ammo. </summary>
/// <returns> This Instance's Ammo Class. </returns>
//////////////////////////////////////////////////////////
virtual const string& GetAmmoClass()const = 0;
};



#endif // !__IAMMO_HEADER__
```

2. Notice how simple this interface is. Only methods that are generic enough to be used by all imaginable ammo types are added to this interface, as our game will need to know how to use the ammo without knowing about what underlying implementation it uses. Any method that is ammo-specific doesn't belong here.

Creating the AAmmo abstract class

Now that our interface is complete, let's go ahead and create an abstract base class. We do this so that we can implement simple methods in the IAmmo interface that won't need to be overriden with custom logic. Doing this significantly reduces code redundancy and allows us to only focus on the key methods that are important. Could you imagine having to implement every method of this interface every time you create new ammunition? We create an abstract class that will implement most of the methods that don't need to be changed for each ammo class, and leave the other methods unimplemented so that specific ammo classes can define them. The steps are as follows:

1. Create a new file called AAmmo.h that will hold our abstract ammo class's declaration. Since all ammunitions will be objects that you can actually place into the world, we will derive them from the IGameObjectExtension interface. The code should look like this:

```
#ifndef __AAMMO_HEADER__
#define __AAMMO_HEADER__


#include "IAmmo.h"
#include <IGameObject.h>
```

```
//////////////////////////////////////////////////////////
/// <summary>
/// The AAmmo Abstract Class.  Implements All Of The
    Trivial IGameObjectExtension Stuff, As To
/// Serve As A Great Base Class For All Ammunition.
/// </summary>
/// <seealso cref="T:CGameObjectExtensionHelper{AAmmo,
    IGameObjectExtension}"/>
//////////////////////////////////////////////////////////
class AAmmo : public IAmmo, public
  CGameObjectExtensionHelper < AAmmo, IGameObjectExtension
  >
{
public:

  AAmmo();
  virtual ~AAmmo();

  ////////////////IGameObjectExtension////////////////

  virtual void GetMemoryUsage( ICrySizer *pSizer ) const
    override;
  virtual bool Init( IGameObject * pGameObject )override;
  virtual void PostInit( IGameObject * pGameObject )
    override;
  virtual void InitClient( int channelId )override;
  virtual void PostInitClient( int channelId )override;
  virtual bool ReloadExtension( IGameObject * pGameObject,
    const SEntitySpawnParams &params )override;
  virtual void PostReloadExtension( IGameObject *
    pGameObject, const SEntitySpawnParams &params )
    override;
  virtual bool GetEntityPoolSignature( TSerialize signature
    )override;
  virtual void Release()override;
  virtual void FullSerialize( TSerialize ser )override;
  virtual bool NetSerialize( TSerialize ser, EEntityAspects
    aspect, uint8 profile, int pflags )override;
  virtual void PostSerialize()override;
  virtual void SerializeSpawnInfo( TSerialize ser )
    override;
  virtual ISerializableInfoPtr GetSpawnInfo()override;
```

```
virtual void Update( SEntityUpdateContext& ctx, int
  updateSlot )override;
virtual void HandleEvent( const SGameObjectEvent& event )
  override;
virtual void ProcessEvent( SEntityEvent& event )override;
virtual void SetChannelId( uint16 id )override;
virtual void SetAuthority( bool auth )override;
virtual void PostUpdate( float frameTime )override;
virtual void PostRemoteSpawn()override;


///////////////////IAmmo///////////////////

virtual bool IsLaunched()const override;
virtual const Vec3& GetLaunchDir()const override;
virtual float GetPower()const override;
virtual const string& GetAmmoClass()const override;

protected:

/// <summary> The Amount Of Damage This Instance Causes.
  </summary>
float m_fPower;

/// <summary> Specifies Whether This Instances Was
  Launched From A Weapon. </summary>
bool m_bLaunched;

/// <summary> This Instance's Class. Used To Identify
  This Type Of Ammo. </summary>
string m_strAmmoClass;

/// <summary> This Instance's Launch Direction And
  Velocity. </summary>
Vec3 m_LaunchDir;

};



#endif // !__AAMMO_HEADER__
```

Notice how we leave the `Launch()` method undefined. This is because most ammunitions will need custom logic to carry out that task.

2. Next, create a new file called `AAmmo.cpp` that will hold our simple implementation of the `IGameObjectectExtention` and `IAmmo` interfaces. We can see now why a nice abstract base class comes in handy, as we now have more than 25 methods for our ammo class. The implementation should look like this:

```
#include "stdafx.h"
#include "AAmmo.h"
#include "CGASGame.h"
#include "CGASGameRules.h"


AAmmo::AAmmo()
{
}




AAmmo::~AAmmo()
{
}



////////////////////AAmmo::IGameObjectExtension//////////////


void AAmmo::GetMemoryUsage( ICrySizer *pSizer ) const
{
  pSizer->Add( *this ); /*Add This Instance's Size To The
    CRYENGINE Performance Monitor.*/
}




bool AAmmo::Init( IGameObject * pGameObject )
{
  SetGameObject( pGameObject ); /*Ensure This Instance
    Knows About Its Owning Game Object. IMPORTANT*/ return
    true;
}
```

```
void AAmmo::PostInit( IGameObject * pGameObject )
{
  pGameObject->EnableUpdateSlot( this, 0 ); /*Enable
    Updates To This Instance (Update() Will Be Called Every
    Frame.)*/
}
```

```
void AAmmo::InitClient( int channelId )
{
}
```

```
void AAmmo::PostInitClient( int channelId )
{
}
```

```
bool AAmmo::ReloadExtension( IGameObject * pGameObject, const
SEntitySpawnParams &params )
{
  ResetGameObject(); /*Ensure This Instance Knows About Its
    Owning Game Object. IMPORTANT*/ return true;
}
```

```
void AAmmo::PostReloadExtension( IGameObject * pGameObject, const
SEntitySpawnParams &params )
{
}
```

```
bool AAmmo::GetEntityPoolSignature( TSerialize signature )
{
  return true;
}




void AAmmo::Release()
{
  delete this;
}




void AAmmo::FullSerialize( TSerialize ser )
{
}




bool AAmmo::NetSerialize( TSerialize ser, EEntityAspects aspect,
uint8 profile, int pflags )
{
  return true;
}




void AAmmo::PostSerialize()
{
}




void AAmmo::SerializeSpawnInfo( TSerialize ser )
{
}
```

```
ISerializableInfoPtr AAmmo::GetSpawnInfo()
{
  return nullptr;
}




void AAmmo::Update( SEntityUpdateContext& ctx, int updateSlot )
{
  //Check To See If We Were Launched By A Weapon.
  if( m_bLaunched )
  {
    //We Were Launched, Keep Us Moving In The Launched
      Direction.
    pe_action_set_velocity SetVelAction;
    SetVelAction.v = m_LaunchDir;
    GetEntity()->GetPhysics()->Action( &SetVelAction );
  }
}




void AAmmo::HandleEvent( const SGameObjectEvent& event )
{
}




void AAmmo::ProcessEvent( SEntityEvent& event )
{
  if( event.event == ENTITY_EVENT_COLLISION )
  {
    //Get Our Games' Instance.
    auto pGame = static_cast< CGASGame* >( gEnv->pGame );

    //Get The Games' GameRules, So That It Can Handle Logic
      For Item/Ammo Pickup.
    auto pGameRules = static_cast< CGASGameRules* >( pGame-
      >GetGameRules() );
```

```
                    //Get The Collision Struct For This Collision Event.
                    auto pEventCollision = ( ( EventPhysCollision* )
                      event.nParam[ 0 ] );

                    //Get The Other Physical Entity Involved In This
                      Collision.
                    auto pPhysOther = pEventCollision->pEntity[ 0 ] ==
                      GetEntity()->GetPhysics() ? pEventCollision->pEntity
                      [ 1 ] : pEventCollision->pEntity[ 0 ];

                    //Check If This Instance Has Been Launched From A
                      Weapon.
                    if( m_bLaunched )
                      pGameRules->OnAmmoHit( this, gEnv->pEntitySystem->
                        GetEntityFromPhysics( pPhysOther ) );//Ammo Has Hit
                        A Target. Notify GameRules About The Ammo Hit.
                    else
                      pGameRules->OnAmmoPickupRequest( this, gEnv->
                        pEntitySystem->GetEntityFromPhysics( pPhysOther ) )
                        ;//Ammo Is Waiting To Be Picked Up (Ammo Was Not
                        Launched). Notify GameRules About The Ammo Wanting
                        To Be Picked Up.
                  }
                }




void AAmmo::SetChannelId( uint16 id )
{
}




void AAmmo::SetAuthority( bool auth )
{
}
```

```
void AAmmo::PostUpdate( float frameTime )
{
}



void AAmmo::PostRemoteSpawn()
{
}



/////////////////AAmmo::IAmmo/////////////////



bool AAmmo::IsLaunched()const
{
   return m_bLaunched;
}



const Vec3& AAmmo::GetLaunchDir()const
{
   return m_LaunchDir;
}



float AAmmo::GetPower()const
{
   return m_fPower;
}



const string& AAmmo::GetAmmoClass()const
{
   return m_strAmmoClass;
}
```

3. Notice the implementation of the `ProcessEvent()` method; try to figure out what is happening. Take a look at the `Update()` method. We simply checked whether we were launched, and if so, we updated our position in the launch direction using physics.

Creating the CFireBallAmmo class

We created our nice `IAmmo` interface and `AAmmo` abstract base class, now what? Well, since all the ground work is complete, it's time to actually create our ammo class.

1. Create a new file called `CFireBallAmmo.h`. This will hold our ammunition's declaration. Make a note of how many methods need to be implemented in order to create a new type of ammunition. The code should look like this:

```
#ifndef __CFIREBALLAMMO_HEADER__
#define __CFIREBALLAMMO_HEADER__


#include "AAmmo.h"


/// <summary> The FireBall Ammo Class. </summary>
#define AMMO_CLASS_FIREBALL "FireBall"


//////////////////////////////////////////////////////////
/// <summary> The CFireBallAmmo Class.  A Projectile Ammo
    That Causes Fire Damage. </summary>
/// <seealso cref="T:AAmmo"/>
//////////////////////////////////////////////////////////
class CFireBallAmmo : public AAmmo
{
public:

  CFireBallAmmo();
  virtual ~CFireBallAmmo();


  ///////////////////IAmmo///////////////////

  virtual void Launch( const Vec3& Pos, const Vec3& Dir )
    override;

private:
```

```
};


#endif // !__CFIREBALLAMMO_HEADER__
```

2. Create a new file called `CFireBallAmmo.cpp` that will hold the implementation of the `CFireBallAmmo` ammunition class. Ok, now let's implement the `Launch()` method:

```cpp
#include "stdafx.h"
#include "CFireBallAmmo.h"
#include "IParticles.h"


/////////////////////CFireBallAmmo/////////////////////


CFireBallAmmo::CFireBallAmmo()
{
  m_fPower = 25.0f;
  m_bLaunched = false;
  m_strAmmoClass = AMMO_CLASS_FIREBALL;
}




CFireBallAmmo::~CFireBallAmmo()
{
}


/////////////////CFireBallAmmo::IAmmo/////////////////////


void CFireBallAmmo::Launch( const Vec3& Pos, const Vec3&
  Dir )
{
  //Find Or Load The Specified Particle Effect.
  auto pParticleEffect = gEnv->pParticleManager->
    FindEffect( "Ammo.Projectile.FireBall" );
  if( pParticleEffect )
  {
```

```
                  //Spawn The Found Particle Effect.
                  auto pEmmiter = pParticleEffect->Spawn( true, QuatTS(
                    IDENTITY, Pos ) );
                  if( pEmmiter )
                    m_bLaunched = true; //Enable Launch Mode (Update()
                      Will Handle Logic From Here).
              }
          }
```

3. If we take a look at the implementation of the `Launch()` method, we can see that all we do is instantiate a particle effect named `Ammo.Projectile.FireBall` and then let the `Update()` method do all the work (by enabling `m_bLaunched`, which is checked in every `Update()`).

Congratulations, you successfully created a complete ammunition system. In the next section, you will learn how to add ammo events to our game. Get ready for some more fun.

Creating ammo events

Now that we have a complete weapon and ammo system, we can shoot and cause some damage. However, how do we know when an object has been hit? If we don't know this information, then how can we know if someone is supposed to take damage or if an object is supposed to break? The answer to this problem, like many, is **events**. We will add a couple of methods to our game's rules that get called when a piece of ammunition hits any object in the game word. From there, it will determine what should happen. Let's get started:

1. Add an `OnAmmoHit()` method to the `CGasGameRules` class and implement it as follows:

```
void CGASGameRules::OnAmmoHit( IAmmo* const pAmmo, IEntity*const
pVictim )
{
  if( "Player" == pVictim->GetClass()->GetName() )
  {
    auto pActor = static_cast< CPlayer* >( gEnv->pGame->
      GetIGameFramework()->GetIActorSystem()->GetActor(
      pVictim->GetId() ) );
    if( pActor )
      pActor->ApplyDamage( pAmmo->GetPower() );
  }
}
```

When any object in the world gets hit by a piece of ammunition, this method is called; pVictim is the object that's hit. We simply check whether pVictim is of the class type CPlayer (which the player and AI are) and if so, we apply damage to that object.

2. Add an OnAmmoPickupRequest() method to the CGasGameRules class and implement it as follows:

```cpp
void CGASGameRules::OnAmmoPickupRequest( IAmmo* const pAmmo,
IEntity*const pRequester )
{
  if( "Player" == pRequester->GetClass()->GetName() )
  {
    //Get The Actor From The Requester.
    auto pActor = static_cast< CPlayer* >( gEnv->pGame->
      GetIGameFramework()->GetIActorSystem()->GetActor(
      pRequester->GetId() ) );
    if( pActor )
    {
      //Get The Requester's Weapon.
      auto pWeapon = pActor->GetWeapon();
      if( pWeapon )
      {
        //If The Requester's Weapon Is Compatible With The
          Specified Ammo Then Pick It Up.
        if( pWeapon->GetAmmoClass() == pAmmo->
        GetAmmoClass() )
        pActor->PickupAmmo( pAmmo );
      }
    }
  }
}
```

If ammunition is touched when it has not been launched, this method will be called; pRequester is the object that touched the ammo. We simply check whether pRequester is of the class type CPlayer (which the player and AI are) and if so, we allow them to pick it up.

If you remember correctly, I told you to figure out what the AAmmo class' ProcessEvent() method did. In the AAmmo class' ProcessEvent() method, we check whether the event that was raised was a collision event (our ammo has collided with another object in the world) and if so, we check our launch state. If we were launched, then the object should possibly take damage. So, we call our game rules' OnAmmoHit() method. If we were not launched, then that means that the ammo was in the game world just waiting to be picked up and the object should attempt to pick it up. Hence, the OnAmmoPickupRequest() method is called.

Summary

In this chapter, you learned how to create a complete weapon and ammo system with the ability to notify the game's rules of ammo events. You also learned how powerful interfaces are when designing extensible OOP systems.

In the next chapter, you will learn how to create a complete AI character that will try to kill the player. Stay tuned.

4
Creating an Enemy AI

Pretty much every game has *bad guys* and it is no different in *GAS*. In this chapter, we will create our very own enemy **artificial intelligence (AI)** that can shoot at the **player**. Here is what you will learn:

- How to register a new AI class
- How to make the AI detect the player and not move
- How to make the AI shoot the player

Registering a new AI class

At the heart of every *character* in **CRYENGINE** is the IActor interface. It provides the mechanism for objects to have AI. When we refer to a player or an AI, we are really referring to something called an **actor**. An actor is responsible for containing and managing all the logic that will be used to bring an object to *life*. This can range from being an animal companion, an AI character, or any other **game object** whose purpose is to represent *living* objects. Since *GAS* is a very simple side-scroller, we will not be using CRYENGINE's AI system. However, we will use CRYENGINE's IActor interface since our character is a *living* object. There is not much difference between our player and the AI; the only difference is how they shoot and who they shoot at. This allows us to reuse the CPlayer class for our AI, and simply register it under a different class name.

Open the CGASGame.cpp file and navigate to the RegisterGameObjects() method. Re-register the CPlayer class under the name AI. It should look like this:

```
//Registers The AI.
REGISTER_FACTORY( m_pGameFramework, "AI", CPlayer, true );
```

Notice that we reuse the `CPlayer` implementation and just register it under a different class name `AI`. This will create another entity class called `AI` that uses the exact same code as the `CPlayer` class.

Detecting the player and preventing mobility

In order for the AI to shoot at the player, it needs to know where it is and how to aim at it. In this section, you will learn how to detect the player and make the AI aim at it:

Open the `CPlayer.cpp` file and navigate to the `Update()` method. Since the AI and player are sharing the same class, we need to branch the logic based on whether we are currently the AI or the player. If we are the AI, we need to aim our weapon at the player. It should look similar to the following:

```
//We Are AI
if( !m_bClient )
{
  //Get The Player.
  auto pPlayer = static_cast< CPlayer* >( gEnv->pGame->
    GetIGameFramework()->GetClientActor() );

  //Get The Direction We Would Need To Aim To Hit The
    Player.
  auto ShootDir = ( pPlayer->GetEntity()->GetWorldPos() -
    GetEntity()->GetWorldPos() ).normalized();

  //Get The Weapon's Entity.
  auto pWeaponEnt = m_pWeapon->GetEntity();
  if( pWeaponEnt )
  {
    //Point The Weapon At The Target.
    pWeaponEnt->SetRotation( quaternion::
      CreateRotationVDir( ShootDir ), ENTITY_XFORM_ROT );
  }

}
```

Notice that we get the direction the AI needs to aim at by getting the difference between the AI's position and the player's position. We then instruct the weapon to set its rotation to the direction that we calculated.

It is important for our game that the AI doesn't move around. Unfortunately, our `Player` class is set up to move when input is detected. To prevent the AI from moving, simply wrap the movement and rotation processing calls with an `if` statement. In the `CPlayer` class's `Update()` method, wrap the movement and rotation processing code with an `if` statement. It should look like this:

```
//Only Process Movement And Rotation If We Are NOT An AI
  (The Player).
if( m_bClient )
{
  //Process Player Movement.
  ProcessMovement( ctx.fFrameTime );

  //Process Player Rotation.
  ProcessRotation( ctx.fFrameTime );

}
```

Notice the `m_bClient` variable; it is the only variable that needs to be considered in order to detect between the player and AI.

Shooting the player

Now that we have added player detection to our AI, it is ready to shoot at the player now. To accomplish this, we will need to use a method that gets called every *n* seconds so as to prevent shooting rapidly during every frame. Luckily, for the purposes of this book, I've created a lightweight *callback* timer that does just this. So let's get started.

Open the `CPlayer.cpp` file and navigate to the `PostInit()` method. Add a *callback* method to the timer that shoots the player. It should look similar to the following:

```
//We Are AI
if( !m_bClient )
{
  //Add Callback To Timer.  Try To Shoot The Player Every 2
    Seconds.
  m_CallBackTimer += [ this ] ( double dDelta )
  {
    //Get The Player
    auto pPlayer = gEnv->pGame->GetIGameFramework()->
      GetClientActor();
```

```
        //Get The Distance The We Are From The Player/
        auto Len = GetEntity()->GetWorldPos().GetDistance( pPlayer->
          GetEntity()->GetWorldPos() );

        //If We Are Less Than 15 Meters, Then Shoot The Player.
        if( Len < 15 )
        {
          //Unlimited Ammo For AI.
          m_pWeapon->AddAmmo( 1 );

          //Shoot At The Target, With A Bullet Speed Multiplier Of 10.
          m_pWeapon->Shoot( 10 );
        }
      };
  }
```

Notice how we first check to see if we are an AI. We then proceed to add a *callback* method in the form of a **C++11 Lambda**, which will get called every time the timer reaches its interval (which is currently set at 2 seconds). In the callback, we simply add ammo to the AI to give it unlimited ammunition and shoot the weapon.

Extending the AI

There are many different ways to extend the AI that would be beyond the scope of this chapter. However, it would be great for you to experiment with ways to improve upon this logic and add your own behaviors. Maybe you want the AI to follow the player wherever it goes. Maybe when the player approaches too close, you want the AI to run away. Whatever it is, it's important for you to experiment with the various possibilities and expand upon the very simple AI coded in this chapter.

Summary

Congratulations! In this chapter, you learned how to create an enemy AI, prevent it from moving, and allow it to shoot the player. As with all chapters, I encourage you to look at the complete source code for a more detailed and nuanced explanation of how all of this works.

In the next chapter, you will learn how to create the game's various **user interface menus**. Stay tuned!

5
Creating User Interfaces

All games need a way to relay information to the player. However, relaying this information through pure gameplay can sometimes be difficult or actually impossible. This is where **user interfaces** come in. User interfaces display information to the player and are only meant for their eyes. This information is typically used to help the player understand the game world or game state and is usually located on the screen. The information displayed can be anything from player and enemy health meters, an RPG's quick slot bar, or even an entire game menu. In this chapter, you will learn how to create the latter: a start and end game menu. Here is what you will learn:

- How to create the Flash UI content for our menus
- Creating UI elements
- Implementing a game menu system in C++

Creating the Flash UI content for our menus

To display the appropriate content to the player, we actually need to create it. In this two-part section, we will do just that.

Creating the main menu

In this part, we will be creating the main menu. It will be the first thing the player sees when they start the game. It will allow the player to start or quit the game. Let's get started:

1. Open Adobe Flash Professional CS6. It should look like this:

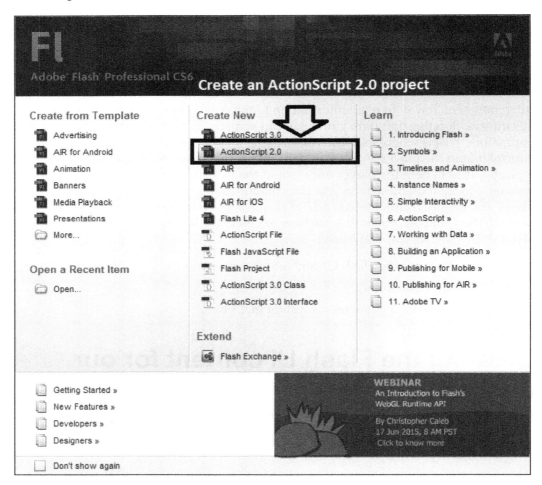

2. Change the scene's resolution to 1920 x 1080 pixels, frame rate to 60 FPS, and Flash Player version to v10.3. The result should look like this:

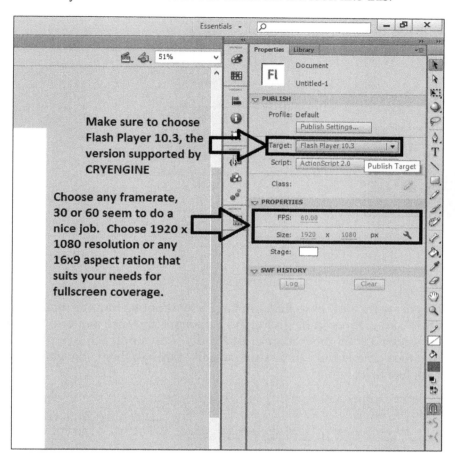

3. Add a button to the scene by first creating a rectangle in the scene using the Rectangle Tool on the right-hand side toolbar; right-click on it and choose **Convert to Symbol**. Make sure to set its new type to **Button**. It should now look like this:

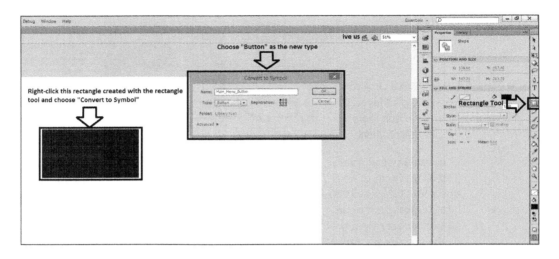

4. Duplicate the button so that you have a total of two buttons: **Start Game** and **Quit Game**. Proceed by giving them a unique instance name so that they can be accessed from the ActionScript 2 code. Then, apply a nice alpha effect so that the game world can be seen partially through them, like glass. It should look like this:

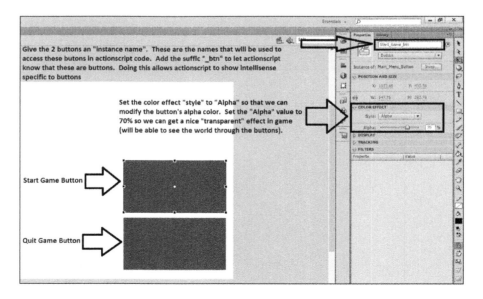

5. Create a title bar by creating another rectangle using the Rectangle Tool. Right-click on the Tool, choose **Convert to Symbol**, set the type to **Movie Clip**, and apply a nice **Alpha** effect. It should now look as follows:

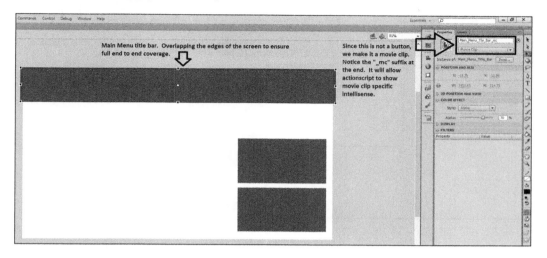

6. Create text to describe the title bar and buttons using the Text Tool on the right-hand side toolbar and embed it. It should look as follows:

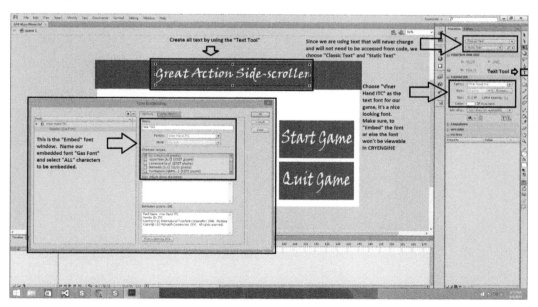

7. We created all the content for the main menu, now it's time to add code to it:

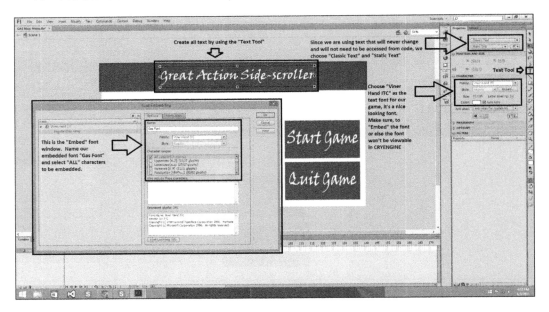

8. Add code to the first keyframe by right-clicking it and choosing **Actions**. It should look as follows:

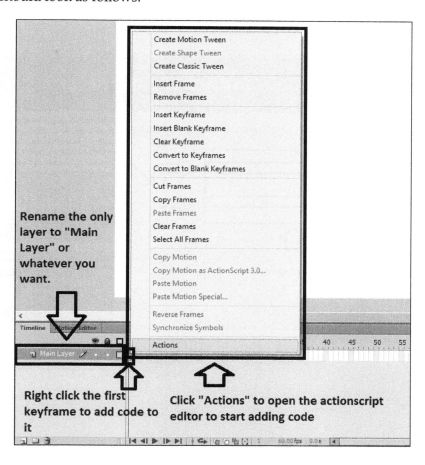

9. Add code to the keyframe that communicates with CRYENGINE that a flash event has occurred. To open the code window, you need to right-click on the first keyframe in the **Timeline** tab and choose **Actions**. The code should look as follows:

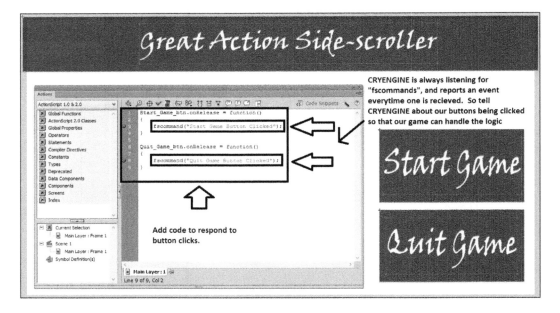

10. That's about it. Let's make sure to save the file in the correct place so that we don't lose our work and CRYENGINE can find it. Save the file in the `CRYENGINE_ROOT/Libs/UI` folder with the name `GAS_Main_Menu.fla`.

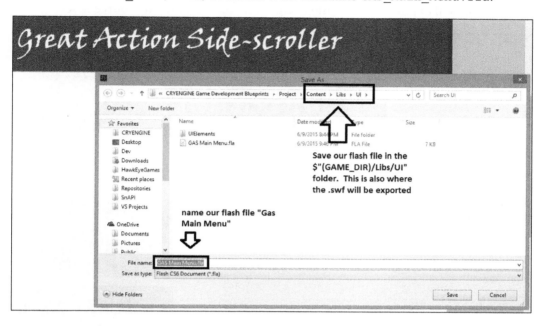

11. We have just saved the source asset. CRYENGINE cannot read the source assets, so we need to export out the Flash file in a game-ready format called `.swf`. Do this by navigating to **File** | **Publish** on the top-left menu bar. This will export the `.swf` file in the same directory as the source asset.

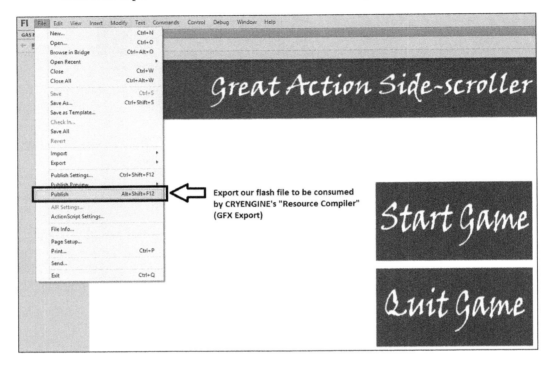

12. In order to test how our user interface behaves and what it looks like, we need to add CRYENGINE's Flash player to Flash Professional CS6 as an extension. Open the Extension Manager by navigating to **Help | Manage Extensions**. Then browse for and choose the CRYENGINE Flash Player extension, which can be found at `CRYENGINE_ROOT/Tools/Scaleform/Extensions`.

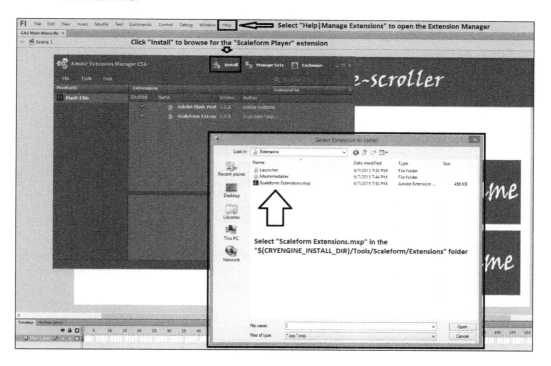

13. Open the new Flash Player extension by navigating to **Window | Other Panels | Scaleform Launcher**:

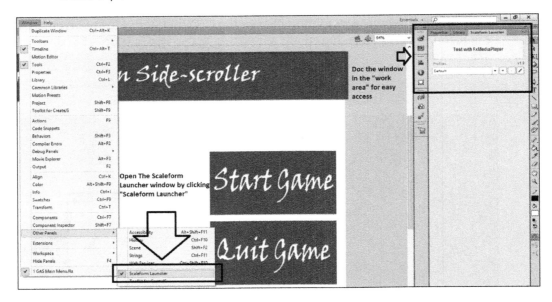

14. To actually use the **Scaleform Launcher** to test our Flash file, we need to add an actual Scaleform player. Luckily, CRYENGINE includes one. Browse for it and open it. It can be found in the `CRYENGINE_ROOT/Tools/Scaleform/MediaPlayer` folder, as shown here:

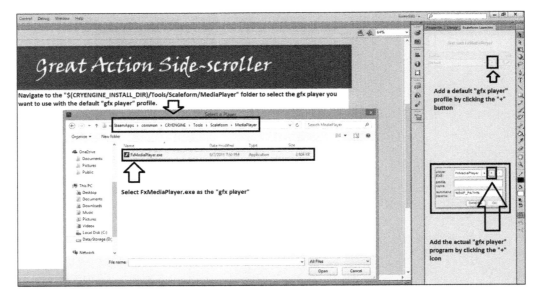

Creating the end game menu

In this section, we will be creating the end game menu. It will be the last thing the player sees when they die. It will allow them to restart the level or quit the game. Let's get started:

1. Create a brand new Flash ActionScript 2.0 project and adjust the resolution, FPS, and other settings as we did for the main menu. Create a full screen quad using the Rectangle Tool so that we can have a full screen and translucent affect. Adjust the **Alpha** effect to 75 percent to give a nice value. The settings should look as follows:

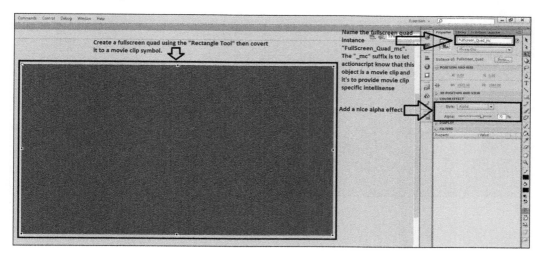

2. Create a dynamic text object using the Text Tool on the right-hand side toolbar. Place it in the top centre of the full screen quad as this will display the designer-specified text when the player dies. Also, create two buttons using the Rectangle Tool that will be used to either return to the main menu or quit the game. The settings should look as follows:

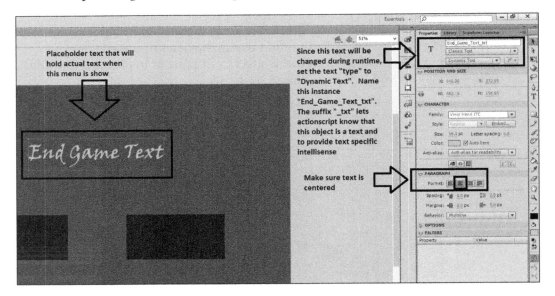

3. Create a static text object for each button and name them `Main Menu` and `Quit Game`, respectively. Proceed by adding code to the first keyframe that will interact with CRYENGINE by sending button click events. The code should look as follows:

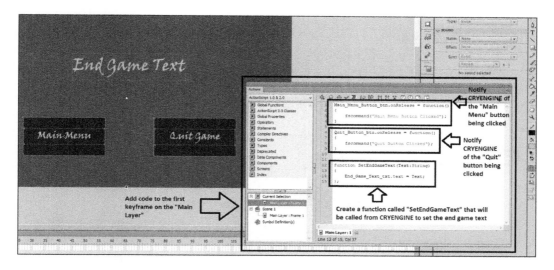

It is time to save our menu so that we don't lose our work and then we can set up the export process. First, embed all text just like we did in the main menu. Then, go to **File | Save As** on the toolbar at the upper left-hand corner of the screen. Save the file in the `$(CRYENGINE_CONTENT)/Libs/UI` folder and name it `GAS End Menu.fla`.

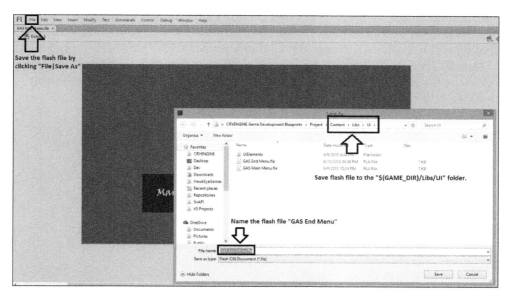

Now that the file has been saved, it is ready for export. Go to **File** in the toolbar at the top left-hand side of the screen and select **Publish**, as shown here:

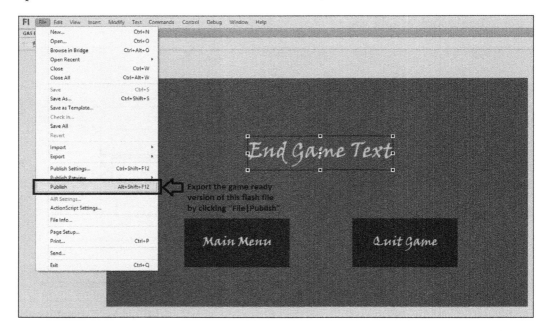

Creating UI elements

So, we created all the UI content needed for our game in Flash, exported it, and converted it to an optimized format for consumption by CRYENGINE. What's next? Well, we need to define **UI elements**. UI elements are CRYENGINE's representation of a Flash UI scene. CRYENGINE cannot directly consume Flash UI content and therefore needs an XML file that defines the entire UI as UI elements. So, in this section, we will be doing just that.

Let's get started:

1. Create a UI element definition file in the `CRYENGINE_CONTENT/Libs/UI/UIElements` folder named `GAS_UI.xml` and open it.

2. Define a UI element for each menu (the main menu and the end game menu):

```xml
<!--Define A Group Of UI Elements Named Menus. This Allows
    Us To Specify Multiple UI Elements In One File And Group
    Them Together For Organization.-->
<UIElements name="Menus">

    <!--Define A UI Element That Will Represent Our Main Menu
        Named "Main_Menu". This Will Be The Name That We Use To
        Retrieve The Main Menu In C++.-->
    <!--Specify That The UI Element Should Catch Mouse,
        Keyboard, And Controller Events And Should Show The
        Mouse Cursor-->
    <UIElement name="Main_Menu" mouseevents="1" keyevents="1"
        cursor="1" controller_input="1">

        <!--Specify The Optimized Exported Flash UI That This
            UI Element Will Represent/Use.-->
        <GFx file="GAS_Main_Menu.gfx" layer="0">
            <!--Specify Various Constraints/Options That This UI
                Element Should Have.-->
            <Constraints>
                <!--Specify That This UI Element Should Be
                    FullScreen-->
                <Align mode="fullscreen" />
            </Constraints>
        </GFx>

        <!--Specify All Of The Event That This UI Element Has.
            (These Are The "fscommands" That The Flash UI
            Calls).-->
        <events>
            <!--Give The Event A Name That CRYENGINE Will Use To
                Identify The Event In C++ Code.-->
            <!--Specify The "fscommand" That Backs This Event.-->
```

```
      <!--Specify The Description That Will Be Visible To
         The C++ Code And Flowgraph.-->
      <event name="Start_Game_Button_Clicked" fscommand=
         "Start_Game_Button_Clicked" desc="Triggered When
         The 'Start Game' Button Is Clicked." />
      <event name="Quit_Game_Button_Clicked" fscommand=
         "Quit_Game_Button_Clicked" desc="Triggered When The
         'Quit Game' Button Is Clicked." />
   </events>

</UIElement>

<!--Define A UI Element That Will Represent Our End Game
   Menu Named "End_Menu".  This Will Be The Name That We
   Use To Retrieve The End Game Menu In C++.-->
<!--Specify That The UI Element Should Catch Mouse,
   Keyboard, And Controller Events And Should Show The
   Mouse Cursor-->
<UIElement name="End_Menu" mouseevents="1" keyevents="1"
   cursor="1" controller_input="1">

   <!--Specify The Optimized Exported Flash UI That This
      UI Element Will Represent/Use.-->
   <GFx file="GAS_End_Menu.gfx" layer="0">
      <!--Specify Various Constraints/Options That This UI
         Element Should Have.-->
      <Constraints>
         <!--Specify That This UI Element Should Be
            FullScreen-->
         <Align mode="fullscreen" />
      </Constraints>
   </GFx>

   <!--Specify All Of The Functions That This UI Element
      Has. (These Are The Functions That The Flash UI
      Contains).-->
   <functions>
      <!--Specify The Name That CRYENGINE Will Use To
         Identify The Function In C++-->
      <!--Specify The Actual Function Name Inside The Flash
         UI-->
      <function name="SetEndGameText" funcname=
         "SetEndGameText">
```

```
        <!--Specify The Function Arguments That This Method
            Has.-->
        <param name="Text" desc="The Text You Want The End
            Game Menu To Display" type="String" />
    </function>
</functions>
<!--Specify All Of The Event That This UI Element Has.
    (These Are The "fscommands" That The Flash UI
    Calls).-->
<events>
    <!--Give The Event A Name That CRYENGINE Will Use To
        Identify The Event In C++ Code.-->
    <!--Specify The "fscommand" That Backs This Event.-->
    <!--Specify The Description That Will Be Visible To
        The C++ Code And Flowgraph.-->
    <event name="Main_Menu_Button_Clicked" fscommand=
        "Main_Menu_Button_Clicked" desc="Triggered When The
        'Main Menu' Button Is Clicked." />
    <event name="Quit_Button_Clicked" fscommand=
        "Quit_Button_Clicked" desc="Triggered When The
        'Quit' Button Is Clicked." />
</events>

</UIElement>

</UIElements>
```

3. That's it, CRYENGINE will now automatically load our UI elements into the memory and make them available to C++.

Implementing a game menu system in C++

Now that we have all of the Flash UI content created and ready to go, it's time to connect it to the C++ layer of CRYENGINE via a game menu system. This system is very basic; however, it is quite powerful when communicating with ActionScript, such as when responding to events (**fscommands**). All we need is a small class that will listen to all of the events that Flash dispatched to us via fscommands. We will then use this listener mechanic to respond to various events, helping us develop a framework to display our various game menus.

So let's see how this is done:

1. Create a new header file called `CGameUIListener.h` that will be used to declare our game's menu system (Flash UI listener). Create a class called `CGameUIListener` that publicly inherits from `IUIElementEventListener`. This will allow us to receive all events from particular UI elements. The code should look as follows:

```
#pragma once

#include <IFlashUI.h>


//////////////////////////////////////////////////////////
/// <summary>
/// A Game UI Listener Class. Used To Listen For Flash UI Events
For Specific UI Elements.
/// </summary>
/// <seealso cref="T:IUIElementEventListener"/>
//////////////////////////////////////////////////////////
class CGameUIListener : public IUIElementEventListener
{
public:
  CGameUIListener();
  ~CGameUIListener();

  ///////////////////////IUIElementEventListener/////////////

  //////////////////////////////////////////////////////////
  /// <summary>
  /// Called Automatically When A UI Element Event Has
  ///     Occurred. Used To Handle Logic For UI Element
  /// Events.
  /// </summary>
  /// <param name="pSender"> [in,out] The UI Element That
  ///     Sent The Event. </param>
  /// <param name="event"> The UI Event That Occurred.
  ///     </param>
  /// <param name="args"> The Arguments That Are Tied To
  ///     The Event. </param>
  //////////////////////////////////////////////////////////
```

```
virtual void OnUIEvent( IUIElement* pSender, const
    SUIEventDesc& event, const SUIArguments& args );

////////////////////CGameUIListener////////////////

private:

};
```

2. Now that we have our listener class declared, lets implement the
   OnUIEvent() method. It should look as follows:

```
#include "stdafx.h"
#include "CGameUIListener.h"


CGameUIListener::CGameUIListener()
{
}




CGameUIListener::~CGameUIListener()
{
}



////////////////////IUIEventListener////////////////


void CGameUIListener::OnUIEvent( IUIElement* pSender, const
SUIEventDesc& event, const SUIArguments& args )
{
  //If The Start Game Button Was Clicked, Then We Should
    Hide The Main Menu And Load The First Map.
  if( string( event.sDisplayName ) == string(
    "Start_Game_Button_Clicked" ) )
  {
  }
  //If The Quit Game Button Was Clicked, Then We Should
    Hide The Main Menu And Shutdown The Game And
    Application.
```

```
    else if( string( event.sDisplayName ) == string(
      "Quit_Game_Button_Clicked" ) )
    {
    }
    //If The Main Menu Button Was Clicked, Then We Should
      Hide The End Game Menu And Show The Main Menu.
    else if( string( event.sDisplayName ) == string(
      "Main_Menu_Button_Clicked" ) )
    {
    }
    //If The Quit Button Was Clicked, Then We Should Hide The
      End Game Menu And Shutdown The Game And Application.
    else if( string( event.sDisplayName ) == string(
      "Quit_Button_Clicked" ) )
    {
    }
}
```

3. As you can see, we now have a game menu system that allows us to respond to various UI events. Now, let's implement the menu display logic. We simply need to show/hide the menus depending on which button is clicked. The code should look as follows:

```
#include "stdafx.h"
#include "CGameUIListener.h"
#include <IGame.h>
#include <IGameFramework.h>


CGameUIListener::CGameUIListener()
{
}




CGameUIListener::~CGameUIListener()
{
}


////////////////////////IUIEventListener////////////////
```

```
void CGameUIListener::OnUIEvent( IUIElement* pSender, const
  SUIEventDesc& event, const SUIArguments& args )
{
  //If The Start Game Button Was Clicked, Then We Should
    Hide The Main Menu And Load The First Map.
  if( string( event.sDisplayName ) == string(
    "Start_Game_Button_Clicked" ) )
  {
    gEnv->pFlashUI->GetUIElement( "Main_Menu" )->
      SetVisible( false );
    gEnv->pConsole->ExecuteString( "map Level_1", false,
      true );
  }
  //If The Quit Game Button Was Clicked, Then We Should
    Hide The Main Menu And Shutdown The Game And
    Application.
  else if( string( event.sDisplayName ) == string(
    "Quit_Game_Button_Clicked" ) )
  {
    gEnv->pFlashUI->GetUIElement( "Main_Menu" )->
      SetVisible( false );
    gEnv->pGame->GetIGameFramework()->Shutdown();
  }
  //If The Main Menu Button Was Clicked, Then We Should
    Hide The End Game Menu And Show The Main Menu.
  else if( string( event.sDisplayName ) == string(
    "Main_Menu_Button_Clicked" ) )
  {
    gEnv->pFlashUI->GetUIElement( "End_Menu" )->SetVisible(
      false );
    gEnv->pFlashUI->GetUIElement( "Main_Menu" )->
      SetVisible( true );
  }
  //If The Quit Button Was Clicked, Then We Should Hide The
    End Game Menu And Shutdown The Game And Application.
  else if( string( event.sDisplayName ) == string(
    "Quit_Button_Clicked" ) )
  {
    gEnv->pFlashUI->GetUIElement( "End_Menu" )->SetVisible(
      false );
    gEnv->pGame->GetIGameFramework()->Shutdown();
  }
}
```

Notice how we retrieve the various menus using the
GetUIElement() method from the IFlashUI interface.
Also, we show/hide menus by simply calling the
SetVisible() method of IUIElement.

As you can see, when either of the "quit" buttons are clicked, we tell
IGameFramework to use Shutdown(). This will shut down the game and close
the application.

4. Now that our game menu system is created, we need to perform one last
    step. In order for our game menu system to actually receive UI events,
    we need to register the UI elements with it. Navigate to the CGASGame.h
    file and add a member variable named m_pGameUIListener of type
    CGameUIListener* to the CGASGame class:

    ```
    class CGASGame : public IGame, public ISystemEventListener,
      public IPlatformOS::IPlatformListener, public
      IGameFrameworkListener
    {
    public:
        .. .. .. .. .. ..
        .. .. .. .. .. ..
        .. .. .. .. .. ..
        .. .. .. .. .. ..

    private:
        .. .. .. .. .. ..
        .. .. .. .. .. ..
    .. .. .. .. .. ..
        /// <summary> The Listener For The Games User Interface.
            </summary>
        CGameUIListener* m_pGameUIListener;
    };
    ```

5. Next, we need to instantiate and delete our game menu system when the
    time comes. Instantiate the game menu system in the Init() method of the
    CGASGame class, and then delete the game menu system in the destructor of
    the CGASGame class. The code should look as follows:

    ```
    bool CGASGame::Init( IGameFramework *pFramework )
    {
        .. .. .. .. .. ..
        .. .. .. .. .. ..
        .. .. .. .. .. ..
    ```

```
//Create The Game's UI Event Listener.
m_pGameUIListener = new CGameUIListener();
//Initialization Was Successful.
return true;
}




CGASGame::~CGASGame()
{
  .. .. .. .. .. ..
  .. .. .. .. .. ..
  .. .. .. .. .. ..

  //Delete The Game Menu Listener If It Exists.
  if( m_pGameUIListener )
    delete m_pGameUIListener;
  m_pGameUIListener = nullptr;

  //Very Important That This Method Gets Called.  Notifies
    All CRYENGINE Systems That Our Game Has Ended.
  GetISystem()->SetIGame( nullptr );
}
```

6. Lastly, we need to register the UI elements to our game menu system and show the main menu when the application starts. The code is as follows:

```
void CGASGame::OnSystemEvent( ESystemEvent event, UINT_PTR
  wparam, UINT_PTR lparam )
{
  switch( event )
  {
    case ESYSTEM_EVENT_GAME_POST_INIT_DONE:
    {
      //Register The Game's UI Event Listener And Show The
        Main Menu.
      auto pUIElement = gEnv->pFlashUI->GetUIElement(
        "Main_Menu" );
      pUIElement->AddEventListener( m_pGameUIListener,
        "Game UI Listener" );
      pUIElement->SetVisible( true );
```

```
        gEnv->pFlashUI->GetUIElement( "End_Menu" )->
          AddEventListener( m_pGameUIListener, "Game UI
          Listener" );
      }
      break;
      .. .. .. .. .. ..
      .. .. .. .. .. ..
      .. .. .. .. .. ..
      default:
      break;
    }
  }
```

Summary

Congratulations! You successfully learned how to create a complete game menu in Flash ActionScript 2 and integrate it into the C++ code of our game. From here on out, you have the knowledge to build amazing user interfaces for any game you choose to make. Everything you learned here will be all you need to know in order to make any UI possible. The code to do so may be more complex; however, it's still just more of the same—creating the UI content, communicating events to CRYENGINE using fscommands, creating UI element definition XMLs for the Flash content, and implementing C++ logic.

6
The Modeling Workflow for Game Characters and Tools

In this chapter, we will discuss character art workflow principles, terminology, and preparing for the tasks ahead. This chapter will cover some of the core fundamentals of character art such as modeling and setting up an efficient workflow and application setup for the software packages used in the following chapters. So, you will learn about Autodesk Maya, Pixologic Zbrush, and Adobe Photoshop.

3D character creation for games is a vast topic and we will cover some of the basic and typical workflows for creating believable characters for your games. The workflow covers a broad overview and takes into account the character creation methods for any high-end gaming systems. So, it's worth noting that depending on what game you are developing the character for, the workflow can be adjusted to suit the needs of the project. In this chapter, we will cover the following topics:

- Getting started with modeling
- Installing the CRYENGINE SDK
- Installing CryTools
- Modeling workflow overview

Getting started

Before getting started with creating a character or any modeling, it's important to make sure that we have installed all the correct tools and applications. For game development, we use a series of industry-standard tools and here is a list of example software that we can use to make characters and assets. Ultimately, the tools are a personal preference as the techniques are transferable between each package.

Software	Used for
Autodesk Maya and Autodesk 3DS Max	Lowpoly and/or highpoly modeling
Autodesk Mudbox and Pixologic Zbrush	Highpoly modeling and detailing
Autodesk Mudbox, Pixologic Zbrush, and Adobe Photoshop	Texturing

In order for the CRYENGINE pipeline to work effectively, please make sure you have one of the recommended software packages installed. For the following chapters, we will use Autodesk Maya, Pixologic Zbrush, and Adobe Photoshop. As we will be using these applications, our focus will be on using these tools but all the techniques are applicable to any of the recommended applications.

Installing the CRYENGINE SDK

When we are working with CRYENGINE, we will need to install the correct plugins for our preferred modeling package. Right now, the plugins are available for either Autodesk Maya or 3DS Max. These plugins allow us to create materials and export our model to work within the engine. There is also a required Adobe Photoshop plugin for texture exporting that we need to install; this exporter uses a Crytek-developed TIFF exporter for compressing the memory size of your textures. If you do not have the SDK, it can be downloaded from the Crytek website or via Steam.

Installing CryTools

When we install the plugins and tools, we have a couple of options available to us. We can either use the CryToolsInstaller application or we can manually install each plugin/tool in the required directory. Here, we will cover the CryToolsInstaller. If you would prefer to do it manually, please refer to the guide for each application on how to do this.

For the following chapters, we need to make sure that the plugins are installed for either Maya or 3DS Max and Photoshop. The steps are as follows:

1. Go to the location where the CRYENGINE directory was installed on your PC. If you used Steam, this will be in ...\Games\Steam\SteamApps\common\ CRYENGINE\Tools, as shown in the following screenshot:

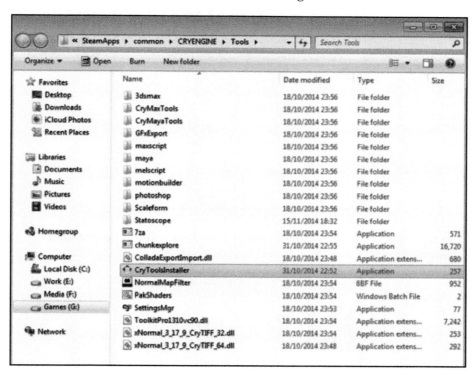

2. Scroll down until you see **CryToolsInstaller**, start the program, and follow the onscreen instructions.

3. In the second window, select which tools you want to be installed and hit **Next**.

As we progress through the following chapters, we will go through how to use each of the Crytools as we use them.

An overview of the modeling workflow

Before we get started, we should get an overview of the character development workflow to familiarize ourselves with any terminology. If you want to delve further into game art workflows, I recommend that you do some additional reading to gain a more in-depth understanding of all the techniques.

The workflow for character modeling can be broken down into five steps that are completed in the logical order with each step taking various amounts of time depending on the needs of the character model.

Blockout

The first step is always to blockout your model with a basemesh. Here, the process is to develop a model that will have the volumes and all the elements blocked out to the correct size and proportions. This step is also sometimes called a **whitebox** model. When we are working in a production environment, this model is used to allow the technical artist to build the rig so that the model can be used in in-game testing.

Highpoly modeling

The second step in the process is to create a detailed model that we will later use to create texture maps that are transferred to the lowpoly model. The process of creating the highpoly can be achieved in a couple of ways depending on what the model requirements are, and it can be achieved in any of the discussed modeling packages. The most common combination is that hard-surface models are created in traditional 3D packages with the details finalized in a sculpting package.

However, with recent advancements in software, this is also achievable in a sculpting package.

Lowpoly modeling

Depending on the brief for the character model and what platform we are working on, lowpoly modeling can be done in a couple of different ways—if we are developing a character that does not require the details of a highpoly. We can box-model the character further from basemesh. In the upcoming chapters, we will look at a process called **retopologizing**, which is where we take the highpoly model and model over it to capture the forms. This process is common in high-end development, as it allows us to transfer the details of the highpoly to the lowpoly via baking a normal map. Normal map baking is where the normals of the highpoly are transferred to the lowpoly with the use of a baking application such as xNormal.

UV mapping

The process of UV mapping creates a laid out version of the model that we can use to texture. The process is similar to skinning an animal and then laying the furs out in a logical way that can be used to apply the textures. This process requires us to be efficient, as we have limited space to get all the elements laid out. It is also important to make sure the UVs are laid out with as little stretching as possible, as shown in the following screenshot:

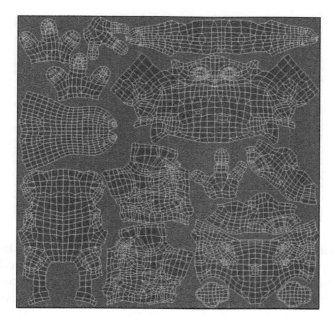

Texturing and materials

The texturing process is a fun part of character creation, as we can now add the colors and add additional details to the model that we were not able to do before. Here, we will also create several texture maps—ranging from the diffuse and specular to the normal map that we get from a process we call *baking from the highpoly model*. As with every step of this process, there is more than one way to achieve the desired map.

When we develop the textures, we will also set up the in-game materials to get the desired effects—ranging from metal to skin—with the use of a subsurface scattering.

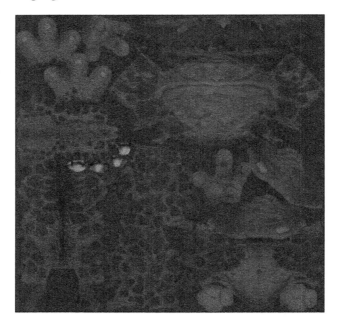

As we can see from the overview, the process is broken down to distinct chunks. Within those chunks, there are multiple ways of achieving the desired effect based on what the intentional use of the model or asset is. Today's workflow is nonlinear in order to allow us, as artists, to be more free with our creative decisions along the way. This nonlinear approach will allow us to go back to any point in the process without causing extensive reworks to other parts of the process, so we are not restricted at any point of the character development process.

Now that we have a broad overview and have all the tools installed, we can start with the details of the modeling workflow. The workflow is typical of what is used today in game studios producing titles across all platforms, ranging from mobile to high-end gaming systems and PCs. Throughout this chapter, we have looked at the overall process and how to install the tools and plugins required to get us started. This broad knowledge will help us to understand the following chapter more clearly and why we are working through the character model in this particular way.

Summary

In this chapter, we saw character art workflow principles, terminology, and how to prepare for the tasks ahead. We also saw some of the core fundamentals of character art, such as modeling and setting up an efficient workflow and application setup for the software packages. We covered some of the basic and typical workflows for creating believable characters for your games; the workflow covers a broad overview and takes into account character creation methods for high-end gaming systems.

In the next chapter, you will learn how to create a highpoly model and determine its uses in-game in current and next-gen game development.

Highpoly Modeling

7

In this chapter, we will look into why we create a highpoly model and its uses in game in current and next-gen game development. Here, we will be working through some of the principles of highpoly modeling and going over a basic workflow for creating the highpoly in Zbrush. Here, we will also cover preparing the model for lowpoly work such as mesh decimation and exporting to an external application. We will also highlight the importance of checking the model at this stage for proportions for rigging.

Blockout

Before we get stuck into the modeling the highpoly, it is important to make sure that your model has the correct proportions and has all the larger elements and forms that appear in any concept art. It is important to make sure the correct proportions are set out to allow for the character to be tested in the game. By making sure we have the correct size, we will avoid the character from being imported into the game at a scale that is out of proportion with the rest of the game.

Depending on your preference, you can do this in either a traditional modeling package or within your sculpting application. What is ultimately important here is that the correct proportions of the character are adhered to, as the last thing we want here is to model the character to the wrong height and dimensions.

If you are using a modeling package such as Maya, this is easily achieved by using the measuring tool. If you were to dive straight in and use Zbrush with DynaMesh, then there is a real possibility that your model will not be the correct size and height. I have a guide that is created for a primitive within Maya. I can take it into Zbrush to get around this problem.

The steps are as follows:

1. First, we need to make sure your measuring units are set to centimeters and not inches. To do this, go to **Window** | **SettingsPreferences** | **Settings**.

2. Open Maya, create a scene, and draw out a cube. Make sure that you align the cube to (0, 0, 0).

3. Switch to the front view, select the measuring tool, and draw out 183 cm. This is the average height of a male human. The measuring tool is located at **Create** | **MeasureTools** | **DistanceTool**.

4. From the 0 of *x*, draw out 25 cm from the center line; as the average width is 50 cm, this will give us a good idea of ideal width.

5. Scale the cube to fit these measurements. Be careful about the *z* depth of the cube; it should not be too excessive.

6. Then, export the file as .obj.

This gives us a basic idea of the size to work with. If you are creating a fantasy character or creature, then you will push these forms; however, it's a good starting point and avoids hassles when creating the lowpoly model and baking the required textures.

The next step is to bring the reference mesh into Zbrush; when bringing the mesh into Zbrush, it is important to remember a couple of steps to make sure the same scale is kept:

1. Open Zbrush and select the star primitive that can be found in the tool rollout.

2. Draw the star onto the canvas and hit *T*.

3. Click on **Import** and bring the reference mesh into Zbrush.

By following this procedure, you will make sure that the reference mesh maintains the same scale as that set out in Maya. It is also worth noting the export rollout at the bottom of the **Tool** menu, as this should be noted and kept at these settings to make sure that when we export the highpoly for creating the lowpoly, the correct size is maintained to avoid any potential scaling issues.

Highpoly

Now that we are in Zbrush, we use the scale reference to aid us as we start blocking out the forms of the body—starting with a sphere primitive utilizing the DynaMesh function. DynaMesh allows us to be more creative and treat the model in the same way as we would a piece of clay, allowing for a much more natural approach to our creations.

DynaMesh will keep adding new geometry to the model as we sculpt, avoiding the need to subdivide the mesh as we work. It will also keep the mesh even, to avoid faceting.

When working with DynaMesh and creating the highpoly, it is important to remember a few simple rules that will make the sculpting experience more fun:

- When starting, keep the mesh as low as possible to allow for quick iteration.

- Increase the density of the mesh only when it's reached the maximum of its integrity. Going too high too soon will slow down the process and make it harder to smooth out the mesh as we are working.

Using DynaMesh

Draw the sphere on the canvas and scale it to roughly the same size as the reference mesh. Expand the geometry rollout in the tool palette to reveal the DynaMesh options, as shown here:

DynaMesh options in the Tools rollout

We will start by keeping the resolution low and turning off the **Project** function, as this will slow us down as we use the tools to blockout the mesh. Hit the **DynaMesh** button and you will notice the mesh on screen has changed.

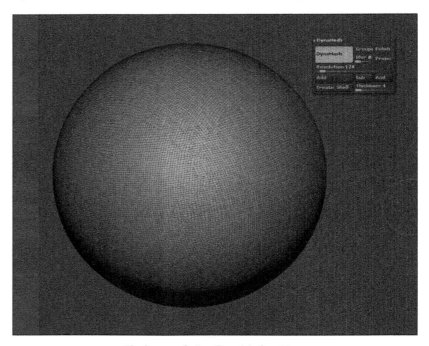

The low resolution DynaMesh settings

Now that we have the DynaMesh set up, we can use a handful of brushes to rough out the basic shape. Here, we will use the Move brush to rough out the torso mass. As you work, you will notice the mesh is becoming broken and faceted as the mesh is pulled and stretched. To bring back the resolution of the mesh, we will hold down the *Shift* key and then drag it in the open space on the canvas, allowing DynaMesh to recalculate the model evenly redistributing the polygons so we can continue working.

We will continue to work pulling out the mesh until we have the basic forms of the character we want to create. When we are working, we can add additional shapes with the Insert brushes and easily create the arms, legs, and head by drawing in the extra shapes. Then, holding down the *Shift* key and dragging in the background, increase the resolution of the mesh.

Highpoly sculpting techniques

Now that we have the base mesh set out, we can start to develop our forms further adding details as we go. When working the highpoly, a small set of brushes is all that is required.

The following is a list of the typical brushes. When working with Zbrush, it is always worth remembering how powerful the brush options are and to experiment to get the best results:

- **Move**: When working with digital clay, we use the Move brush to push and pull the clay around to find the larger forms. The standard Move brush is the one we mostly use but there are others that I recommend experimenting around with, as they all work slightly differently.

- **ClayTubes**: When defining the sculpted forms from the base mesh, this brush in one of the most useful as it will allow us to build up the overall volumes quickly. When you are in the early stages of the highpoly, we will use this brush the most. As you become more familiar with sculpting in Zbrush, this will become one of the most valuable brushes in your toolset.

- **Standard**: This is another essential brush to use and is extremely versatile when combined with the brush actions and an alpha. This brush will be the first one you encounter and will give us a clean simple sculpted effect on the surface of the model.

- **Dam_Standard**: Once this was an optional brush and had to be downloaded, but it now comes as standard with the more recent versions of Zbrush. We will use this brush to cut and carve into our mesh to help define specifics of our model. This is another brush that will become invaluable in your day to day work.

We will use other brushes, but the ones listed are the ones that personally I find I return to when doing the largest amount of the highpoly sculpting work.

Sculpting out the forms

Before diving straight into the modeling, we will need to make sure our mesh is set up in way that we will find easy to work with. For this, we will need to set up polygroups. By setting up some basic polygroups, this will allow us to quickly select or hide parts of the model that we want to work on or will need to easily mask.

To set up the polygroups, we can use a quick technique to get this done:

1. Use the mask tool to masking out the arms up to and include the shoulders.

2. Press *Ctrl + W* to create a polygroup from the mask, you will notice that the mask has disappeared.

3. To check the polygroup, press *Shift + F* and then repeat the steps until you have the model broken up into easy to use chunks.

Now that we have the polygroups set out, we can use these to hide parts of the mesh in order to make working with the model easier. To hide any part of the model, press *Ctrl* and left-click on the polygroup we want to be visible. When we want to unhide other polygroups, we can press *Ctrl* and left-click again in the background of the canvas.

Adding the forms

Taking the base mesh base, we start to find our major forms using the ClayTubes and the Move brush. As you build up the forms, use the Smooth brush to knock back the forms and keep repeating these steps in order to find the larger forms.

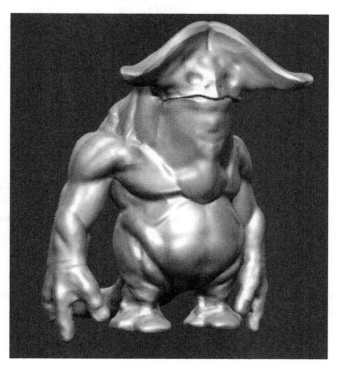

Basic forms added

When working with a fantasy character, keep in mind how your anatomy works. This is because keeping the model grounded towards this will help make the character more believable.

Blocking out the larger forms

 For this, I would recommend keeping an anatomy book or reference handy at all times.

Once we have the major forms blocked out, we can look to add more details to the mesh. As we are using the DynaMesh function as we model, when the mesh starts to look broken, we can use the DynaMesh algorithm to recalculate the mesh by holding *Shift* and dragging it in the open area of the canvas.

This basic and simple workflow is what we use when developing the mesh. It allows us to be creative, while not getting overly bogged down in technical areas. This is one of the joys of creating characters. Technology over the past few years has allowed for a more creative process that has empowered us as artists.

Adding more details

As we add more detail, we can step up the resolution of the DynaMesh.
To add more details, such as wrinkles, we use a combination of a few brushes
and Zbrush's surface options. Here, we use the Dam_Standard brush on a low
setting to create further details. By using a combination of carving and adding,
we can add some interesting details:

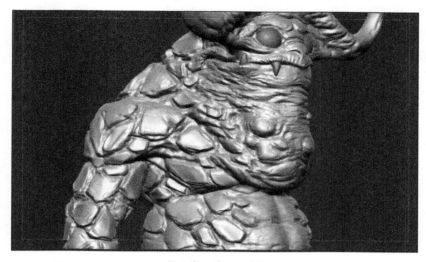

Detailing the model

For the more armored/stony elements of the character, the technique of carving and
then adding around the plated edges allows us to quickly build up the extra details.
As we do this, we then use the Trim dynamic brush to flatten out the extrusions to
create a more stone-like surface. Repeat the process until you are happy with the
way the detail is looking.

Adding fine details

There are a few different ways in which we can add details to the mesh for things such as skin pores or even the bumpy elements of the rock-like plates on the model's skin. When creating these details, we could use Alpha combined with the Standard brush, with drag set as the draw option. But I think we should explore the possibilities of the NoiseMaker for this.

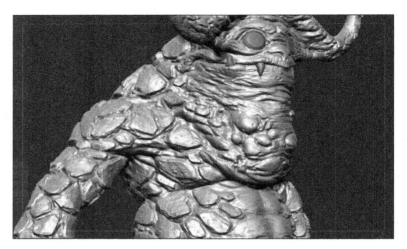

The model with details added

Let's start by opening NoiseMaker, which can be found in the **Surface** rollout of the **Tool** menu. On opening the rollout, we get a small selection of options.

The Surface menu

The NoiseMaker comes with a few examples that are included with Zbrush. However, we will explore making our own pattern with the powerful noise plug toolset.

Click on **Edit** and a pop-up window will appear; it includes a window that displays our model. This shows us how the model will look with the details applied. Right now, we can see the default details but we can open up the options further to create what we are looking for.

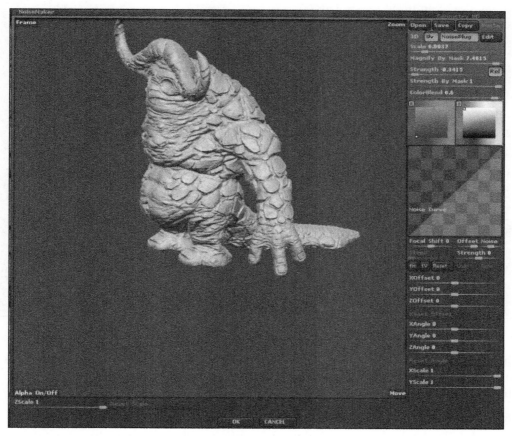

The NoiseMaker menu

We now have the options that will allow us to create our own specific details based on what we are looking for. The options here allow us to be as creative and make some unique details. I recommend experimenting with each of the different surface types to get familiar with the different ones available.

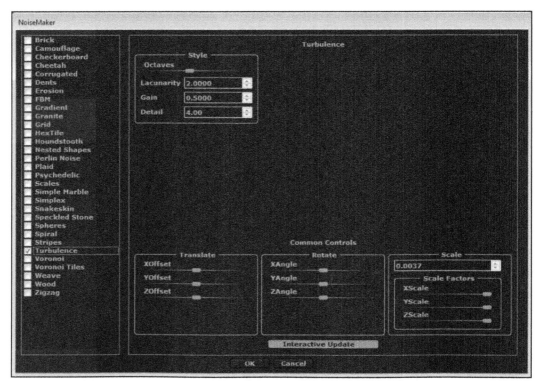

The Edit menu in NoiseMaker

Once we have found the one that fits our needs, we can click on **OK** and move back to the previous window. Don't worry if it's not exactly what is required, as we can still play around with the settings in the main option window.

Using these options, we can adjust the size, strength, and many other elements of the details. Again, I recommend experimenting with the options to see what each of them does.

Once we find what we are looking for, we can click on **OK** and return to the main workspace. However, before we apply this to the model, we need to consider a few things. Make sure that the density of the mesh is high enough to support the frequency of the details; if the mesh is too low, the details will get lost and blurred out.

We also need to consider where we would like the details to be applied. Right now, the details will be applied to the whole of the model. If we utilize the masking features, we can selectively choose where the details are applied.

Now that we have masked out the areas we wish for the details not to be applied, it is recommended that we create a layer to allow us to keep the details as nondestructive as possible.

This will also allow us to build up the details on separate layers and adjust them accordingly to reach the desired effect we are looking for. By making sure that we use layers, we enable ourselves to play with the details and avoid committing to what we have already set in place.

Keeping details on layers

Once the desired areas are masked and the layer is set up, the final step is to commit the details to the mesh. This is done by clicking on **Accept** so that the details are projected into the surface.

The hair system

For the character, we want to make a simple hair system that we can then bake to the lowpoly hair cards later. Before doing this, we will experiment with the fiber mesh to get a good understanding of how the hair will look and allow us to create the highpoly hair strands.

There are many tools and systems available to us but as we are only looking for a simple short fur, we can use fiber mesh to quickly give us a good result. The steps are as follows:

1. The first thing to do is to mask the areas we would like the hair to grow from; fiber mesh uses the masking as a way to isolate the hair growth.

2. Open up the **Fiber Mesh** rollout in the **Tool** menu. Instead of starting from scratch, we will use one of the supplied presets to give us a good base to work from.

3. I imagine the hair would be quite coarse and spiky. So, we can select the **Grass** preset as a base and work it up from there to get the desired hair.

Now that we have the grass fiber mesh in place, we can play with some of the settings to get the right kind of hair. When exploring what the hair should look like, we play around with a few of the settings. As with the NoiseMaker, please experiment to find various looks and styles.

The following are the main settings I experimented with to get the desired look:

- **Length**: This controls the overall length of the strands. You can also add variation to the length with the variation slider.

- **Amount**: With this, we can increase the number of hairs.

- **Coverage**: This will increase the overall coverage of the hairs. It is worth noting that if the amount of hairs is set low and the coverage is increased, the strands are wider.

- **Gravity**: The slider and the curve affect the way the hairs are affected by gravity, playing with this can give interesting results.

- **Spans and sides**: As we want to later export the hair as geometry for baking, we will need to make sure that each strand has at least four sides and enough spans to allow for a relatively smooth curve along the stands.

- **UVs**: It is important to make sure that this is active so that the fibers are given a UV of 0 to 1. Then, we can add a hair texture later when baking the textures.

By using the settings and building the hair up in segments, a simple hair system can be built that we can later use to create the lowpoly hair. In *Chapter 9, Texturing and Materials*, I will cover how to export and use this hair to help us build the textures.

Exporting the highpoly mesh

Now that we have created a highpoly model, we need to export it to create the lowpoly model. To prepare the mesh, we will use Decimation Master so that the model we export will not be too heavy when we bring it into our preferred application for creating the lowpoly model.

To find Decimation Master, we need to look in the **Plugins** rollup. This tool will allow us to reduce the polygon density of the model, while retaining the detail we will need for baking the maps later. Before using Decimation Master, we must make sure that all the layers we have created are baked down into the mesh.

When using Decimation Master, we can use the default settings. Click on **Pre-calculate** so that the mesh can be analyzed. Once it is done, click on **Decimate** to create a model that has lower polygons yet retains the details of the higher resolution mesh.

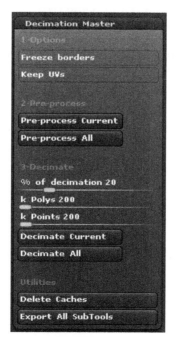

The Decimation Master menu

Now, all that we have to do is export. Before doing so, make sure to double check your export settings in the rollout to make sure the mesh maintains the original size.

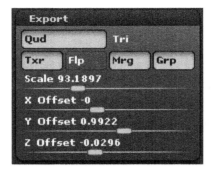

Checking export settings

Click on **Export** and export the mesh as an `.obj` file.

Summary

We discussed some of the techniques used to create an organic highpoly model. As with all areas of 3D character creation, there are varying techniques and I would always recommend playing around and being creative when looking for a solution for something you are looking to create.

Now that we have the highpoly done, we can move forward to the next chapter and look at creating a lowpoly model that we can take into the CRYENGINE.

8
Lowpoly Modeling

In this chapter, we will look at lowpoly generation and some of the more important areas to remember, such as efficient topology and areas to remember for deformation, other important topics such as efficient UV mapping, and how to generate LODs from the original lowpoly. Here, we will highlight what tools should be used and go through the workflow that is used for the example. We will also go over the importance of clear naming and scene setup to make the transition to skinning smoother.

Creating the lowpoly model

Now that we have the highpoly, we need to make a lowpoly model that can be used with the engine efficiently. Right now, the model is too dense, so it will not be able to be rigged and ultimately used for any game. In order to achieve this, we must build a lowpoly mesh over the highpoly, create UVs, and then bake down the details for the highpoly to the lowpoly so that we can get the same level of detail without the burden of the highpoly polycount.

Tools

As with all parts of this process, there is no set tool that you must use to achieve the end result and you are free to choose whichever application you wish to do it in as the process fundamentals are the same.

For the process of retopologizing, you can use standalone applications such as Topogun or you can achieve the same result with any of the traditional modeling packages such as Maya or 3DS Max. Here, we will not cover the technical differences between the packages, but focus on the requirements of a good topology model with efficient UVs that will be efficient for rigging and skinning. As we move through this chapter, I will be using Topogun to make a lowpoly and Maya to create the UVs.

Getting started

The first thing we need to do is bring the highpoly model into Topogun and use this as our reference model. We use the decimated version of the highpoly that we exported at the end of the previous chapter. As stated in the previous chapter, it is ideal to bring in a decimated version of the mesh to make life easier for our hardware and to avoid a sluggish process that will frustrate us.

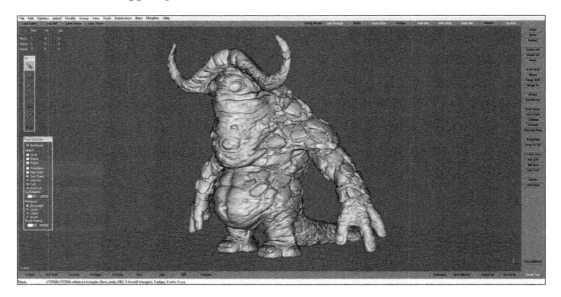

Now that we have our reference model loaded, we can start to draw on the lowpoly model. This process can take some time and it is important not to rush it, as we are aiming for a clean lowpoly model.

Topology and edgeflow

The edgeflow of the model is important as the model will be rigged and skinned for engine use, so we have to consider the deformation of the model and make sure it has a good topology and edgeflow.

If we do not, then the model could deform incorrectly when animated.

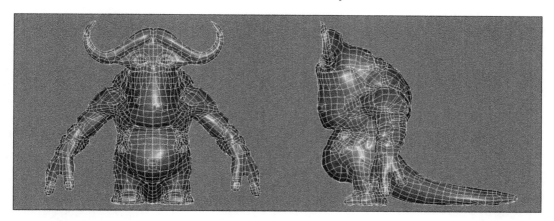

This is where it's good to have some understanding of anatomy and topology to allow for a successful model. When working with a technical artist, it is always worth getting feedback on the lowpoly as you progress to avoid any potential issues that would mean going back and doing considerable rework.

As we can see, here the topology follows the flowing lines of the model. If you are unfamiliar with doing topology for deformation, it is worth considering using the polypaint functionality of Zbrush to draw on the edgeflow before exporting the model for lowpoly work.

Good and bad topology

Looking at the character, we have to assess what the key areas of deformation would be. For this character, as well as the usual areas of deformation, we have to consider how his belly, neck waddle, and tail would deform and behave.

A key thing to remember when creating the mesh is to stick to quad polygons as much as possible; if you have to include triangles, then try to place these in areas of little deformation or areas of little visibility.

Here is an example of the topology used:

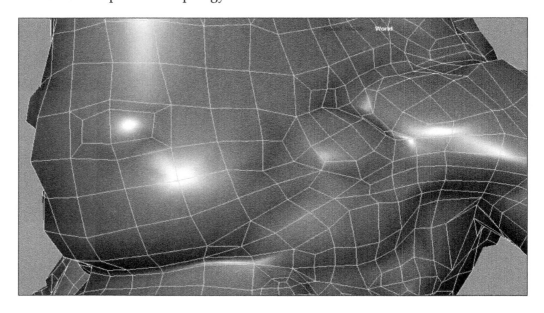

Here is another example of the topology used:

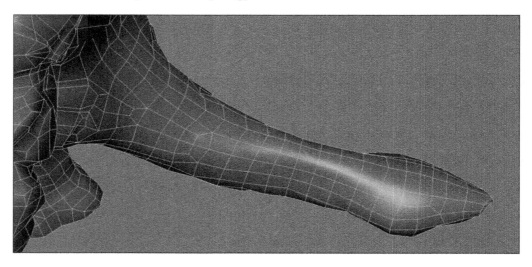

Building the lowpoly

For developing this topology, we will be using Topogun. It is a powerful and simple application for getting great game meshes quickly and cleanly, but a similar workflow can be used with either the Maya quad draw or Max graphite modeling tools.

When we are creating a lowpoly, we always need to consider the polygon budget for the model. The budget is always in triangles and can vary greatly between projects depending on what platform the project is being developed for. For this model, we will have a budget of around 10,000 triangles as this would be a rough ideal number for Xbox 360 or PS3, but newer hardware could have a higher polycount.

Topogun has some great features for creating complex topology; for what we need to do, we can focus on a few of the key tools that will also be very similar to other applications in how they perform. Before we start to build the mesh, if you have painted on your edgeflow lines, you can make them visible by selecting **Make Vertex Colors Visible** in the menu.

If you want to use vertex colors, select **Options | Use Vertex Colors**.

For this model, we can use the mirror function as the majority of the model is symmetrical in volume and the medium to smaller details take care of the asymmetrical look of the character. When working the symmetry, there are two ways of working and this is a personal preference on how you work. I prefer to work with the symmetry function switched to off and mirror over the geometry once I have created the larger forms; once mirrored, I refine the mesh further by adding the extra polygons where the asymmetrical details are.

If you want to use symmetry, use the *X* hotkey.

Now, we can start to build the mesh over the highpoly. When creating the mesh, I prefer to start on a larger area where there will be deformation when the character is animated. To start drawing the mesh, we simply place vertices on the model and draw a face and edges when a polygon is formed.

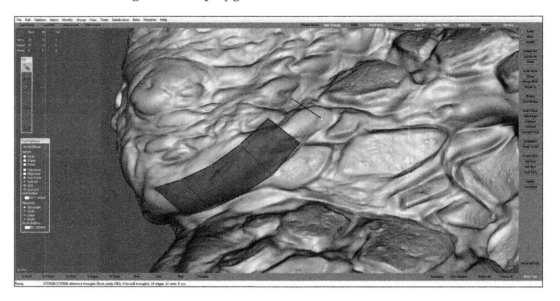

We will continue to draw out the mesh on the model while keeping in mind the topology of the anatomy moving around the model from area to area, making sure that important areas of deformation such as elbows and knees have efficient edgeflow to allow good deformation when the model is animated.

Once we have fully modeled the character, the next step is to mirror it over so that we have a nearly complete mesh.

The next step is to add any asymmetrical details. For this character, we can add a couple of extra polygons to the neck waddle to emphasize the details.

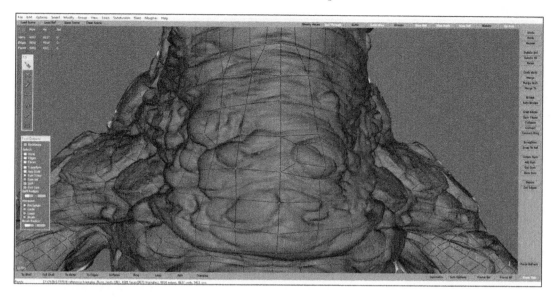

Right now, the model is 8,248 triangle polygons, which seems like a good number as we are yet to add the eyes or the polycards for the details of the fur.

Creating UVs

Before we add the other elements, we need to create the UVs for the body. For this character, we will break the model into separate UV tiles and the body mass will be one of them. Even though we will use one multimaterial in the engine, we can use multiple maps for the one character.

The first thing we need to do is to make sure the model has some UVs. If it does not have any, then we can quickly create some in Maya by going to **Create UVs | Create UVs Based On Camera**.

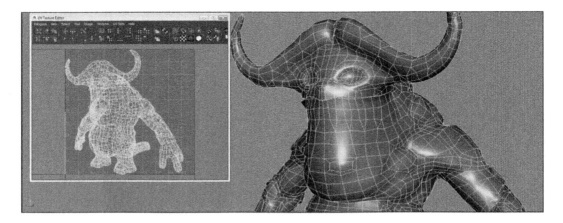

This will give us some UVs, but right now, they are not usable for texturing.

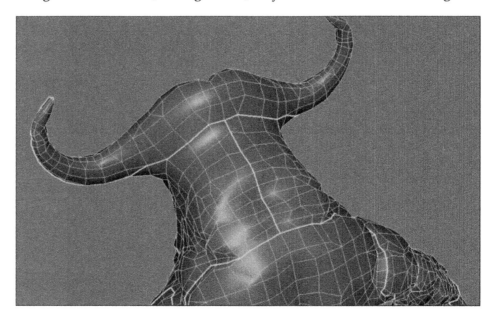

When creating the UVs, we need to make sure that the seams are in areas that will be least visible to the player in order to minimize (as much as possible) visible seams.

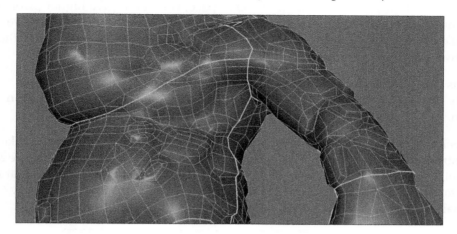

When cutting up the model, we will separate the model into an efficient set of UV islands such as arms, legs, and the tail.

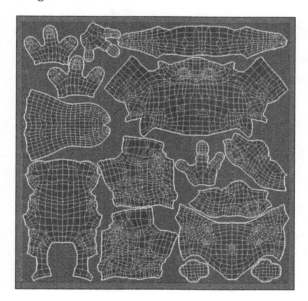

When laying out the UVs, we have to consider how the character model will be used and viewed by the player. For instance, when laying out the UVs for an NPC for a first-person shooter in the UV space, we would give higher priority to the head—working down the smaller UV space for the boots. The reason we should consider this (where the player camera may fall) is because, as a rule, there will always be more focus on anything that is at eye level.

For this character, we will work on the premise that the model will be viewed equally from all angles and, as such, we need to make sure the UV distribution is even.

To check this, we use a simple checker texture and scale the UV islands to make sure the distribution is even. When arranging the islands, we have to make sure we are as efficient as possible with the spacing between them. It is also worth noting that it is important to consider the texturing process and lay the UVs out in such a way that will make sense when we start the texturing.

 It is also important to note that CRYENGINE does not support multiple UV channels.

Adding the eyes

The eyes are simple to create and consist of three elements: the ball, the cover, and the wetness. The eyeball will carry the color information, while the cover will take care of the gloss or wet look of the eye and the final element of the wetness helps to give the impression that the eye is connected to the body.

To create the eye, we need to take the body mesh into Maya:

1. If you have been creating the lowpoly in another program, we will use this mesh as a guide.

2. Next, we create a cube with equal sides and then hit 3 on the keyboard. This will turn off subdivision modeling and the cube will turn into a sphere. Once we have done this, we will need to convert the subdivision preview mesh into a workable mesh.

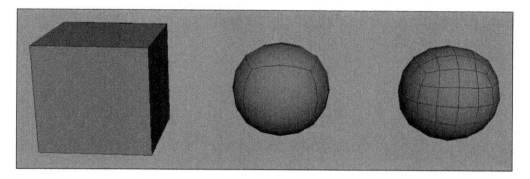

3. To do this, go to **Edit | Convert | Subdivision preview to polygons**.

4. We now have a sphere with equal ploys and we do not have the issue of a pointed star that we would have had if we had used a sphere primitive.

5. As we will use the same mesh for the cover, we need to give the mesh some UVs. For this, we swap to the front view and frame the mesh by hitting *F*. Next, we create the UVs and select **Create UVs Based On Camera** to give us good workable UVs that we can use for the eye texturing.

6. Next, we duplicate the mesh and slightly scale it to create our eye cover. It is also recommended that we group the two meshes together to make life easier.

7. The next part we need to create is the wetness that goes around the eye. This is simple to create, as we select the face loops that go around the eye socket and duplicate them; as we made the UVs earlier, the duplication will come with the UVs that we can keep for this purpose.

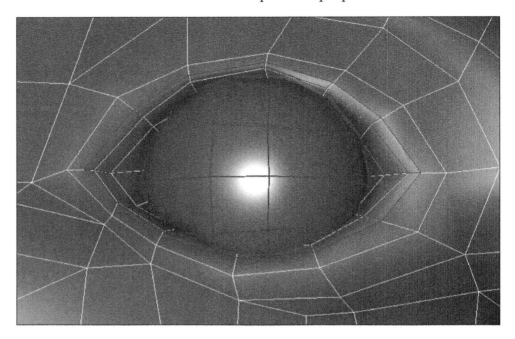

Naming and organizing a Maya scene

Now that we have nearly all the elements in the scene with the exception of the hair cards, it is time to make sure the scene is organized. When it is handed over for rigging and skinning, it will become easier for the artist to pick the file up.

Naming

The first thing to do is to delete any unwanted meshes or materials before we move forward. Once this is done, I use the naming and grouping illustrated in the following screenshot.

By keeping key elements (such as the eyes) grouped, it will make the scene easier to navigate.

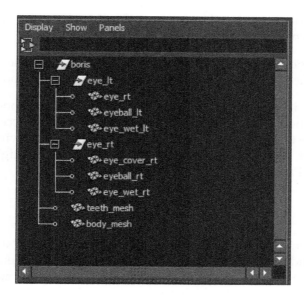

In Maya, select the meshes and then use *Ctrl + G* to group meshes together. You can place groups within a larger group as I have done here with the eyes.

As Maya does not allow name reproduction between different scene elements (such as meshes, materials, and layers), we can use a simple suffix to solve this.

Here's a set of examples:

- `_grp`: This is used for group naming
- `_lyr`: This is used for layer naming
- `_mesh`: This is used for geometry naming
- `_mat`: This is used for material naming

So, for example, a mesh could have the naming convention, `head_mesh`, and the material for that head could have `head_mat`.

Layers

For scene navigation, we can also place elements into layers so that we can quickly hide parts that we don't need in the viewport. To add meshes to a layer, simply select the meshes and then click on the icon.

You can add and remove elements from the layers by selecting the mesh and then right-clicking on the layer, which will bring up a set of layer options.

Scene organization is an important habit to get into. In a professional working environment, you never know when someone else will need to access your work in your absence for tasks, such as bug fixing. In a complicated environment such as game development, being confronted with a messy scene with a tight deadline is both confusing and frustrating.

LODs

During development, we will have to optimize the game in order to avoid performance-related issues that could potentially spoil the experience for the player. One way we help this is by creating lower versions of the model called LODs, short for Level of Detail, which can be swapped at a certain draw distance from the camera.

As a rule of thumb, each LOD should be around 50 percent lower in polycount than the previous model, but this will always be dependent on what is required for the game. If we take this rule, we could see the following count:

- **LOD00**: 10,000 triangles
- **LOD01**: 5,000 triangles
- **LOD02**: 2,500 triangles
- **LOD03**: 1,250 triangles
- **LOD04**: 600 triangles

The primary LOD will be used close to the camera, but **LOD04** would never be any more than a few pixels high on the screen and, as such, would not need the level of detail seen in the mesh closest to the camera.

Creating LODs

Generating LODs can be a time-consuming task, but we can do a few things to make our lives easier. For each LOD, we could take the approach of retopologizing each LOD from the highpoly from scratch, but this would be both demotivating and not a very efficient use of our time.

If we consider our current lowpoly to be **LOD00**, we can optimize this mesh through careful consideration and, through a series of deleting edgeloops and collapsing edges, we can create the next LOD.

To start, duplicate the mesh and correct the naming of the mesh so that it has the suffix lod00, also for the ease of working, add this mesh to its own layer.

Before we start working we should make sure to have the edges of the UV islands visible on the mesh as we do not want to damage these. If we keep the same UV islands then we can use the same texture maps for all the LODs and let the engine control the resolution of the textures through MIP mapping.

Now that we have the scene set up we can proceed to carefully collapse and delete edges until we are near our target triangle count.

When creating the LODs the primary considerations must always be toward maintaining an efficient mesh for deformation and making sure we keep the silhouette of the character. If we fail to keep the silhouette intact, we will potentially see a LOD popping when the game is running. This should be avoided as much as possible because even though CRYENGINE can smoothly translate between the LODs, if the meshes do not do this effectively, then this effect will be broken.

Summary

Now that we have our lowpoly model we can look to texture the model and bake the required textures; when we are creating the lowpoly, it is important not to rush and make sure we take our time because doing it right first time will be far less frustrating. Even though lowpoly generation can be a fun task, the creation of the LODs can be tedious but it is important to remember that, as a character artist, your role is to create efficient lowpoly models for in-game use as well as beautiful highpoly sculpts.

In this chapter, we did not cover how to create the hair and add that to the model but we will cover that in the next chapter as this is primarily a texturing task.

9
Texturing and Materials

In this chapter, we will go over techniques to create and bake textures. We will look at tools such as Photoshop and Zbrush for creating texture maps. We will discuss how to bake the highpoly information to the lowpoly model using xNormal, and how these baked maps are used in texture creation. We will also look at the basics of **Physically based rendering (PBR)** techniques and what to consider when texturing for the CRYENGINE SDK. We will also cover exporting a CGF of the model to import into the engine to check the textures and how to create and set up the shaders in Maya and the SDK.

As with all parts of this process, there is more than one way to achieve the texturing due to the variety of tools that are available today. For this chapter, we will be using a workflow that uses a system of baking a set of maps and then texturing in Photoshop. While we will not cover a process from an artistic perspective, we will look at some of the technical aspects and processes that can be easily be implemented into any workflow.

Baking

For baking, we are going to use xNormal. It is a free application and is widely used within the gaming industry due to its ability to produce clean normal maps. You can download it from `http://www.xnormal.net`. The steps for baking are as follows:

1. Once the application is installed, the first thing we need to do is load in our highpoly and lowpoly meshes into the correct locations.

2. Once we have loaded them, we can select the maps we would like to output. We can select to output a normal map, ambient occlusion map, and a vertex color bake that will be our material ID map, to create quick masks in Photoshop later.

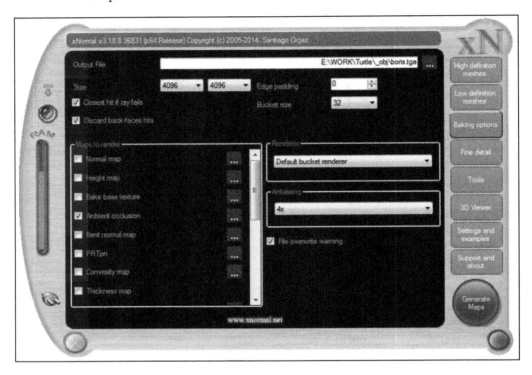

3. To create the material ID map for this character, we paint this in Zbrush onto the highpoly. When we export the highpoly, it will keep the color information that we can bake down.

 In order to bake the vertex colors, we have to check the box to allow vertex colors. When this is selected, we cannot bake the ambient occlusion map at the same time.

4. Now that we have everything set up, we can input an output folder for the maps and select our map baking size, edge padding, and various other options. The edge padding is important as this will negate seams when the model is seen in the engine. As we will be baking at a high resolution of 4096 x 4096 pixels, I would recommend setting this to around 15 pixels. If we bake at lower resolutions, we can half that number. For example, if we bake at 2048 x 2048 pixels, we should set edge padding to 7 to 8 pixels.

5. For the final texture size output, we will select 4096 x 4096 but it is recommended to complete the test bakes at a lower resolution as the larger the map the longer the bake will be.

Baking maps is not a process that can be rushed, so it is important to experiment with the settings until a good bake is achieved. Sometimes, it is required to complete multiple bakes and then combine the maps in Photoshop for cleanup.

Baking the fur and alphas

To make the fur, we have to transfer the details from the highpoly hair system we created in Zbrush to a selection of UVed polygon plains that will enable us to create the impression of hair when laid out. To do this, we first take our hair system in Zbrush and create a group of variations. The steps are as follows:

1. Inside Zbrush, we create a primitive plain and draw a circular mask. This will allow us to grow our variations.

2. Once we have the variations, we need to export them to Maya as `.obj` files. Before we do this, we need to make sure that each variation has UVs applied. This can be done by going to the UV rollout and clicking on **FiberUV**. This will lay out the UV in a 0 to 1 form so that we can apply a simple gradient for the hair color.

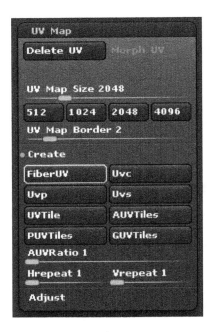

3. Once we have the highpoly meshes in Maya, we need to organize them into a single row, keeping space between each cluster of hair. We also need to create and align a set of polygon plains and assign and layout UVs for them.

4. Once we have everything aligned, we need to re-export the highpoly hair to one file and export the polygon cards as one file so that we can bake across the information.

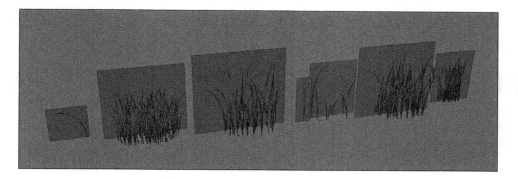

5. Now we need to load the meshes into xNormal, as we did before, but this time we can load in a texture onto the highpoly mesh. Therefore, we can bake down the diffuse map. For the texture, we open up Photoshop and create a gradient that will be assigned as the texture.

6. When we bake down the diffuse map, there will be an alpha map created that we use to cut out the shape of the hair strands.

7. Once we have all of the maps baked, we can start to build our textures. For the fur, as we now have the textures baked, we can build up that fur on the character. The process of laying out the hair is time-consuming and will require patience. Here, it is simpler to build up the general look before loading the mesh into the engine. Once we have the character loaded in the engine, we can come back and refine later.

Efficient psd setup

When texturing, the most commonly used application is Photoshop due to the powerful image manipulation tools. The workflow consists of building up the texture in layers in a nondestructive way that will allow us to experiment.

As we work, it is important to keep the scene organized. For this, a system of color coordinated groups with a clear naming convention is required that will not only allow anyone to pick up your work, but also to make sure that we don't get confused whilst we work.

Here's an example of setting out the psd:

Looking at the structure, we can load all of our maps in and set them into groups. As we don't have a gloss or a secular map at this time, we can set up dummy groups. We can keep textures such as the ID map and the ambient occlusion map in another group. In this group, we will keep all or odd textures that we create while making our final textures.

Using masks

Using masks is an efficient way to texture, as they allow us to isolate the specific areas we want to texture. To create them, we use the ID map we created by doing quick color selections in Photoshop. To make the selection, go to **Select | Color Range** and then pick the first color from the ID map.

Now that we have the color selected, we will see a selection mask. To turn the mask into a layer, first create a layer and then click on the layer mask icon.

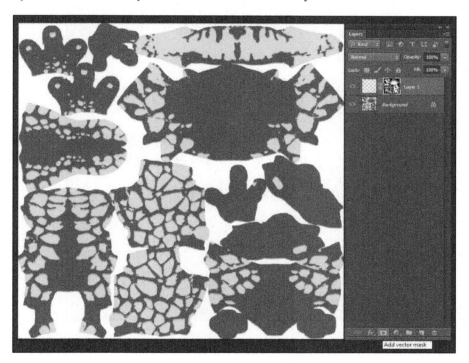

We continue to do this for all the different IDs, making sure to name them as we go. By working this way, we can quickly select the layer we need based on the part of the texture we are working on. With layer masks, we can use tiling textures so that we don't have to worry about manually deleting out parts of the texture every time.

Basics of PBR texturing

PBR is a rendering model that is now incorporated into CRYENGINE. This allows us to adopt a slightly different approach to texturing, allowing our textures to function in a realistic way in any lighting environment.

With this way of texturing, we have to make a few changes to the way we work:

- **Diffuse map**: A diffuse map is shown here:

The diffuse or albedo map is created just how a map is always created, with a few exceptions to the previous workflow. When creating this map, we must keep these rules in mind:

  - The map must have no lighting information baked into it
  - The map must be flat with no ambient occlusion or cavity overlaid

- When creating metals, all pure metals must have an almost black color as pure metals have no physical color

- Impure metals, for instance painted metals, can have color as they are treated as nonmetals because the paint is now covering the metal

By applying these simple rules we can create our map using similar methods we have used in the past.

- **Specular maps**: A specular map is shown here:

The specular map is used to define the materials, the actual values used are based upon real work physical specular attributes. We need to consider what values we place in the map.

- **Nonmetals**: There should be no color in the values and anything between 47,47,47 and 70,70,70 can be used. For skin, we can use a value around 50,50,50 but for inorganic materials, such as plastic, we can use values more towards 70,70,70.

There are exceptions to the rules when it comes to precious stones as they have a specular value over 170,170,170, but this is worth experimenting with.

- **Metals**: Metals have a specular range much higher than that of nonmetals. As a rule, most metals are from 170,170,170, but some metals have a color value such as gold and copper.

  One consideration that must be used for the diffuse map: all metals are almost black in color, avoid using pure black. But as a rule, we should use a dark value.

- **Gloss maps**: A gloss map is shown here:

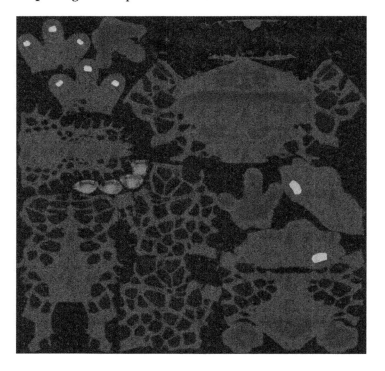

In the gloss map, we can add variations to the material and add interesting features to the surface of the model. Now that the specular map is used to define the materials, we use the gloss map to a much larger extent than we used to.

Similar to the diffuse or albedo map, the gloss map is where we will spend a large amount of our creative time. The creation of the gloss map is fun, and it is worth experimenting with to see what different effects you can get.

Exporting maps

CRYENGINE comes with a Photoshop plugin that we can use to export the textures for use in the engine. This plugin will define the compression of the texture to the desired size for the engine to read, without the need to change the size of our original psd. The exporter is simple to use and was installed when we completed *Chapter 6, The Modeling Workflow for Game Characters and Tools.*

To export the textures, we need to follow the following process:

1. Have the diffuse texture layers selected and alphas placed into the alpha channel.

2. Then, select **Save as** from the **File** menu and select the file type as **Crytiff**. This will then open up the exporter window.

   There are a few options in the window, but the main two that we need to make sure we adjust are the size of the texture, to meet what the requirements are, and also making sure the dropdown is set to the right type of texture we are looking to export.

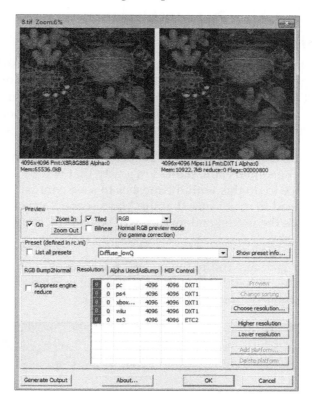

For each texture export, we will need to do this and make sure we have selected the right one from the dropdown. When exporting, it is worth experimenting with the size of the various textures. For instance, lowering the size of the specular map to half of the diffuse or normal map will not affect the textures, but it will reduce the amount of texture memory required for the character.

When exporting the maps, we use a set of standard naming conventions. Here's a list of examples:

- **Diffuse map**: For this, we use `_diff`
- **Specular map**: For this, we use `_spec`
- **Normal map**: For this, we use `_ddn`
- **Normal with Gloss in alpha**: For this, we use `_ddna`
- **Height/displacement map**: For this, we use `_displ`
- **Detail map**: For this, we use `_detail`

Exporting a mesh and materials into CRYENGINE

As we are making the textures, it is always advisable to check these in the engine to make sure we are getting the desired result we are looking for. In order to do this, we will need to export both the mesh and the materials we are using in a way that the engine will be able to read them. To do this, we will use the Crytools exporter that we installed in *Chapter 6, The Modeling Workflow for Game Characters and Tools*.

Before we export the model, we need to make sure that the right materials are applied to the correct geometry and named in a way that will be understandable. It is also good practice to do this with the meshes to save confusion. Once we have this organized, we need to make sure that the Maya scene is saved in our desired engine location where the model and texture will be read by the engine. The steps are as follows:

1. The first step is to make sure the meshes we are looking to export are grouped in a way that the exporter will recognize. To do this, we first open up the tools button from the Crytek shelf.

2. We have an option that will automatically set up the correct group naming for the mesh that we want to export. This saves us time and automates the grouping process for us. Without selecting meshes, press on **Create CryExportNode**.

3. To check the group, open up the outliner.

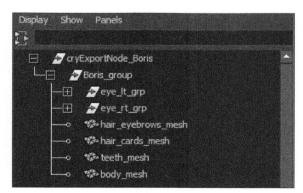

4. Next, we need to set up the materials for export. Within the engine, we will need to create a multimaterial that will contain all or separate materials for each element. To set this up, we use the material creation tool named Mat Ed that is available on the Crytek shelf.

5. The first step is to name the group. Once this is done, select all of the meshes and then click on **Get Materials From Selection**. This will add all of our materials to the group.

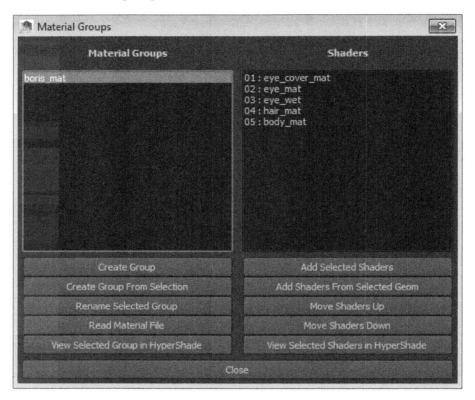

6. Now that we have all of this set up, we can use the exporter. Select the **Exporter** button from the shelf and then set the desired export path for the materials and the mesh.

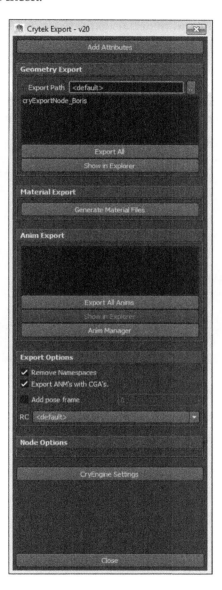

Importing the mesh by using CRYENGINE Material Editor

Now that we have the mesh and materials exported, we can start CRYENGINE. The engine is a fully functioning game building tool, but we only have to access a few of the features available to us for our requirements. The steps are as follows:

1. First, we need to import our model. To do this, we need to access the **Rollup** menu that can be found on the right-hand side of the editor. If this is not visible, you can access it by going to the **View** tab and selecting it.

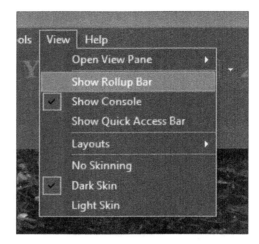

2. To bring our mesh, we need to select **Geom Entity** and scroll down to the location where the .cgf file was saved. Click on it and then place it into the editor window.

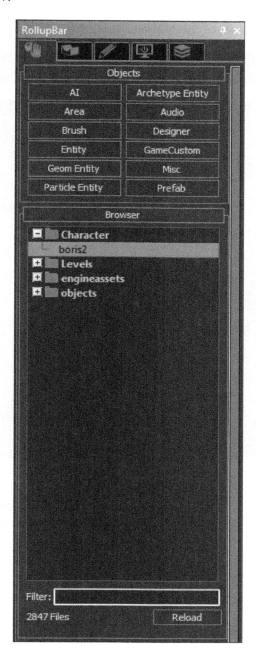

3. With the model still selected, we can open up Material Editor. To do this, click on the material icon on the top shelf. This will open up a new window that will be a powerful Material Editor. Now, we need to load in the textures that we exported and apply the material to the model by clicking on the icon in the top-left corner of the **Material Editor** window.

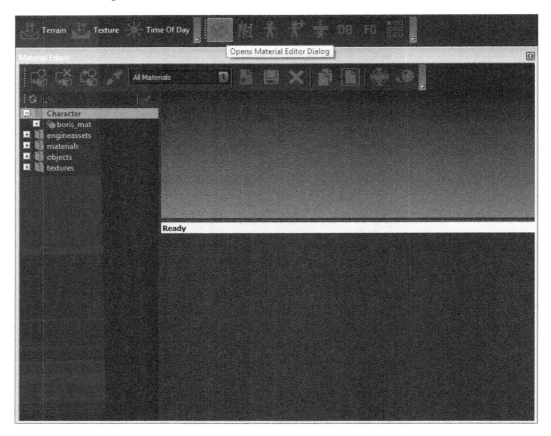

4. As the materials were allocated correctly in Maya, the right material will be applied to the right material IDs allocated to the model. Now that the textures are loaded, it will update the textures on the model every time we alter the textures and re-export.

5. Material Editor is simple to use and allows us to make a variety of visual changes and enhancements to our model. There are options that allow us to use subsurface scattering and also functions that allow us to use the alpha map we created for the fur.

 I recommend playing around with Material Editor to find out what it can do for your characters.

As we can see, the process of texturing and setting up the material is a fun part of the character creation process. The process of developing the textures takes time and it is important to remember to constantly check the results in the engine and experiment with the results that can be achieved with the powerful combination of the texture and the materials.

File check and handover

Once we have our final textures, it is time to get all the files organized and ready to be handed over for skinning. It is time for us to go through our Maya scene and make sure it is organized and named in a logical way that is easy to follow for the tech artist who will rig and skin it.

It is important to make sure we have all the work files organized and named correctly. It is a good practice to organize the file types into their own folders. We can also place an underscore at the beginning of the folder named `workfiles`.

Summary

Now that we have been through the character development process to model and texture our character, we can hand it over to tech art so it can be used and animated in-game. As with all aspects of this process, it is important to find a creative workflow that works for you and to constantly keep improving on your skills and techniques, as the games industry is constantly evolving based on new technologies and hardware.

10
Building the Character Rig

Now that the character model is ready, we will go over the steps to make it ready to be used in game, starting from setting up the character in Maya to exporting the asset and its animations to the engine. In this chapter, we will cover the following topics:

- Scene settings in Maya
- Authoring a deformation skeleton in Maya
- Setting up the hitboxes or phys proxies in Maya
- Creating a simple, efficient rig for animating the character

Getting started

Before we get started, please go to the accompanied website and extract the gettingStarted zip folder contents to the GameSDK folder that should be in your CRYENGINE installation folder. If you used Steam, then it should be something similar to this: (Steam install location)\Steam\SteamApps\common\ CRYENGINE\GameSDK.

Now, you should have two new folders in the GameSDK folder: the Objects and Animations folders. Check the next screenshot:

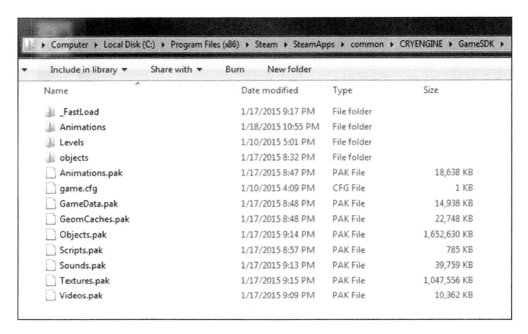

Inside the Objects folder, you will find another character folder called Boris (the name of our character). This is where we will be exporting our assets and saving our Maya files. In the Animations folder, there is also another Boris folder where we will be exporting the animations.

Scene settings in Maya

It is recommended to follow the same scene setup of CRYENGINE in Maya where the up axis is z and the forward axis is y. We will also need to set the frame rate to 30 fps. To apply these settings in Maya, go to **Windows | Settings/Preferences | Preferences**.

In the **Preferences** window, go to **World Coordinate System | Settings** and set the **Up axis** option to **Z**. In the **Working Units** tab, set the **Time** option to **NTSC (30 fps)** as shown in the following screenshot:

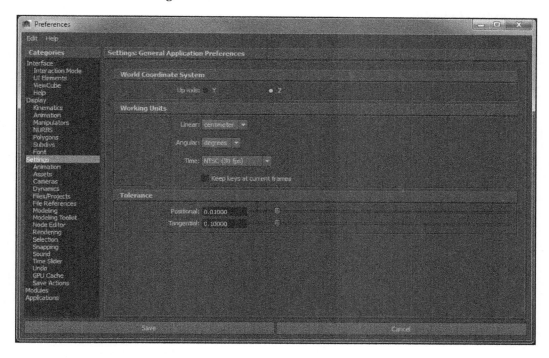

You still can work in Maya with *y* axis as up, but it requires a workaround that we will cover in the next chapter.

Authoring the deformation skeleton in Maya

Before we go ahead and work on the character rig in Maya, I would like to go over some rules you can use for building any character skeleton that is meant to be used for CRYENGINE.

There are some rules when it comes to creating a deformation skeleton for a CRYENGINE character. That's why we like to keep our animation and deformation skeletons separate.

The **deformation skeleton** is what we will use for skinning the character and it is the one that we will export to the engine in the CHR format. Because this skeleton needs to follow certain rules, we use another skeleton for building the rig, which is the **animation skeleton**.

The animation skeleton will drive the deformation skeleton via constraints or direct connections. There are no rules for laying out your animation skeleton; you can have whatever **hierarchy** you prefer for your rig as long as you understand that the end result needs to be hooked to the deformation skeleton.

The deformation skeleton rules

The following are the rules for the deformation skeleton:

- You need to create a parent joint for all the joints in the skeleton at the origin of your scene. We usually refer to that joint as the **Root bone**. Whether you are working in Maya with z up or y up, you need to have the Root bone z axis pointing up and y forward. So, double-check the joint orientation.

- No scaling is allowed. The export process will fail if you have any scale values on your joints. If you need to have squash and stretch set up, you can simply apply that to your animation skeleton and let it drive the translation values on the deformation skeleton.

- Using underscore in the beginning of the joint names excludes them and their children from the skeleton hierarchy in the engine. So, make sure you don't have any of the excluded joints in your skin cluster. Otherwise, it will break your skinning in the engine.

Building the rig

Rigging a character in Maya is quite a vast topic that could be a book on its own. Although we will be creating a rig for the character, this chapter is not meant to teach you everything about rigging. We'll discuss just what you need to make sure you have a stable and friendly rig with all the items necessary to export the character to engine.

This is the order we will follow for building the rig:

- Creating the hitboxes
- Rigging the arm

- Rigging the spine
- Rigging the leg
- Finalizing the rig

Setting up the hitboxes

In this section, we will go over the **hitboxes** setup for CRYENGINE in general and then apply the information we have to create the hitboxes for our character.

The hitboxes (we also refer to them as **phys proxies** or **capsules** in CRYENGINE) are invisible primitive shapes that roughly resemble the shape of the model in game. They are used for collision and hit detection in the game instead of the real geometry of the asset, which would be expensive to perform real-time hit calculations on.

The common shapes we use for phys proxies are poly cylinders, spheres, and cubes. You can scale them or change their shape input properties, such as the radius and height.

However, if you scale the proxies nonuniformly or change the primitive shape, the exporter may export it as a mesh proxy instead of a physics proxy, which is more expensive based on the resolution of that mesh. Check the following screenshots for examples.

The following screenshot shows a good capsule:

The following screenshot shows a bad capsule:

That being said, you can use the **user defined property** (**UDP**) to force a proxy to be a primitive in the engine. You can do that through the UDP window in the Crytek shelf. In the UDP window, you can simply type the primitive shape you want to convert your proxy to. You can choose between box, cylinder, capsule, and sphere:

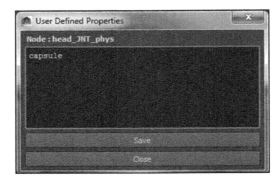

When you click on **Save** in the UDP window, a string attribute on the proxy is added with the typed value.

We will have a detailed look at the phys proxies and how to prepare them for the engine when we start creating them for the character in the next section.

Creating the phys proxies for the character

In the Boris folder in Objects, you will find the boris_skeleton Maya file. The file has the character model and the deformation skeleton. The mesh is already bound to the skeleton and all we need is just to create the phys proxies now.

In the **Polygons** tab, go to **Create | Polygon Primitives**. To make it easier to go through the upcoming steps, turn off **Interactive Creation** and click on **Cylinder**.

Now, we have a cylinder that we will use as a capsule for the left arm joint. To display the cylinder as a capsule in Maya, we will enable the **Round Cap** option in the **PolyCylinder** node of the cylinder shape in the channel box and increase the **Subdivision Caps** option to 5, as shown in the next screenshot.

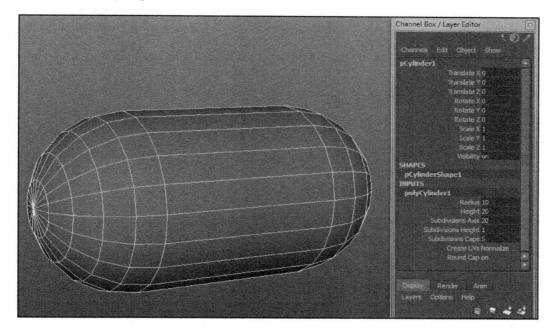

Move, rotate, and scale (uniformly) the capsule to roughly match the shape of the upper arm. When you are happy, parent the capsule under the **L_arm** joint and rename it to L_arm_phys. All phys proxies need to have the name of the parent joint plus a suffix _phys.

To parent an object (child) to another object (parent) in Maya, select the child followed by the parent and go to **Edit | Parent**, or just use the shortcut *P* key.

You can apply the same steps for the rest of the skeleton using cylinders as capsules or spheres or cubes. You don't need to create a capsule/phys proxy for every joint in the skeleton, just enough to cover the body mass of the character. The following screenshot shows an example of what your setup might look like. You can find the following setup in the `boris_phys_skeleton` Maya file in the `Boris` folder.

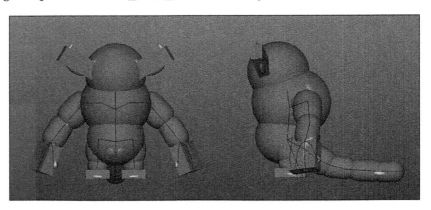

Applying the phys proxies material

We are almost there; all we need now is to follow the next steps to apply a **proxyNoDraw** material to the phys proxies. The steps are as follows:

1. Select all the phys proxies in the scene, and then right-click and select **Assign New Material**.
2. Choose **Blinn** from the **Assign New Material** window.
3. Rename the newly created **Blinn** material `boris_phys_mat`.
4. While the material is selected, go to the Crytek shelf and click on **Export**.
5. In Crytek **Export** window, click on the **Add Attributes** button.
6. Make sure you have the material selected and go to **Attribute Editor**.

7. In the **Extra Attributes** section, set the **Physicalize** attribute to
   ProxyNoDraw.

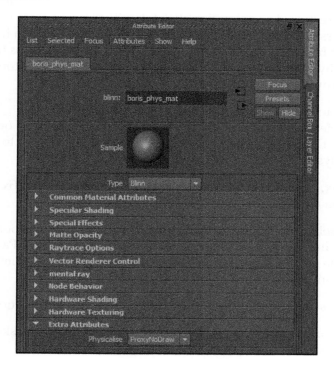

Building the character's animation rig

As I have mentioned before, rigs can get very complex based on the character.
For the sake of this book, we will stick to simplicity and stability. However, you can
use the same concepts to rig any character no matter how complex it is—a biped,
quadruped, or even a prop—and export it easily to CRYENGINE.

For your convenience, you should hide the phys proxies so you can easily see and
select the joints. You should also enable **X-Ray Joints** from the shading menu in the
view port so that you can see the joints inside the mesh.

Creating the animation skeleton

We talked briefly about the animation skeleton in the *Authoring the deformation skeleton in Maya* section. The animation skeleton will give you more freedom in the hierarchy versus the deformation skeleton. For example, we can have other transform nodes besides the joints, such as locators or empty groups in the animation skeleton hierarchy, but we can't do that with the deformation skeleton because the exporter will throw errors about those nodes.

The easiest way to create the animation skeleton is to duplicate the deformation skeleton and give it a prefix. Select the root joint in the outliner and go to **Edit | Duplicate**, or use the shortcut *Ctrl + D*. Make sure to remove the duplicate phys proxies from the new skeleton.

To add the prefix, select the duplicate skeleton, go to **Modify | Prefix Hierarchy Names**, and type ANM_.

In the outliner, select the **ANM_root** joint first and then select the root joint. Make sure to be in the **Animation** menu set and go to **Constrain | Parent**. This will constrain the root joint position and orientation to the **ANM_root** joint position and orientation.

Repeat the same steps for every joint in the animation and deformation skeletons.

Now that we have the animation skeleton driving the deformation skeleton, you can save the file as boris_rig_ready in the Boris folder.

Creating the controllers

It is preferable to use controllers for selecting and posing the joint chain rather than the joints themselves. These controllers control our rig via constraints or direct parenting. Before we create our first controller, go to **Create | NURBS Primitives | Interactive Creation** and make sure this option is **OFF**.

We will use a nurbs circle for the shape of our controller. To create the circle, go to **Create | NURBS Primitives | Circle**. In the shape inputs in the channel box, you will find the **makeNurbCircle1** node. This node controls the shape attributes of the circle, such as the radius, the normal direction, and the degree.

After you tweak the shape, to go to **Edit | Delete by Type | History**. This will delete our **makeNurbCircle** node, as the rig (depending on its complexity) can get heavy if we left that node for every controller in the scene.

Now, we need to align the controller to the object we will control. A fast way to do this is to simply create orient and point constraints from the object to the controller, and then delete the constraints.

Let's quickly create an object as a target to explain what we have been talking about here. Create a polygon **Cube** and rename it to `targetCube`. In the channel box, set **Translate Z** (up) to **10** and the **Rotate X** to **45**.

Rename the **nurbs** circle to `targetCube_CTRL`. Select **targetCube** and **targetCube_CTRL** in that specific order, and make sure you are in the **Animations** menu set. Go to **Constrain | Point | Options** (the little square next to **Point**) and make sure **Maintain Offset** is OFF. Repeat the same steps as before, but now choose **Orient** instead of **Point**. You can see that **targetCube_CTRL** is aligned in position and rotation to **targetCube** and also constrained to it.

Now that we have our proper alignment for the controller, we can get rid of the point and orient constraints. You can find them in the outliner under the **targetCube_Ctrl** transform node, as shown in the following screenshot:

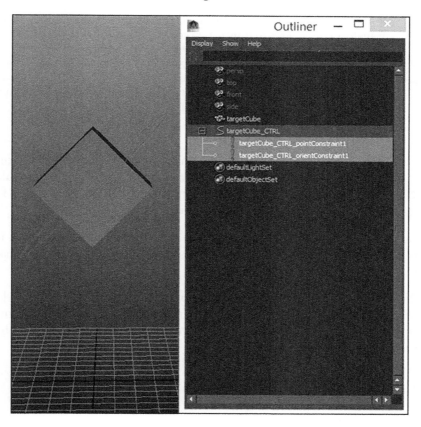

The last step we need to do before we create the connection between the controller and the target is to zero out the controller's channels. Animators are used to just zero out the channels on the controllers to go to the default pose, and it is really recommended to have that as a standard on all of your controllers.

Currently, we have values on the **Translate Z** and the **Rotate X** channels of our controller. To get rid of these values and at the same time retain the position and the orientation on the controller, we will create an offset group.

To create the offset group, make sure nothing is selected in the scene and create an empty group either by going to **Edit | Group** or using the shortcut *Ctrl + G*. Rename the newly created **null1** group `targetCube_CTRL_offset`.

Apply the same transformation values of our controller to the offset group, that is, **10** in the **Translate Z** channel and **45** in the **Rotate X** channel. Now if you parent **targetCube_CTRL** under the **targetCube_CTRL_offset** group, you will see that the channels on our controller are zeroed out.

> Some artists use freeze transformations to zero out the channels on a transform node. Freeze transformations is not really recommended because it resets the orientation to world, so the controller will not have the same orientation as the target object any more (if this is the desired behavior then by all means use freeze transformations). Also, it can cause problems later when you try to create more complex setups, and need to snap this controller to another one (such as what we usually do when switching from FK to IK setups).

Now that we have our controller ready, we can create any kind of connection between it and the target object. You can tell by now that this process can take some time and because we want to be consistent in creating our controllers for our character, we have a Python script to do the job for us very quickly.

Go to the accompanied website and extract the `scripts` zip folder contents to your Maya `scripts` folder. The default script path is `\Users\<username>\Documents\maya\scripts`.

Let's try the script out! Go to Maya Script Editor by navigating to **Window | General Editors | Script Editor**. In the **Script Editor** window, go to the **Command** menu and select **New Tab**. A pop-up window will show and ask you to specify executer source language, choose **Python**.

In the **Python** tab, type in these lines of code:

```
import cryEngine_BP as CE
CE.createController(name=None, shape="circle", alignPos=True,
alignRot=True, color="yellow")
```

This is shown in the following screenshot:

Now, we will go over these lines one by one.

```
import cryEngine_BP as CE
```

In the preceding line, we are importing our cryEngine_BP Python module that has all the functions we will be using in this chapter. The as keyword allows us to assign a shorter or more friendly name to our module. Consider the next line:

```
CE.createController(name=None, shape="circle", alignPos=True,
alignRot=True)
```

Here, we are calling the createController function from the cryEngine_BP module, with some keyword arguments that we will go over one by one:

- name: This argument is a string name for the controller we are creating. If the value is None, then the controller name will be like the target object with a suffix of _CTRL, such as the naming convention we had for our targetCube_CTRL.

- shape: This argument tells the createController function what shape to create. We can choose between circle (which is the default value), arrow, star, cross, square, and arrowCircle as shapes for our controller.

- alignPos: This argument is a Boolean value to align the controller position to a target object.

- alignRot: This argument is a Boolean value to align the controller orientation to a target object.

There is a detailed description for the code inside the cryEngine_BP module, if you need to have a better look at the commands used to build this function. Now let's try to run our code.

Delete the **targetCube_CTRL_offset** group, then select the cube, and (while it is selected) execute the script in the Script Editor.

 To execute a script in the Maya Script Editor, click anywhere in the **Python** tab and press *Ctrl + Enter* or just hit the *Enter* key on the numeric keypad.

Now, you should have the same controller we created manually for **targetCube**.

Rigging the arm

Open the boris_rig_ready file in the Boris folder. Since we will be working mainly on the animation skeleton for this and upcoming sections, there is no need to see the deformation skeleton for now. To hide the deformation skeleton, we just need to hide the top parent node which is the **Root bone**.

For the arm, we will create a very simple **FK** rig. FK is short for forward kinematics. Forward kinematics provides a direct control over each joint rotation, which makes it easier for creating nice and clean arc motions.

To create the FK controllers, select the **ANM_L_arm** joint in the animation skeleton hierarchy; while the joint is selected, execute these lines of code in the same **Python** tab we created before:

```
CE.createController(name="L_arm_CTRL", shape="circle", alignPos=True,
alignRot=True)
```

The only thing we changed here is the name of the controller. Repeat the same steps for **ANM_L_elbow_JNT** and change the name argument value in our createController function to L_elbow_CTRL. So it should look like this:

```
CE.createController(name="L_elbow_CTRL", shape="circle",
alignPos=True, alignRot=True)
```

Repeat the same steps for **ANM_L_hand_JNT**, and change the name to
L_hand_CTRL.

You probably cannot see the controllers because they are hidden inside our
character's model. If you press *4* to enable the wireframe view, you will be
able to see them inside the mesh, as shown in the next screenshot.

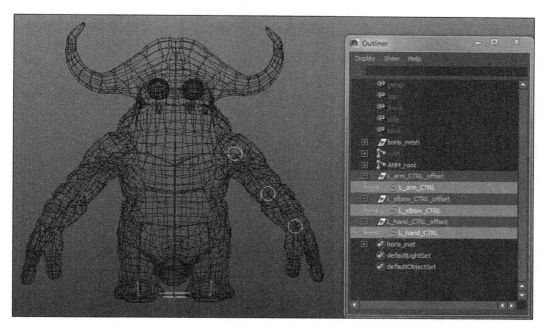

Repeat the same steps for all of the controllers' curves. When you are done, you can
toggle back to object mode by pressing *F8* again.

Now, we are ready to constrain the arm joints to the controllers via orient constraints.
Select **L_arm_CTRL** followed by **ANM_L_arm**, make sure you are in the **Animation**
menu set, and go to **Constrain | Orient**. Repeat the same steps to constrain **ANM_L_
elbow_JNT** to **L_elbow_CTRL** and **ANM_L_hand_JNT** to **L_hand_CTRL**.

Our final step is to parent the controllers to each other accordingly. Parent the **L_elbow_CTRL_offset** group under **L_arm_CTRL**, and then parent the **L_hand_CTRL_offset** group to **L_elbow_CTRL**. The next screenshot shows what the arm controller hierarchy should look like:

The fingers

You can look at each digit as an arm on its own. We will use the same setup we used before for the arm starting with the thumb.

Select the **ANM_L_thumb_01_JNT** joint and execute our createController function in the Script Editor to create a controller aligned in position and orientation to that joint. We will name our controller L_thumb_01_CTRL:

```
CE.createController(name="L_thumb_01_CTRL", shape="circle",
alignPos=True, alignRot=True)
```

Repeat the same steps for the second and the third thumb knuckles. Remember to change the name to represent the number of the knuckle before the _CTRL suffix.

Now, you should have the **L_thumb_01_CTRL, L_thumb_02_CTRL**, and **L_thumb_03_CTRL** controllers for our thumb. As with what we did for rigging the arm, you should now create orient constraints to constrain the thumb joints to their corresponding controllers.

Parent the **L_thumb_02_CTRL_offset** group to **L_thumb_01_CTRL** and parent the **L_thumb_03_CTRL_offset** group to **L_thumb_02_CTRL**.

The final step in rigging the thumb is to parent the **L_thumb_01_CTRL_offset** group to **L_hand_CTRL** so that the thumb follows the movement of the hand.

Repeat the same process for the rest of the fingers and you should have your hand setup ready.

The clavicle

For the clavicle, we will use a pretty straightforward setup: just a simple controller!

Select the **ANM_L_clavicle_JNT** joint and create a controller called **L_clavicle_CTRL** aligned in position and rotation to the clavicle joint. We will also use the **arrow** shape this time for the controller. This is what the createController function should look like:

```
CE.createController(name="L_clavicle_CTRL", shape="arrow",
alignPos=True, alignRot=True)
```

Create an orient constraint to connect **ANM_L_clavicle_JNT** to our clavicle controller. Now, we can parent our **L_arm_CTRL_offset** group to **L_clavicle_CTRL** so that our arm and hand rigs follow the clavicle motion. The next screenshot shows what the controller hierarchy should look like in the outliner:

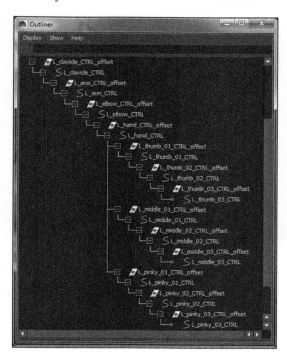

Cleaning up the arm controllers

Now that we have all of our arm, fingers, and clavicle controllers in the scene and parented in the right order, we should now lock and hide all the channels that we will not use for these controllers.

Since we used only the forward kinematics setup for our arm rig so far, we don't need to keep any translation channels on the controllers (unless you intentionally want to break the joints). We should also hide and lock the scale and the visibility channels for all the controllers that we have for the whole rig.

To lock and hide those channels, select all the arm, fingers, and clavicle controllers. In the channel box, select the translation, scale, and visibility channels, and then right- click and select **Lock and Hide Selected**. This is shown in the next screenshot:

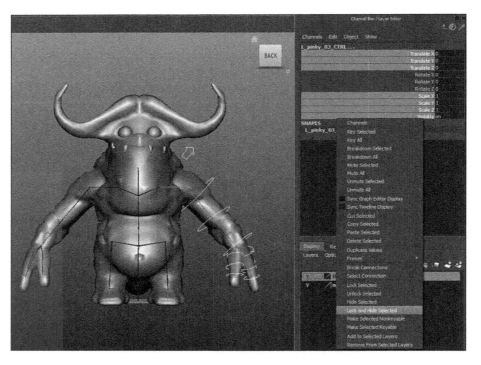

Rigging the spine

If you analyze where the most action of the spine happens, you will find it mainly happens in the chest and the hip areas. Ideally, we would like to pose these two areas separately without them affecting each other but at the same time we have that smooth interpolation on all the joints between them.

There are many ways to rig the spine. In our case, we will simply create our two main controllers for the hips and the chest and average the position of the rest of the joints between them.

To create the chest controller, select the **ANM_spine_03_JNT** joint and run our `createController` function to create a controller named **chest_CTRL**, which is aligned in position to the joint:

```
CE.createController(name="chest_CTRL", shape="square", alignPos=True,
alignRot=False)
```

Parent-constrain the joint to our new controller, and make sure in the parent constraint options to enable **Maintain Offset**.

To create the controller for the hips, select **ANM_spine_01_JNT** joint and create a controller named **hips_CTRL** that is also aligned only in position to the joint. Use our `createController` function.

After you create the controller, create a parent constraint with **Maintain Offset** set to on to constrain the **ANM_spine_01_JNT** joint to the **hips_CTRL** controller. We also need to constrain **ANM_pelvis_JNT** to **hips_CTRL** using another parent constraint with **Maintain Offset** set to on so that it follows the controller's movement.

Now that we have our two main controllers for the spine, it is time to take care of the joints in-between. In order to be able to average the position of the middle joint between both controllers and achieve that natural twist when we rotate one of them about its aim axis (in our case *z*), we will need to use a little bit of advanced rigging methods. It's nothing complicated, I promise.

Let's start with averaging the position of **ANM_spine_02_JNT** between the chest and the hips controllers in the next few steps:

1. Create three locators with the following names: **ANM_spine_02_LOC, ANM_spine_02_UP** and **ANM_spine_02_AIM**.

    To create a locator, go to the **Create** menu at the top and select **Locator**.

2. Move the **ANM_spine_02_UP** locator 25 units in the x axis.

3. Parent **ANM_spine_02_UP** and **ANM_spine_02_AIM** under **ANM_spine_02_LOC**, as shown in the following screenshot:

4. Snap **ANM_spine_02_LOC** to the **ANM_spine_01_JNT** joint position.

    You can snap one object to another using the temporary point constraint technique we explained before in the *Creating the controllers* section. Alternatively, while using the Move tool, hold V (shortcut for the Snap to Points tool), click on the middle mouse button, and move to the object you want to snap to.

5. We will use these locators to control the **ANM_spine_02_JNT** joint. Create a parent constraint with **Maintain Offset** set to on from the **ANM_spine_02_AIM** locator to the **ANM_spine_02_JNT** joint. Now if you move and rotate the top locator **ANM_spine_02_LOC**, you will see that our joint is following.

6. Finally, select **chest_CTRL**, **hips_CTRL**, and **ANM_spine_02_LOC** (in that order) and create a parent constraint with **Maintain Offset**.

Now if you move the chest or the hips controller, you will see that the position of the middle joint is averaged between both of them. However, in order to get that smooth line between the hips and chest, we also need to make the spine joints aim towards each other and we should also be able to twist like a normal spine. We can get this result using the **aim constraint**.

The aim constraint constrains an object's orientation so that it aims at other object/objects. To create an aim constraint, we need to provide three vectors: the **aim** vector, the **up** vector, and the **world up** vector. The aim vector is the constrained object's local axis that you want to aim towards the target object. The twist orientation of the object is controlled by the up vector and the world up vector. Please refer to the Maya documentation at `http://help.autodesk.com/view/MAYAUL/2015/ENU/?` if you need more information about the aim constraint.

Let's see how we can use all of this information to achieve the result we want. Select **chest_CTRL** and then the **ANM_spine_02_AIM** locator, and go to **Constrain | Aim Constraint Options**. In the **Aim Constraint Options** window, apply the following settings:

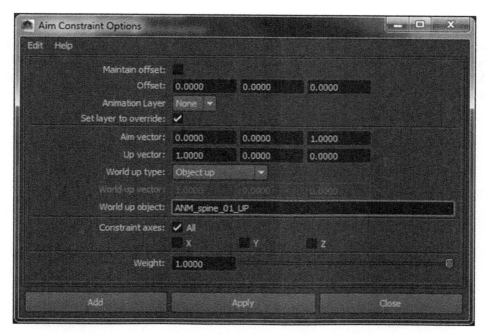

In the options box, we used the **Aim vector** field to tell the aim constraint to constrain our **ANM_spine_02_AIM** locator's positive z axis to point to our **chest_CTRL**. In the **Up vector** field, we decided to use the **ANM_spine_02_AIM** locator's positive x axis as it's up vector. In the **World up object** field, we tell our up vector to try to point in the same direction as the **ANM_spine_02_UP** locator.

If you move the **ANM_spine_02_UP** locator in the y axis now, you should see that it is controlling our **ANM_spine_02_JNT** joint, and if you move and rotate the **chest_CTRL**, the **ANM_spine_02_JNT** joint is aiming to it and twisting properly.

We are almost there! The final step for that setup is to also make our **ANM_spine_01_JNT** joint aim towards our mid spine joint too. To do this, we will repeat some of the steps we followed before.

Duplicate **ANM_spine_02_LOC** and replace **spine_02** in the name of the duplicate locator and its children with **spine_01**. Snap **ANM_spine_01_LOC** to the position of the **ANM_spine_01_JNT** joint and parent it under **hips_CTRL**. Delete the parent constraint we created before on **ANM_spine_01_JNT** and create a new parent constraint with **Maintain Offset** set to on to constrain **ANM_spine_01_JNT** to the **ANM_spine_01_AIM** locator.

Now, we will create an aim constraint to constrain the positive z axis of the **ANM_spine_01_AIM** locator to point towards the **ANM_spine_02_LOC** locator. Select **ANM_spine_02_LOC**, select the **ANM_spine_01_AIM** locator, and go to the **Aim Constraint Options** window to apply these settings:

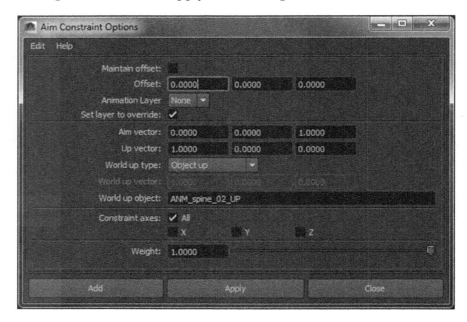

Now, we have our spine rigged and our controllers aiming towards each other properly. The advantage of this setup, besides the flexibility, is you can also squash and stretch without creating any problems exporting because we are relying on translation only.

The upper body controller

Besides the hips and the chest controllers, we will need another controller we can use to move and rotate the whole upper body. We will use our `createController` function to create a controller aligned in position to the **ANM_pelvis_JNT** joint and name it **upperBody_CTRL**:

```
CE.createController(name="upperBody_CTRL", shape="arrowCircle",
alignPos=True, alignRot=False)
```

Tweak the shape of the new controller so that it is visible and selectable. Then, parent the **hips_CTRL_offset** and **chest_CTRL_offset** groups and the **ANM_spine_02_ LOC** locator under **upperBody_CTRL**.

Now if you move **upperBody_CTRL**, you will see the whole body is following. If you rotate it, you will notice the clavicle and the arm are not following the body orientation. To fix this, we need to parent the **L_clavicle_CTRL_offset** group under our **chest_CTRL**. Now when we rotate the upper body controller, the whole body is moving and orienting as it should.

The head

For the head and the neck joints, we will use simple FK controllers. Select the **ANM_neck_JNT** joint and run our `createController` function with the following parameters:

```
CE.createController(name="neck_CTRL", shape="circle", alignPos=True,
alignRot=False)
```

Create a parent constraint with **Maintain Offset** set to on to constrain the **ANM_ neck_JNT** to the **neck_CTRL** controller.

We will do the same for the head joint, just change the name of the controller to **head_CTRL**. Select the **ANM_head_JNT** joint and run the `createConntroller` function:

```
CE.createController(name="head_CTRL", shape="circle", alignPos=True,
alignRot=False)
```

We will also use a parent constraint with **Maintain Offset** to connect the **ANM_ head_JNT** joint to our head controller. Now, parent the **head_CTRL_offset** group under **neck_CTRL** and parent the **neck_CTRL_offset** group under our **chest_CTRL** so everything now follows the upper body controller and our neck and head controllers follow our chest controller.

Cleaning up the spine controllers

So far, we should be able to move and rotate all the spine and head controllers. We just need to lock and hide all the scale and visibility channels on the controllers in the channel box, as we did before for our arm controllers (check the *Cleaning up the arm controllers* section). It is worth mentioning that you should also lock and hide the channels on the rigging locators we used for the spine, since we don't want the animators or yourself to select or delete them by mistake.

This is a screenshot of what the setup of the upper body can look like with some tweaking on the controllers shape:

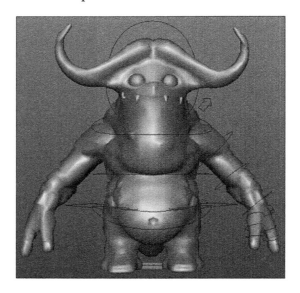

Rigging the leg

It can get a little difficult to use the FK to pose the legs against the upper body. So, we will use **inverse kinematics (IK)** to rig the legs. When you move an **IK handle**, the solver calculates the rotations of all the joints between the start joint and the end joint based on the position of the **end effector** that is usually located at the end joint.

There are different types of IK solvers that are available in Maya. The most common one used for rigging the limbs is the **Rotate-Plane IK solver (ikRPsolver)**. Please refer to the Maya documentation at `http://help.autodesk.com/view/MAYAUL/2015/ENU/?guid=CSN_ikHandle` for more information about the IK solvers available in Maya.

To apply the IK handle to our leg joints, go to **Animation | Skeleton | IK Handle Tool**. In the **Tool Settings** window, select **Rotate-Plane Solver** for the **Current solver** option, as shown here:

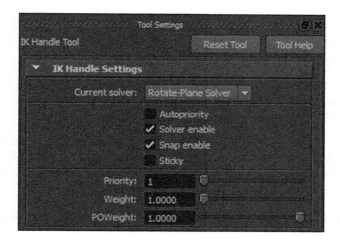

Click on our start joint **ANM_L_thigh** and then click on our end joint **ANM_L_ankle_JNT**. You should see our new IK handle in the outliner; rename it as `L_leg_IKH`. If you start moving the IK handle, you will see how it drives the rotation of our IK chain. We don't want to select the IK handle to move our joints, so we will use the `createController` function to create a controller for that. Select the **ANM_L_ankle_JNT** joint and run the function with the following parameters:

```
CE.createController(name="L_foot_CTRL", shape="square", alignPos=True,
alignRot=False)
```

Now that we have a controller for our IK handle, we just need to create the connections so we are able to pose the leg only using **L_foot_CTRL**. Create a point constraint to constrain the position of **L_leg_IKH** to our foot controller and then create an orient constraint with **Maintain Offset** set to on to constrain the orientation of the **ANM_L_ankle_JNT** joint to the controller.

To control the twist of the joint chain, we need to create a **pole vector** controller for the IK handle. To do so, select the **ANM_L_knee_JNT** joint and run our `createController` function:

```
CE.createController(name="L_leg_PV_CTRL", shape="star", alignPos=True,
alignRot=False)
```

This will create a star-shaped controller positioned exactly at the knee joint. Select the **L_leg_PV_CTRL_offset** group and move it an additional 40 units in the *y* axis, so that the controller is out of the mesh and in front of the knee joint.

Select **L_leg_PV_CTRL**, select the **L_leg_IKH**, and go to **Constrain | Pole Vector**. This will create a pole vector constraint on the IK handle, so we can control the twist or the orientation of our joint chain with **L_leg_PV_CTRL**.

It is important to mention that if the **L_leg_IKH** crosses our pole vector controller or faces the opposite direction, the leg joints can flip. To fix this, we can simply move the pole vector controller so it is always in front of the leg.

The last step to finish our leg rig is to create a toe controller. You can simply create the **L_toe_CTRL** controller that is aligned in position and orientation to the **ANM_L_toe_JNT** joint using the `createController` function. Then, create an orient constraint to connect the **ANM_L_toe_JNT** joint to the controller.

Parent the **L_toe_CTRL_offset** group under the **L_foot_CTRL** controller so that it follows the leg movement.

Cleaning up the leg controllers

Select all the controllers we created for the leg, and then lock and hide the scale and visibility channels from the channel box. We will not need to rotate the pole vector controller, so lock and hide the rotation channels on **L_leg_PV_CTRL**. For the toe controller, you should lock and hide the translation channels (unless you want to break the toe).

Rigging the tail

We will create a very simple **FK** setup for the tail. You should be familiar with the process now. Starting with the first joint of the tail, select the **ANM_tail_01_JNT** joint and run the `createController` function:

```
CE.createController(name="tail_01_CTRL", shape="circle",
alignPos=True, alignRot=True)
```

Then, create an orient constraint to constrain the **ANM_tail_01_JNT** joint to the **tail_01_CTRL** controller. Repeat the same steps for every joint in the tail, parent the offset groups of the child controllers to their preceding controller, and parent the **tail_01_CTRL** offset group under the **hips_CTRL** controller so the tail follows the hips movement. This is what the hierarchy for the tail controllers should look like:

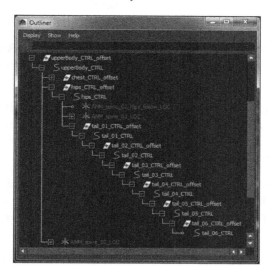

Cleaning up the tail controllers

Like most FK controllers, we will lock and hide all the scale, translation, and the visibility channels on the tail controllers.

Enhancing the deformations

You can do lots of stuff to enhance the deformations on this character. Armored with the knowledge of the do's and the don'ts for rigging a character to export to CRYENGINE, you can now freely be creative to correct some of the deformations on this character. For the purpose of this chapter, we will keep things simple and merely talk about fixing the twist on the upper and the lower arm.

The forearm twist

If you take a look at any reference material for how the forearm moves around, you will notice that when the wrist twists, it occurs down the entire length of the forearm. The forearm is made up of two joints the **radius** and the **ulna**, and during **pronation** the distal end of the radius rotates around the ulna from its position on the lateral side of the wrist to the medial side of the wrist. This action turns the hand, wrist, and forearm almost 180 degrees.

You can achieve this kind of behavior with different methods, such as using the **spline IK** in Maya to drive a twist chain or utility nodes to directly distribute the twist value along the forearm joints.

Using a similar technique we used for rigging the spine, we will use the aim constraint to drive the twist on our **ANM_L_hand_twist_JNT** joint. To average the twist between the hand and the elbow joints, we will need to create three locators.

Create a locator with the same position and orientation as the **ANM_L_hand_JNT** joint. Rename the locator L_hand_twist_UP and parent it under the **L_elbow_CTRL** controller.

Move the locator about 20 units in **Translate Y**, then duplicate it twice. Rename the first duplicate locator L_hand_twist_elbow_follow_LOC and rename the second duplicate locator L_hand_twist_hand_follow_LOC. Parent the **L_hand_twist_hand_follow_LOC** locator under the **L_hand_CTRL** controller.

Select both the **L_hand_twist_elbow_follow_LOC** and **L_hand_twist_hand_follow_LOC** locators, parent the **L_hand_twist_UP** locator, and create a parent constraint. This will average the position and orientation of the **L_hand_twist_UP** between the hand and the elbow joints.

Select the **ANM_L_hand_JNT** joint, select the **ANM_L_hand_twist_JNT** joint, and go to the **Aim Constraint Options** window to apply the following settings:

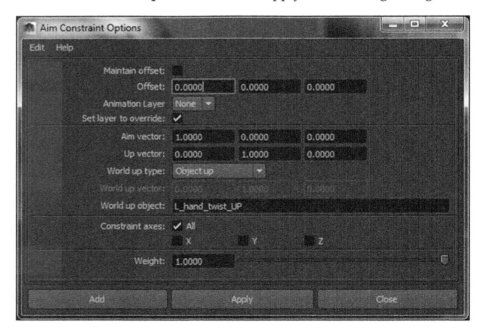

Now, the twist rotation of the **ANM_L_hand_JNT** joint is controlled by the **L_hand_twist_UP** locator and averaged between the hand and the elbow joints. To keep the scene clean, hide all the locators we have created and lock their channels since we don't want to move or delete them by mistake.

The upper arm twist

If you look at a reference or yourself when you twist your arm, the shoulder bone itself doesn't rotate. Instead, the effect takes place gradually down the length of the arm.

To achieve that kind of twist behavior, we need to lock the first upper arm twist joint so it doesn't rotate when we use our FK controller for twisting the arm.

We will need to create a set of locators to achieve that kind of setup for the upper arm. Create an empty group and name it **L_upperarm_offset_GRP**. Align the group's position and orientation to the **ANM_L_arm** joint. Create a locator, name it **L_upperarm_driver_LOC**, and parent it under the **L_upperarm_offset_GRP** group. Zero out all the translation and rotation channels on the **L_upperarm_driver_LOC** locator so that it is snapped to its parent group.

Duplicate the **L_upperarm_driver_LOC** locator and rename it L_upperarm_aim_LOC. Move the new locator about 5 units along its local *x* axis.

Duplicate **L_upperarm_driver_LOC** locator twice and rename the first duplicate L_upperarm_lock_LOC and the second one L_upperarm_twist_LOC. Parent **L_upperarm_twist_LOC** under the **L_upperarm_lock_LOC** locator.

We will use **L_upperarm_aim_LOC** to lock the twist axis on the **L_upperarm_lock_LOC** locator using an aim constraint. Select **L_upperarm_aim_LOC**, select **L_upperarm_lock_LOC**, and go to the **Aim Constraint Options** window to apply the settings shown in the next screenshot.

The **L_upperarm_twist_LOC** locator will be used to extract the proper twist value to be used on the upper arm middle twist joint. By adding an orient constraint from the **L_upperarm_driver_LOC** locator to the **L_upperarm_twist_LOC**, we will get the rotation difference between **L_upperarm_driver_LOC** and the **L_upperarm_lock_ LOC** locators.

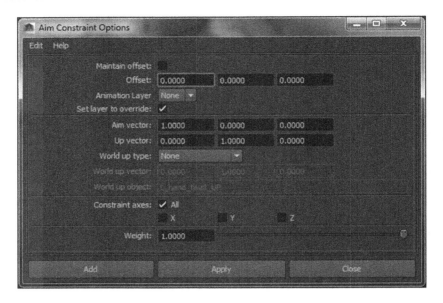

Setting **World up type** to **None** in the **Aim Constraint Options** window will orient L_upperarm_lock_LOC such that the aim vector points to the **L_upperarm_aim_ LOC** world position, but no twist calculation is performed by the constraint.

Now, we need to connect our locators' setup to the left arm rig. Start by parenting the **L_upperarm_offset_GRP** group under **L_clavicle_CTRL**. Create a parent constraint to constrain the **L_upperarm_driver_LOC** locator to the **ANM_L_arm** joint. To lock the twist on the first arm joint, orient-constrain the **ANM_L_arm_twist_01_JNT** joint to **L_upperarm_lock_LOC**.

Now if we rotate the **L_arm_CTRL** controller, the **ANM_L_arm_twist_01_JNT** joint follows in every axis except the *x* axis, which is exactly what we wanted. The last step in our upper arm twist setup is to distribute the twist on the middle twist joint **ANM_L_arm_twist_02_JNT**. Select both **L_upperarm_lock_LOC** and **L_upperarm_ twist_LOC**, select **ANM_L_arm_twist_02_JNT**, and create an orient constraint.

Finalizing the rig

Now that we have all the rig components ready, we just need to create the last controller for this rig: **Locomotion_CTRL**. Select the **ANM_root** joint and run our `createController` function:

```
CE.createController(name="locomotion_CTRL", shape="arrow",
alignPos=True, alignRot=True)
```

Create a parent constraint to connect the **ANM_root** joint to **Locomotion_CTRL**. This controller is used in the engine to describe the logical movement and orientation of the animation.

It is recommended that you organize the rig into groups. You can have one group for the controllers and another one for the joints in the scene, and use a group on top of both to globally move the rig. Keep in mind that you can't have the skinned meshes in the same group as the group you will use to move the rig; otherwise, you will have double transformations. Have a look at the final rig structure in the `boris_rig.ma` file in the `Boris` folder.

As mentioned before, this chapter is not meant to teach you everything about rigging. However, we covered very important concepts to create a very light and stable rig that is also compatible with CRYENGINE. There are many additions you can explore on your own to add to the rig if you want to take it to the next level, for example, a reverse foot setup and IK FK switch.

Summary

Equipped with a better understanding of the rules for creating and authoring skeletons for rigging characters designed for CRYENGINE, you can now export any skeleton-based character rig to the engine.

Depending on your preferred rigging techniques and the fidelity of the characters you are working with, you can definitely use the same techniques we used for rigging our character to add to and use in your rig.

In the next chapter, we will see the rig in action when we explore exporting characters animations to CRYENGINE.

11
Exporting the Character to CRYENGINE

Now that we have the character rig file ready, we have everything to get this character in the engine along with its animations. We will also go over debugging the character in the Character Editor and see how to create all the necessary engine files to export and see the character's animations in the engine. In this chapter, we will cover the following topics:

- CRYENGINE asset types
- Export groups in Maya
- The Character Editor
- Exporting the character's animations
- The animation pipeline of the engine
- Physicalized attachments

Getting started

For this chapter, we will work on exporting the character's animations into the engine. Therefore, we will need to unpack the animation files found in `Animations.pak` in the `GameSDK` folder. The `Animations.pak` file is a compressed folder of all the **compressed animation files (cafs)** and other animation files that we will need to edit to be able to export new animations to the engine. Like any other ZIP folder, you can unpack the contents of `Animation.pak` with any archive program.

Art asset file types

In this section, we will cover the different visual art assets that can be created within Maya or other digital content creation tools. Before the Resource Compiler converts the assets to the desired Crytek file format, they get exported into an intermediate **collada** file format where the asset information such as the material ID, vertex colors, and physics properties are written.

The Crytek Geometry Format

The **Crytek Geometry Format** (**CGF**) is the CRYENGINE file type used for static geometry. You can also create phys proxies for the CGF meshes using the same steps we explained in the previous chapter. Instead of parenting the proxies under a skeleton, here we will parent them directly under the CGF's parent group under its CryExport group.

It is worth mentioning that the CGF asset and its phys proxy's material IDs need to be in the same material group; otherwise, you will get an error exporting the asset. This is a requirement that we don't need to follow for exporting the **Character Format** (**CHR**) skeleton and its phys proxies.

The Character format

The **Character** (**CHR**) format is used to export all the skeletons and phys proxies' data through a skinned mesh. We can't export an object as a CHR that is not bound to bones via a **skin cluster** node in Maya, which makes the CHR in that aspect similar to the **skin** (**skinned Render mesh**) file format.

In some older assets, the CHR actually represents both the skeleton and the skinned mesh. However the recommended pipeline now for creating characters in CRYENGINE dictates a separation between the two. Think of the CHR as simply just the skeleton and its proxies, while the skins are the mesh attachments for it.

The most common practice for creating the CHR in Maya is to create a simple mesh, usually in the shape of a triangle, and smooth bind it to an upper body joint such as the pelvis joint. The material used for the CHR mesh is a **ProxyNoDraw** material, usually the same one applied on the phys proxies. We will cover the process for creating a CHR in detail in the *Creating the export groups in Maya* section.

The Skinned Render mesh

The **Skinned Render** mesh or **skin** represents a CRYENGINE compatible skinned assets file type. A skin can be any mesh that is smooth bound to our character's skeleton, which is represented by the CHR.

In older CRYENGINE versions, you would get a crash if you tried to load a character definition file in Sandbox, where there is an extra bone used in the skin cluster of the skin attachment and not found in the CHR. This has changed in SDK 3.6. If you add a skin attachment with extra bones to the character definition file now, those bones are extended to the CHR skeleton. We call that system the **skeleton extensions**.

It is important to understand that these extra bones are not being added to the CHR file itself. The process of extending the skeleton is done at the character definition file load time. The CHR file hasn't been modified, and neither has the character definition file.

Skeleton extensions provide great flexibility when it comes to a character's pipeline. It is common to use one CHR/skeleton for multiple characters in a game. However, it can get problematic if you have a more complicated asset where you need to add extra corrective bones to get the desired result. Without the skeleton extensions, you would need to add all of these bones onto the same skeleton. If you get even more complicated assets to skin to the same skeleton, imagine how cumbersome the process would be to have all of these joints that belong to different skins added in the same CHR.

The Crytek Geometry Animation

The **Crytek Geometry Animation (CGA)** assets are simply animated rigid meshes where the animations are applied directly onto the geometries. CGA animations can be exported as .anm and .caf file types, while skeleton-based animations only use .caf files. By default, you export one default animation with the CGA asset. To have additional animations, you will need to export them to the same folder where the CGA asset is saved. The animations get linked to the CGA by using the name of the CGA asset as a prefix for the name of those animations.

Creating the export groups in Maya

We will use the `boris_rig` Maya file in the `Boris` folder to export our assets. Let's start with creating the export groups for our skins. In the **Outliner** window, expand **boris_character_GRP** and select **boris_body** mesh in the **boris_mesh_GRP** group, as shown in the following screenshot:

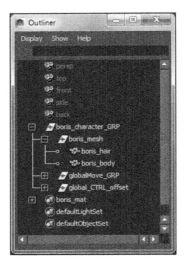

With the object selected, go to the **Crytek** shelf and click on the **Tools** icon. The **Cry Tools** window should open like this:

Click on **Create CryExportNode** to open the options window like this:

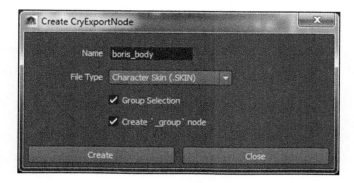

Select the **Character Skin (.SKIN)** option from the drop-down menu of the
File Type field and ensure that both the **Group Selection** and **Create '_group'
node** options are checked. Now, we have our **cryExportNode_boris_body** group
ready. Repeat the same steps for the **boris_hair** mesh too. If you wish at any time to
change the file type of the asset, you can select the **cryExportNode** group and go to
the Attribute Editor. In the **Extra Attributes** section, you can change the file type as
shown in the following screenshot:

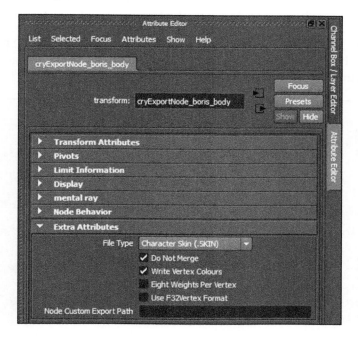

Let's go ahead and create our CHR. To create the CHR mesh, go to **Create | Polygon Primitives | Plane Options** and apply the following settings:

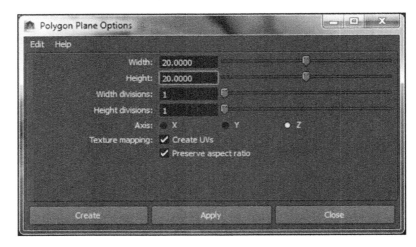

Rename the polygon plane `boris_skel`. To make the plane look like a triangle pointing towards the front of the character, make sure you are in the **Polygons** menu set and select the front two vertices in component mode then go to **Edit Mesh | Merge To Center**. Make sure to delete the history on the plane afterwards.

Move the **boris_skel** plane to the **pelvis_JNT** joint position. Select the **pelvis_JNT** joint, select the **boris_skel** plane, switch to the **Animation** menu set, go to **Skin | Bind Skin | Smooth Bind** options, and apply these settings:

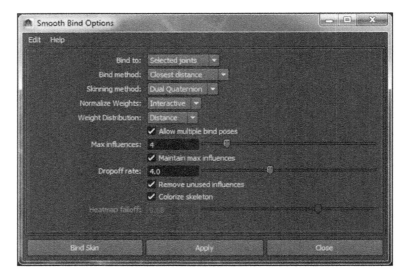

You can unhide the deformation skeleton in the **globalMove_GRP** group under the **boris_character_GRP** group.

Now, we have the skeleton information on our CHR and it is time to create the **CryExportNode**. Follow the same steps we used to create our character skins, but this time we set the file type to **Character (.CHR)** in the **Create CryExportnode** options. Let's go ahead now and try to export our meshes. In the Crytek shelf, click on the **Export** icon to open the **Export Options** window. The following screenshot has been cropped intentionally to focus on the **Geometry Export** and **Material Export** sections:

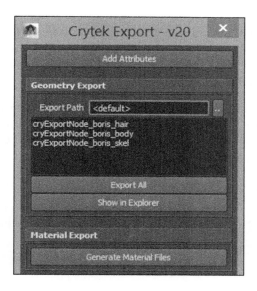

As you can see, the **Export Path** option is set to **default**, which is the folder where the current Maya file is saved. You can browse to another folder for exporting the assets just by clicking on the small button next to the export text field. For our purposes, leave the export path as default then click on **Export All**. Now, you should see the **Cry Validate** window with the following errors:

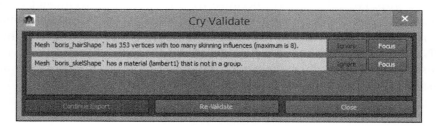

The first error says **Mesh 'boris_hairShape' has 353 vertices with too many skinning influences (maximum is 8)**. It can sound confusing since you probably expected that the maximum skinning influences is four… well, you are right!

Eight skinning influences is the limit that can be used for exporting skins with morphs or blend shapes from Maya. Skins using eight skinning influences have to also use software skinning, which is a flag that can be added manually in the CDF. Without that flag, the skins will not use software skinning and the 8 skinning influences will be clamped to four by the engine.

We use this trick to have more flexibility in skinning our characters. It is totally up to you if you want to work with four maximum influences to be 100 percent sure this is the result you will see in the engine, but you can also take the advantage of using eight maximum influences for skinning your objects and let the engine deal with the conversion. So far (since implementing this feature and till the time of this writing), the results have been pretty accurate and smooth in the engine without using the software skinning since it can be expensive.

We can use Maya's **Prune Small Weights** tool to get rid of the small weights that have no visible effect on the skin. Make sure to be in the **Animation** menu set, select the **boris_hair** geometry, go to **Skin | Edit Smooth Skin | Prune Small Weights**, and apply the following settings:

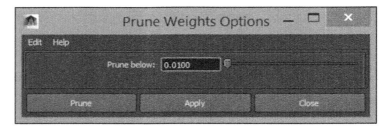

This will prune all the weights below 0.01. If you still have the **Cry Validate** window open, press on the **Re-Validate** button and you will see that this error disappeared.

The only error left now says: **Mesh 'boris_skelShape' has a material (lambert1) that is not in a group**. We got that error because we forgot two important steps in the creation of our CHR. The first one is to assign a material ID to our triangle and the second one is to add that material ID to a material group. Because the CHR needs a **ProxyNoDraw** material similar to the one we used for our phys proxies, we can simply use the same material. Select and right-click on **boris_skel** geometry and select **Assign Existing Material**. Choose **boris_phys_mat** material.

Now, we need to add that material ID to a material group. If you click on the **MAT. ED** icon in the Crytek shelf, you will see all the material groups we have in the scene and all the submaterials included in them, as shown in the following screenshot:

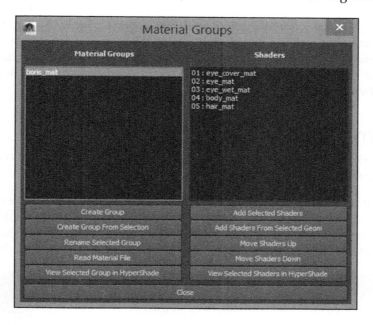

You can add **boris_phys_mat** to the existing **boris_mat** group by selecting the **boris_skel** triangle and clicking on the **Add Shaders From Selected Geom** button in the **Shaders** panel in the **MAT.ED** window. The **boris_phys_mat** will be added to the **boris_mat** as submaterial number 6. However, it is preferable to create a separate material group for the ProxyNoDraw material so you can reuse it as much as you want without worrying about the sub materials order in the group.

Let's create our own material group for the CHR and the phys proxies material. In the **Material Groups** panel, click on the **Create Group** button and rename the group phys_mat. Now, add the CHR material to the **phys_mat** group the same way as before. It is worth mentioning that you can't have the same material in more than one material group.

If you click on the **Re-Validate** button again in the **Cry Validate** window, you will see that the error has disappeared and the **Continue Export** button in the window is available. You can use it to continue exporting our assets.

Now, we need to create the material file for the **phys_mat** group. In the Crytek **Export** window, there is an option to export the material files using the **Generate Material Files** button in the **Material Export** section. Unfortunately, we can't choose which material files we want to export. The button will export all the existing material groups in the scene. We don't want to export the **boris_mat** material file, since it was already provided by the character artist with the proper textures path and the material settings that don't necessarily correspond to the material setup we have in Maya. A quick workaround is to set the file to read-only, so it doesn't get overwritten by the exporter.

Exporting with y axis up

If you are working with *y* as the scene up axis in Maya, you will need to follow a few steps to make sure your assets are exported properly to the engine:

1. As we have mentioned before in the *Deformation Skeleton rules* section in the previous chapter, the **Root bone** local rotation axis should always point up in the *z* axis and the *y* axis points forward. These are the orientation values you should have on your **Root bone** if you are working in Maya with *y* up.

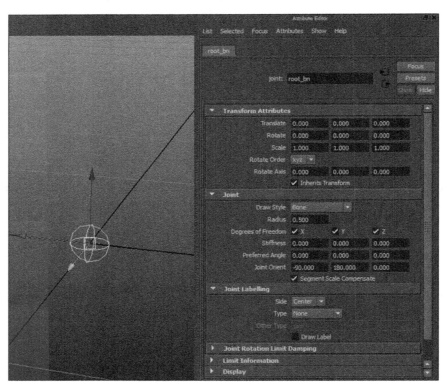

2. Create an empty group and name it SceneRoot.

3. Apply the same orientation values we had for the **Root bone** to the rotation values of the **SceneRoot** group, as shown in the following screenshot:

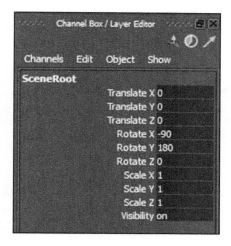

Now that we have all the assets ready and in place, it is time to assemble the character in the Character Editor.

The Character Editor

The **Character Editor** is the editor that you will use the most for creating the characters and testing their animations in the engine. We use the Character Editor to create the character definition files and preview all the available animations for our characters. We can also use the **Debug Options** tab to debug our assets in the editor and create physicalized attachments to add that nice and free secondary motion to our assets in the **Attachments** tab. To open the Character Editor in Sandbox, go to **View | Open View Pane | Character Editor**.

There are many other usages for the Character Editor that we will not be able to cover in this section, such as the animation layers and the blend-space control. You can check out the CRYENGINE documentation (http://docs.cryengine.com/display/SDKDOC2/The+Character+Editor) for full explanation on those two topics.

Debugging in the Character Editor

You can find the **Debug Options** tab if you scroll down to the bottom of the Character Editor's **Rollup** panel on the far right. You can also click on the **Advanced Animations Settings** tab to minimize it; then you will see the **Debug Options** tab. When you click on the **Debug Options** tab, you will see a long list of debug options you can use:

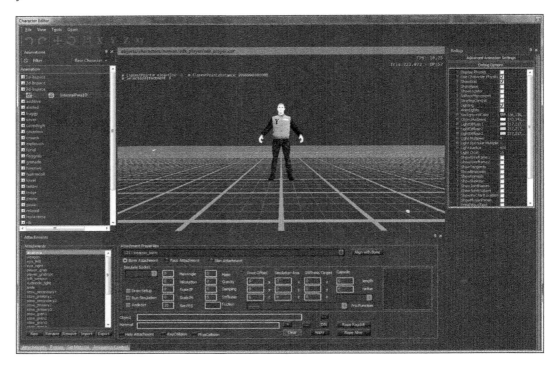

You can go ahead now and check some of the options to see the results on the SDK character. For example, you can check the **showSkeleton** option to see the skeleton of the character or check the **Display Physics** option to see the phys proxies. We don't need to have a character definition file to debug our character in the Character Editor; we can also use these options to debug CHRs.

Let's go ahead and test our **boris_skel** CHR to see if everything is exported properly using the debug options in the Character Editor. Go to **File | Open**, and load the `boris_skel.chr` file from `GameSDK\objects\characters\Boris` folder in the file browser. You will not see our exported triangle because we assigned a ProxyNoDraw material to it, which makes it invisible. Check the **showSkeleton** and **showJointNames** options to see our skeleton with names in the editor. This is shown in the following screenshot:

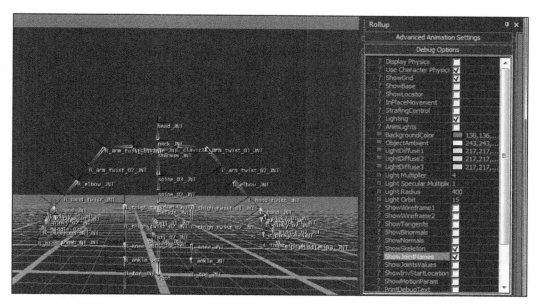

One thing you need to keep in mind when using the debug options in the Character Editor is that you are actually setting global variables! For example, if you check the **showSkeleton** option in the Character Editor, it will show the skeleton of all the characters you have in the level. Be careful when using those options and make sure to set them back to their original state before closing Sandbox. This is because the next time you open the Character Editor, it will keep the changes you made from the last session, and there is no button to restore defaults.

Creating the character definition file

The **character definition file** (CDF) is what ultimately will end up being used in game. It is the file type that level and cinematic designers use to place the characters in their levels and animators use this to check their animations. The whole process of creating the CDF is done in the **Attachments** tab in the Character Editor. Let's go ahead and create a **boris** CDF, starting with these few steps to create our first skin attachment:

1. Open the `boris_skel.chr` file in the Character Editor.

2. In the **Attachments Properties** group box, make sure to select **Skin Attachment** to attach our skin files to the CHR. This is highlighted in the following screenshot:

 Both the **Bone Attachment** and **Face Attachment** options are used only with CGFs and don't support Skin file type.

3. In the **Attachments** panel, click on the **New** button. This is highlighted in the following screenshot:

4. A pop-up window will appear. Type in the name of the attachment, which is `body`, and click on **OK**.

5. Select the **body** skin attachment in the **Attachments** group box. In the **Attachment Properties** section, click on the button next to the **Object** field and choose `boris_body.skin` from the `GameSDK\objects\characters\Boris` folder. Then, click on the **Apply** button. This is highlighted in the following screenshot:

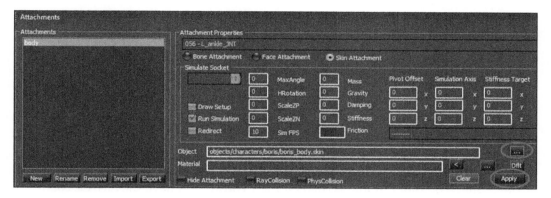

6. Go through the steps from 2 to 5 to create our **boris_hair** skin attachment.
7. Finally, save the file as `boris.cdf` in our `Boris` folder.

Now, you should be able to see the full character in the Character Editor:

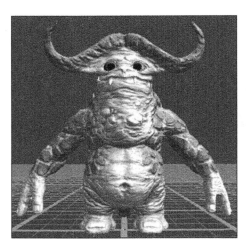

 The Character Editor will not give you an accurate representation of the textures and shading of your model. However, in **Debug Options**, you can tweak some options like the **ObjectAmbient** and **lightDiffuse** values to get better shading on your model in the editor.

Exporting the animations to the engine

Before we go ahead and export our animations from Maya, we need to create our animations' folder structure. Assuming you already extracted the contents of the `Animations.pak` folder in the `GameSDK` folder, you should have the `Animations` folder with the following folders inside:

Share with ▾	Burn	
Name	Date modified	Type
animals	2/25/2015 8:04 AM	File folder
human	2/25/2015 8:04 AM	File folder
Mannequin	2/25/2015 8:04 AM	File folder
objects	2/25/2015 8:04 AM	File folder
weapons	2/25/2015 8:04 AM	File folder
Animations.img	2/12/2015 9:14 PM	IrfanView IMG File
DbaTable.xml	9/15/2014 2:43 PM	XML Document
DirectionalBlends.img	2/12/2015 9:14 PM	IrfanView IMG File
SkeletonList.xml	12/2/2014 9:44 AM	XML Document

Create a new folder named `Boris`. This will be the folder where we export all of our character's animations to. Now, we have everything in place to export our animations from Maya in the following steps:

1. In the `Boris` folder in `Objects`, open the `boris_walkCycle01` Maya file. You should see a 35-frame walk cycle. Make sure that your playback range starts at frame 1 and ends at frame 35.

2. In the Crytek shelf, click on the **Export** icon to open the Crytek **Export** window.

3. In the **Anim Export** section, click on the **Anim Manager** button to open the **Cry Animation Manager** window.

4. In the **Cry Animation Manager** window, click on **New** to add our walk cycle to the Animation Manager. Now, you should see the **Add Anim Range** window with multiple fields.

5. In the **Name** field, type `boris_walkCycle01`. This will be the name of our exported animation file.

6. Click on the **Use Range From Time Slider** button at the top of the window to fill in the **Start Frame** and **End Frame** fields.

[If you don't want to set your time slider to the start and the end of your animation exactly, you can fill those fields manually.]

7. Select our **root_bn** joint in the deformation skeleton and then click on the **Select** button next to the **Root** field to add the **Root bone**.

8. In the **Path** field, browse to the `Boris` folder we created in `Animations`. This is the path where we will export the animation to. Here is a screenshot of the complete fields in the **Add Anim Range** window:

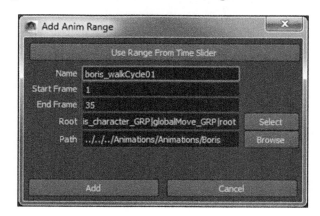

9. After filling the information about our walk cycle, click on the **Add** button at the bottom of the window to go to back to the **Cry Animation Manager** window. You should see our **boris_walkCycle01** animation added in there:

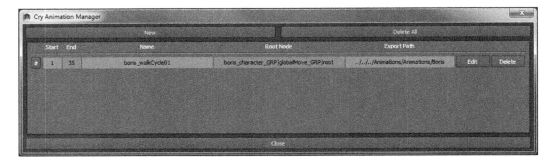

10. Finally, select **boris_walkCycle01** in the **Anim Export** panel and click on **Export Selected Anims** to export the animation. After exporting the animation, you can click on **Show in Explorer** to open our Boris animation folder. You should see the boris_walkCycle01.i_caf animation file there. The name i_caf is short for **Intermediate Character Animation File**. This file holds the character's bone animation in an uncompressed format. There are a few other steps we need to follow in the upcoming order to be able to see our animations in the engine.

Any time you would like to change the animation settings, you can click on the **Edit** button next to the animation in **Cry Animation Manager**. Back in the Crytek **Export** window, you should be able to see our animation in the **Anim Export** section:

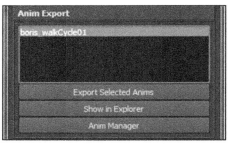

The Character Parameters file

In order to map our exported animation to our character we will need to create a **Character Parameters** file (**chrparams**). The chrparams XML file is where we can define the animation set our character will use in the engine. There are also other definitions you can add to the chrparams file of your character, such as the **level of detail** (**LOD**), **Look and Aim IK** definitions, and more. For a full list of all the available definitions you can add to the chrparams file, please refer to the CRYENGINE documentation at http://docs.cryengine.com/pages/viewpage. action?pageId=1310814.

There are a couple of rules we need to follow when creating the chrparams file. First, the file needs to be saved where the CHR of the character is located. Second, the name of the file needs to match the name of the character CHR. In our case, that would be boris_skel.chrparams. Since we can't export chrparams files from the engine, we will create the file manually. Using any text editor, add these few lines of code:

```
<?xml version="1.0"?>
<Params>
 <AnimationList>
   <Animation name="#Filepath" path="animations\Boris"/>
   <Animation name="*" path="*\.caf"/>
 </AnimationList>
</Params>
```

The #Filepath command points the engine to the folder where the animations of this character are exported to. In Animation name, you can assign any game name to your animation file. Using the asterisk symbol (*) to represent the animation name will allow you to use your animation file names in the game. Otherwise, you would have to add every animation in the animation folder or its subfolders and give each one of them a unique name. If we are going to use this method for our walk cycle, then the code would look like this:

```
<Animation name="walkCycle01" path="boris_walkCycle01.caf"/>
```

Here we assigned an in-game name `walkCycle01` to the `boris_walkCycle01.caf` file. Although in our case it is not a big deal to add our animation and give it an in-game name in the engine, you can imagine how much time you can save using the wildcard mapping if you have lots of animation files for your character. Adding line by line each animation you have can lead to an unnecessarily long and messy chrparams file.

Setting the `path` parameter to `*\*.caf` will include all the animations in the `animations\animations\Boris` folder and also its subfolders if you decided to have any. Finally save the file as `boris_skel.chrparams` in our `Boris` folder in `Objects`. As mentioned before the **chrparams** file needs to be saved in the same location as the character's CHR file.

The Skeleton List file

As you have probably noticed, we are loading CAF files in our chrparams file, which are simply the compressed `i_caf` files. Our final step to be able to load the **boris_walkCycle01** animation in the engine is to compress it using the **Animation Import** pane. In Sandbox, go to **View** | **Open View Pane** | **Animation Import**. On the right-hand side of the **Animation Import** window, you will see a list of CHR skeletons in-game and on the top-left side you can see our `boris_walkCycle01.i_caf` file.

The skeletons section is simply a representation of the `SkeletonList.xml` file that you can find in the `Animations` folder. We will need to add our **boris_skel.chr** skeleton to the **SkeletonList** file as well so we can compress our character's animations. You can add CHR skeletons to the file manually, but we will use the **Animation Import** window instead. Make sure the `SkeletonList.xml` file is writable. At the bottom of the **Skeletons** section, in the **Animation Import** pane, click on the **Add** button. Browse to our `boris_skel.chr` file in the `Boris` folder in `Objects` and select it.

Now, you should see our skeleton added to the list, as shown in the following screenshot:

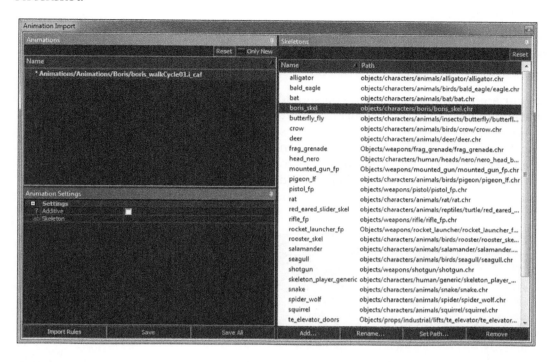

Select our animation in the **Animations** section on the right and double-click on **boris_skel** entry in the skeletons list. You should see our skeleton added to the **Skeleton** field in the **Animation Settings** panel, as shown in the following screenshot.

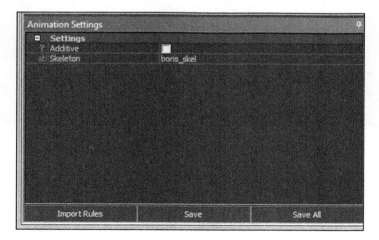

Now, click on the **Save** button at the bottom of the panel to save our settings and we should be done compressing our animation. If everything goes correctly, you should see these lines in the console:

```
Task Completed: Compression of 'Animations/Animations/Boris/boris_
walkCycle01.caf'
```

```
Task Completed: Reload CHRPARAMS
```

In our `Boris` animation folder, you should now see the `boris_walkCycle01.caf` file and the `boris_walkCycle01.animsettings` file. The animation settings file is created for each animation and holds its compression settings that we saved in the **Animation Import** pane. To see the animation, open the Character Editor and load our `boris.cdf` file from the `Boris` folder in `Objects`. In the **Animation** panel on the right-hand side of the **Character Editor** window, you should see our `boris` animation folder and our `boris_walkCycle01.caf` file inside, as shown in the following screenshot:

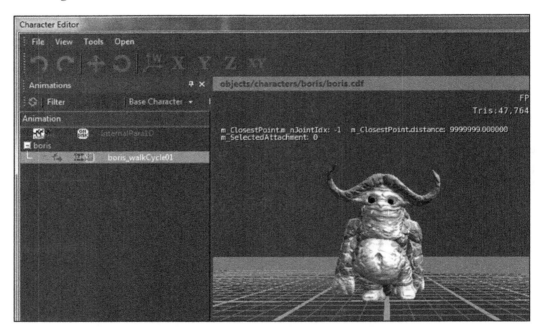

The physicalized attachments

The physicalized attachments in CRYENGINE provide a simple, easy-to-setup, and stable way to create secondary motion to characters. You can use the physicalized attachments to dynamically simulate characters' accessories, such as necklaces, earrings, and cloth, or body parts, such as tails, tentacles, and fat jiggle. Physicalized attachments work on both bones and static meshes. Depending on your pipeline, you can decide how to use them, but we advise to use bones as much as possible to save **draw calls**.

In our example, we will simulate our character's belly. Sounds fun, right? Go back to the `Boris` folder in `Objects` and open the `boris_export_groups` Maya file. In the view port, go to **Shading** and make sure that **X-Ray Joints** option is checked. You should see our **belly_JNT** parented under **pelvis_JNT**. In the **Animations** menu set, go to **Skin | Edit Smooth Skin | Paint Skin Weights Tool**. You should see all the skin influences in a list in the **Tool Settings Editor**. Select the **belly_JNT** bone in the **Influences** list and have a look at its smooth influence on our body mesh. It should look like the following screenshot:

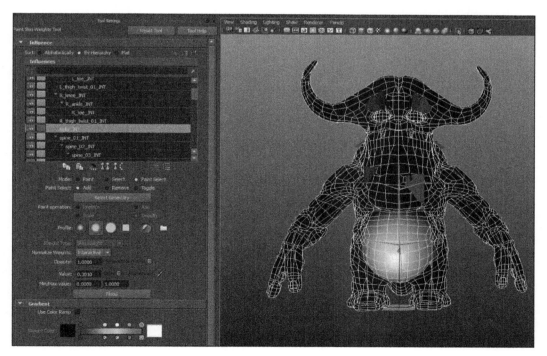

Feel free to move and rotate the joint to have a better feeling of how it affects the skin, but make sure to set it back to its default position and orientation. Please keep in mind that the skinning is a very important step in our setup. Skinning along with the physicalized attachments setup in the engine can define how strong your simulation can be. So it is a back and forth process between modifying the skinning in Maya and the attachment settings in the engine until you get the results you want. The last thing we need to do is to update the **boris_body** skin attachment by exporting it from Maya again.

In Sandbox, open the Character Editor and load the `boris.CDF` file. Now, we will go through the steps to create a bone attachment, which we will use later to physicalize the **belly_JNT** bone using either the **springs** or **pendula** properties in the engine:

1. In the **Attachment** properties tab, check the **Bone Attachment** button.
2. Select **belly_JNT** from the joints list.
3. In the **Attachments** section, create a new attachment and rename it `belly_phys`.
4. Click on **Apply**.
5. Click on **Align with Bone**, so our attachment has the same position and orientation as the **belly_JNT** bone.

In the **Simulate Socket** drop-down list, you will see five options: **No physics**, **Cone**, **HalfCone**, **Hinge**, and **Ellipsoid**. The **No physics** option renders the attachment as a normal bone attachment. The **Cone**, **HalfCone**, and **Hinge** options use the **pendulum** physics properties, while the **Ellipsoid** uses the **spring** physics properties. Because the Pendulum simulation creates a simple harmonic motion, it is better in general for physicalized chain setups, such as ropes, tentacles, and tails. The swinging of the object attached to the pendulum can be controlled by the physical parameters and constrained by the geometrical shape of the **Cone**, **HalfCone**, and **Hinge** primitives. The spring physical properties are similar to the pendulum properties. The difference between these two is that the spring can *stretch* and the spring system implemented in CRYENGINE allows stretching in any direction, unlike the helical spring. The object motion attached to a spring can be constrained by the limits of the geometrical shape of an **ellipsoid**. The great thing about the ellipsoid is that it is scalable. So, using a few parameters we can transform the shape of the ellipsoid to a line, a plane, and half a sphere.

We will use the spring simulation in our example, so select the **Ellipsoid** from the **Simulate Socket** list. Make sure to check the **Re-direct**, **Run Simulation**, and **Draw Setup** checkboxes. The **Re-direct** option activates the simulation on the attachment. The **Run Simulation** option allows you to see the run time simulation in the Character Editor. The **Draw Setup** option will draw the geometrical shape of the ellipsoid, as shown in the following:

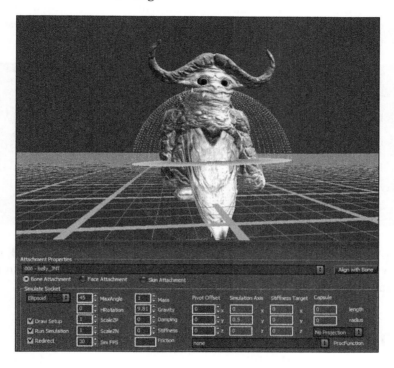

This is of course not what we want the belly to look like. The first thing you probably thought of is decreasing the size of the ellipsoid, you are right! However, you need to keep in mind when you reduce the size of the ellipsoid to get the desired results, it will end up probably (based on the size of your character of course) inside the mesh and it will become more difficult to tweak its shape. So let's try first to think about the final shape we would like to have for our ellipsoid and then reduce its size. First of all, let's rotate the ellipsoid so that its y axis faces towards our character. Set the **HRotation** value to 90. We don't want our joint to rotate 360 degrees at any time. So it makes sense we use only half of the ellipsoid by setting the **ScaleZP** value to 0. Now we can reduce the size of our ellipsoid (or half ellipsoid now). Set the **MaxAngle** attribute to 10. Now we are starting to see better results just by adjusting the shape and size of our ellipsoid, but we still have some more parameters to adjust.

Leave the **Mass** value at 1 so that the gravity doesn't pull the pendulum more downward in the way that you see it now. Increasing the **Mass** value will increase that affect but increasing the **Stiffness** value will reduce it. So set the **Stiffness** parameter to 100. You probably will see now the pendulum moving pretty fast inside the ellipsoid. To get much smoother results set the **Damping** value to 7. If you still want less gravity, you can set the **Gravity** value to 5 instead of 9.8, just make sure to have a higher value than one. Otherwise, you will end up getting a very damped and floating effect, which we don't want. The following screenshot represents all the values we set to our spring attachment for your reference:

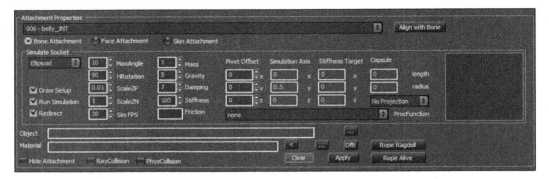

Feel free to play more with these parameters or the shape of the ellipsoid, so you have a better idea of their effect on the simulation and where else you can use them in your character setup.

Summary

In this chapter, we covered the different asset types that can be used to assemble a character inside the Character Editor and how to use that editor to debug our character and make sure it is exported properly. We also went through the process of exporting our animations from Maya to the engine and all the files you need to edit or create in order to see these animations in the engine, and have a better idea about the potential errors you may face while exporting your animations from Maya and how to solve them. Using the Character Editor we were able to set up a physicalized attachment using the spring properties in the engine. You also saw how you can tweak the properties to get a better result for creating a secondary motion to your character.

12
Initial Level Blockout and Setup

Single player level design is a complex and multilayered process that requires a broad understanding of everything from environment construction to scripting events. To kick off our deeper look into constructing single player content in Sandbox, we will cover the following topics:

- Cover the design theory used to build a typical **action bubble** in Crytek's *Crysis* series, giving us a basic outline to proceed with as we move toward building the many facets of a single player level in CRYENGINE3

- Adapting the premade SDK content

- Look at how we can use the work created for the existing SDK environments to speed up our level creation, as well as optimal editor setup, to make sure our level production experience is as pain-free as possible

Action bubble level design

Level designers for the *Crysis* games lived by a simple mantra: *VVV*, which stands for *Veni Vidi Vici* (I came, I saw, I conquered). This was a simple way to constantly reinforce to designers that levels should be designed around this flow: the player arrives at the space, observes the challenge and available options, and then executes their plan. These spaces were known as action bubbles, a name for the pockets of gameplay within a level that form the peaks of level pacing. The very first main action bubble in *Crysis 1* is a perfect example of this in action: the player emerges from a jungle overlooking a beach, and they are presented with a set of enemies and a number of visible options for approaching the challenge. This gives the player the ingredients they need to make choices about how to proceed.

Before we start getting into technical details and building the level proper, I am going to give a basic introduction to building action bubbles. This will not be a requirement for following the rest of the chapters, but simply a template using existing assets that you can follow if you want to learn more about scripted Sandbox setup without committing to the action RTS or medieval platformer that you might have in mind.

References and 2D layout

A useful first step for creating any level is collecting a reference for our desired location. This could be anything from photos of the real world to concept art. We want to ground the location in some form of reality from the outset. Assuming we are only using the SDK asset libraries for now, I have picked a remote forest fishing village as the location in order to minimize any requirements for further art work.

If you're able to generate level art yourself, have artists in a team at your disposal, or are simply looking to prove out gameplay without high visual fidelity, then an alternative choice would be to create very basic whitebox geometry to support our level design. This is where very simple geometry (typically white boxes) is used to generate a fun gameplay space without a strong emphasis on aesthetics; the Designer Tool in CRYENGINE is well suited to this task. However, given that the SDK is kitted out with enough art assets to generate a more polished environment, we'll use the fishing village for now as a backdrop to learn more about single player level setup.

With this location in mind, I've generated a rough topdown map to give me a foundation for level design moving forward:

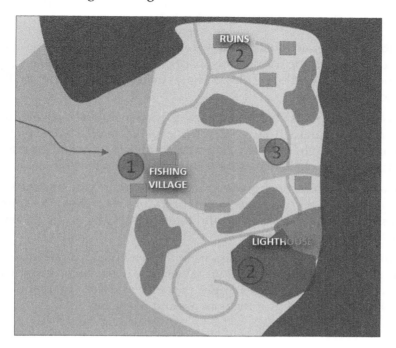

Along with the map, I've also generated an initial set of objectives that correspond to key map locations. This will give us ample opportunity to demonstrate a broad set of single player setup principles in CRYENGINE and produce something fun in the process:

- **Objective 1 – Land On The Island**: This is a small scripted boat sequence that opens the level, giving an exciting introduction to the level and an initial combat sequence

- **Objective 2 – Clear The Enemy Encampments**: The two objectives are playable in any order, allowing more freedom and player-driven exploration of the map

- **Objective 3 – Destroy The Reinforcements**: Having learned about most of the playspace, the player must then scavenge the environment for weapons that are able to take out the heavy enemy reinforcements

Design considerations

While generating this initial layout and flow, a few aspects were considered in order to make sure the space fulfills a few level design requirements:

- Multiple smaller action bubbles were used instead of one large combat space. This gives the overall playspace a more open feel, and also gives us the ability to add some player choice in objective ordering for the middle section of the level.

- Traversal space was considered between action bubbles, pacing the experience so not to throw all that the level has to offer at the player in the first encounter. The objective flow should ideally vary both in the type and difficulty of the challenge as the player progresses through the level.

- The action bubbles were given enough space to provide multiple attacking options. Again, this escalates as part of the objective flow. We start the player in a smaller combat encounter, and then increase the size of the encounter towards the final objective.

- Distinct theming and landmarks were implemented for each action bubble. This aids navigation and adds visual variety. It also helps give each combat area a strong identity, for example, players could say, "first I took out the lighthouse guys and then the ones around the caves."

This layout is not set in stone and is likely to change as we iterate on the level, but it can be useful to work out the layout problems on paper before committing to more time consuming engine work. For example, as part of this process, I was able to ensure that both of the second objectives were spaced correctly to encourage usage of the second path away from the coastline. My initial map positioning had these areas closer to the fishing village's path, which would have had encouraged a less interesting backtracking route when moving between the two.

Level content

The final aspect to consider when designing the space is which gameplay elements we plan to populate the area with.

To do this, we need to take a look at what challenges and tools the SDK build contains so we can best support these with our level design:

- **Core mechanics**: Due to the stripped-back nature of the SDK build, stealth mechanics such as hiding in vegetation or AI distraction are not a part of the player's arsenal. However, the player is equipped with a selection of weaponry and a regenerative health system, facilitating basic combat. As a result, we should look to provide interest through the cover layouts and broader level design, and try to avoid situations where the player feels like they are able to stealth their way through the whole level without conflict. The *Halo* series does a particularly good job of this kind of encounter design, using elements such as having AI initiate combat before the player arrives to set the tone for the upcoming gameplay.

- **Interaction**: The SDK build offers simple interaction in the form of usable objects (for example, doors) and pick-and-throw abilities. Utilizing these to create simple obstacles or gameplay opportunities would add an extra element to the gameplay.

- **Enemies**: A number of entity archetypes exist that should provide good variety in the combat AI within the level. Additionally, there is a boat, a jeep, a tank, and even a helicopter if you're feeling especially adventurous and inspired by Black Hawk Down.

- **Traversal**: The player is able to move, crouch, sprint, slide and jump. Obstacles that encourage the use of these abilities can help add interest to the traversal of the level.

- **Destruction**: The SDK offers a sizeable library of destructible props. While these don't help or hinder the player necessarily (unless used as dynamic cover), they add extra interaction into the environment, which can increase interest in an otherwise static scene as a result of player or AI actions.

Now we have a rough 2D plan to move ahead with, along with ideas of how we are going to make it fun, we can move toward achieving this goal in Sandbox.

Setting up user preferences, hotkeys, and toolbox macros

Before we jump into making level content, first we should make sure our work environment is set up to make producing that content as efficient and stable as possible. Working this way will make us quicker at iterating on the level design and make sure we keep our work backed up and safe.

User preferences

There is a vast number of user preferences that exist in Sandbox, which can be modified to suit each individual's tastes. However, there are a few options which I would recommend changing. These preferences can be found at **Tools | Preferences**.

The Auto Backup action

The Auto Backup action is available through **General Settings | Files | Auto Backup**. Auto backup can perform a few functionalities that help protect your work. When enabled, it will create copies of the `.cry` file and any `.lyr` files, place them in the same directory as the source file, and rename their extension to `.bak`. In order to utilize these backups if you lose work or just want to go back to an earlier version, simply rename the `.bak` extension to the original extension. Along with this, it will also periodically back up the whole `level` folder and place it in the `YOURLEVELNAME/_Autobackup` folder.

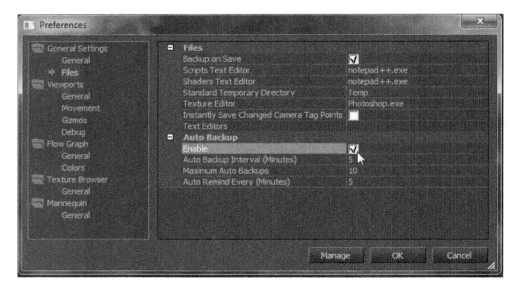

The **Auto Backup** section of the user preferences contains a number of options that you are able to customize:

- **Enable**: This option turns the feature on. This is the box to tick and never untick.

- **Auto Backup Interval (Minutes)**: This specifies how often the feature will create auto backups.

- **Maximum Auto Backups**: Increase the value of this option to increase the number of back up iterations that are stored, for example, changing this to 5 will back up five consecutive versions of the level files, with the oldest one given a .bak5 extension.

- **Auto Remind Every (Minutes)**: This will prompt you to save the level at every time period specified, which can also be useful if you feel particularly save-happy.

The Fill Selected Shapes action

The Fill Selected Shapes action is available through **Viewport | General | Viewport Displaying | Fill Selected Shapes**. When we start creating logic based on the shapes placed in the level, it can be useful to visualize the boundaries of these shapes more adequately by having the faces of the shapes filled in. Checking this box enables this setting; on the edited screenshot that follows, you can see the left side without the fill, and the right side with the option enabled:

The Display Dimension Figures action

The Display Dimension Figures action is available through Viewport | **General** | **Viewport Displaying** | **Display Dimension Figures**. This feature is invaluable when creating anything to specific metrics; the dimension figures show the length, width, and height of any selected object. The results of this setting are displayed in the following screenshot:

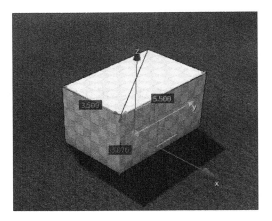

The View Pane layout

A final preference option that you won't find in the previous menus is the View Pane layout. CRYENGINE offers a few different subeditors in order to work with many different facets of the game production and to keep them organized. Sometimes, getting an easy access to the panes can be a pain (pun intended), especially if you don't have much free screen real estate. To combat this, in Sandbox, you can *dock* panes to each other, allowing you to click on multiple tabs in one view pane instead of cycling through many view pane windows. To do this, simply, click and drag a view pane (for example, a Flow Graph) and select the middle *tab* option when hovering over another view pane, as shown in the following screenshot:

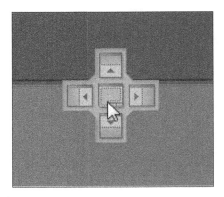

Hotkeys

While the choice of hotkeys is another option specific to each user, there are some relatively hidden features in CRYENGINE that deserve to be exposed to hotkeys to make your general editing workflow more efficient. Hotkeys can be assigned by navigating to **Tools | Customize Keyboard | Keyboard Tab**:

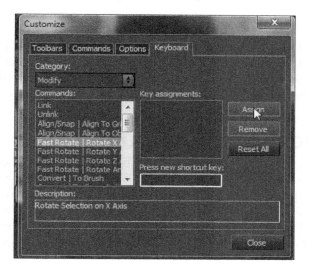

The Fast Rotate action

The Fast Rotate action is available through **Modify Category | Fast Rotate**. If you've ever wanted to rotate an object by 180 degrees and have sat there twiddling the rotation gizmo until it's correct, then these hotkeys are for you. You can assign a key for each axis to rotate an object by 45 degrees per key press. This is incredibly useful for fast iteration on object placement.

The Convert action

The Convert action is available through **Modify Category | Convert**. The **Convert** set of operations is very useful whenever working with a lot with geometry assets. If you often find yourself converting rigid bodies into brushes or want to quickly create a Designer object version of an existing brush, it's worthwhile setting these hotkeys up.

The Simulate Objects action

The Simulate Objects action is available through **Modify Category** | **Physics** | **Simulate Objects**. This is a nice little functionality that makes placing entities in a realistic manner particularly fast. Using this hotkey will physicalize the selected entities, wait for them to come to rest, and then save their new positions.

The Switch Camera action

The Switch Camera action is available through **Display Category** | **Switch Camera**. If you find yourself working a lot within Track View to create cinematic sequences, this set of hotkeys will allow you to quickly jump in and out of your selected camera's view without having to do so via the **Context** menu in the perspective view.

The Toolbox Macros feature

The final power user option that's worth investigating is the Toolbox Macros feature, which is located at **Tools** | **Configure Toolbox Macros**. Using this system, we are able to group together multiple CVARs or scripts which can then be assigned to a button within a toolbar, allowing us to automate the process of manually opening the console and entering the CVAR values by hand. To demonstrate this, we'll go through the motions of adding the physics mesh debugging CVAR (p_draw_helpers) to a button:

1. In the **Configure Toolbox Macros** window, press the **New** button in the **Macros** section. Here, you can enter your desired name for the macro.

2. Next, press the **New** button in the **Commands** section. Don't enter a name (this will be represented by the CVAR) and press *Enter*.

3. Deselect the command and then reselect it; this is required to make the parameters of the command editable.

4. In the **Command** field, enter p_draw_helpers. You should see this autocompleted as you type.

5. Once it is entered, enable **Toggle Variable**. This tells the macro that the value will toggle between 1 and 0 when it is run.

6. Finally, click **Assign** with the command selected; the command should now be assigned to your associated macro command. It will also rename itself to **p_draw_helpers** and be displayed in a purple color, as shown in the following screenshot:

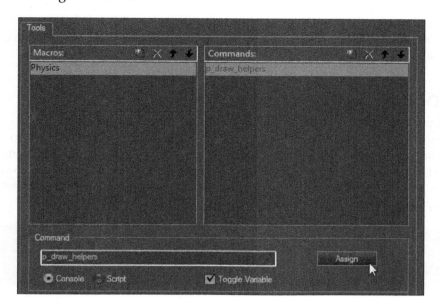

From here, you can now add extra functionality such as a hotkey or an icon for the toolbar. For now, we'll exit this dialog. Now, all you need to do is go to **Tools | Toolbox Macros** and drag the window out by using the handle at the top of the list. Then, this becomes a toolbar that you can dock in the main window like any other. This is a powerful feature that enables the automation of a lot of frequently performed steps. This is something to keep in mind if you find yourself often entering CVARs or running scripts that could take the form of a preset macro.

Adapting the premade SDK content

It can often be very daunting to go to **File | New** and look at a blank ocean. However, unless you are starting your project entirely from scratch, many games (and in our case, the SDK) include levels with huge amounts of content already created. Thankfully, there are a number of ways that this content can be repurposed or simply used as a reference for creating your very own level.

Level duplication

One way to ease the workload of production, especially if you plan on making a level with a similar style or location to an existing map, is to simply duplicate the level in Windows explorer, rename the level folder *and* the .cry file to your new level name, and load this level instead. You can then tear this level apart and modify it to fit your own needs—easily moving around existing content while the original level is safely backed up.

Exporting objects

If you'd prefer to work in a clean .cry file from scratch, you can export lightweight groups of objects between levels, which means you don't have to copy individual geometry paths across maps if you want to grab some objects from one level and import them into another. Simply select all the objects you want to copy and then press **Save Selected Objects** on the **Edit** mode toolbar, as shown in the following screenshot:

This can then be loaded by using the adjacent **Load Selected Objects** button in a different level. This will load the objects into the new level at their old position, select them, and assign them to your current layer.

Exporting the world

You can also export the various files used by the systems that represent the rest of the world in the level. This includes terrain, vegetation, and lighting. This can be useful if you want to reuse particular world settings that worked well in a different level, but apply this to your new map.

The heightmap

The heightmap is the basic 2D image data that represents the terrain in the world. Go to **View** | **Open View Pane** | **Terrain Editor** and then navigate to **File** | **Export Heightmap** within this editor. From here, you can choose multiple formats to export to, which will allow you to edit the file with different third-party applications such as World Machine (a terrain generation tool) or even Photoshop.

The option is shown in the following screenshot:

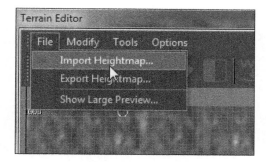

Terrain layers

Terrain layers are the data used to paint textures onto the heightmap via the **Layer Painter** tool in the **Terrain** tab within the **RollupBar** menu. To export these, go to **View | Open View Pane | Terrain Texture Layers** and navigate to **File | Export Layers**:

This creates a .lay file that contains both the surface types defined in the **Terrain Texture Layers** editor and the layer settings defined per layer in **Layer Painter**.

Vegetation instances

You may also want to use premade vegetation instances that work well within the existing level. To do this, go to the **Vegetation** menu in the **RollupBar** menu's **Terrain** tab (which is the second from the left), select all the vegetation categories you want to export, and then press the **Export Vegetation** button.

This is shown in the following screenshot:

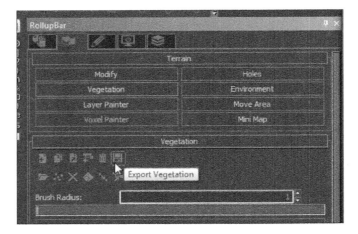

This functionality exports both the categories and instance locations. This means that when imported, the editor will import the categories and their settings, and then place instances of those vegetation categories at every position they existed in before.

Time Of Day and Lighting

Finally, there are the two systems that make up the lighting in CRYENGINE: the **Time Of Day** editor and the **Lighting** tool. The Time of Day file stores all the data that controls the various components of the lighting system such as the sky, fog, and shadow properties across the 24 hour day-night cycle. To export this for use in your new level, go to **View** | **Open View Pane** | **Time of Day** and press the **Export File** button. This will produce a .tod file that you can import with the adjacent button into your new level. This is shown in the following screenshot:

In addition to this, the `.lgt` file exportable from the Lighting tool controls higher level lighting properties such as the position and orientation of the sun in the sky, which can be tweaked in order to place the sun (and consequently, shadows) in your desired position in the world. To export this, go to **View | Open View Pane | Lighting Tool** and press the **Export** button situated below the sun path over the terrain preview. This is shown in the following screenshot:

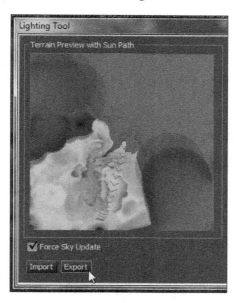

Using and understanding source files

Finally, it's worth going through the various ways in which we have access to the raw data in CRYENGINE source files, and how this enables us to perform operations from finding and replacing asset paths to tracking down numbers of entity references across your game.

Layers

Like most level files in CRYENGINE, layers (`.lyr` files) are simply XML files with a different file extension. This means you can open every layer file in a text editor and dive into the guts of the source code that makes up your level. This is powerful in a number of ways.

Mass editing content

If you've ever been in a situation where you want to change a geometry path or archetype ID across the entire game, bulk edits of raw layer files are a fast and effective solution to this. Using the Find and Replace feature found in text editors (such as Notepad++), you are able to find every instance of any value across potentially hundreds of source files and correct them to a new one.

Stat tracking

How many ammo crates have I placed across the game? Is that heavy enemy class being used in levels 3 or 4? If you have a search term, you can use bulk search features to find exact answers for many of these types of questions.

Fixing broken content

In the very unlikely event that the level files are corrupted, it's often possible to salvage the vast majority of work within the source files by simply editing out the bad entries in the XML file by hand if it's the fault of a bad entity.

The .cry and .pak files

The .cry file is the primary level editor file accessed by the Sandbox editor, whereas the level.pak file is where all the exported data lives which is then run by the game. However, despite their extensions, both are in actual fact archive files. This means they can be opened with any archive manager such as 7Zip or WinRAR, giving us even more access to the level source. The .cry file contains editor-only information such as references to all the loaded libraries and layers, while the .pak file contains all the various files exported by the editor such as AI navigation data, terrain files, and CGFs for any designer objects. Armed with this knowledge, it's possible to track down any bugs or discrepancies inside these files across multiple users and ascertain the exact information about the nature of the problems.

 You are unable to export to the engine with the level.pak file open in an archive manager, so make sure you close any instances of these before you export.

Summary

In this chapter, we covered the fundamentals of action bubble level design and how we can quickly get our Sandbox workflow up and running in order to jump into single player level creation.

In the next chapter, we'll familiarize ourselves with the Flow Graph working practices as we look toward constructing a variety of interactive scripted events that will populate our level.

The Flow Graph Workflow

13

Flow Graph is CRYENGINE's visual scripting interface, and it will be one of our primary tools for creating single player content in Sandbox. It is a powerful tool that offers a huge amount of control over the world, and it's easily possible to create interesting and flexible gameplay setups that respond believably to player interaction. Before we start scripting actual events, we are going to see how to create clean and flexible Flow Graphs that are easy to read, maintain, and iterate on as we develop our map. We will cover the following topics:

- Using Flow Graph containers
- Using Game Tokens to create cleaner Flow Graphs
- Laying out Flow Graphs to aid readability
- Thinking modularly to future-proof our work

Using Flow Graph containers

When authoring any work in CRYENGINE, the resulting data has to be saved somewhere. In most cases when working with editor objects in Sandbox, this data is stored on entities: Flow Graphs are no exception. Every entity in Sandbox has a **Flow Graph** section in its **RollupBar** parameters, where you are able to host Flow Graph scripting on that entity. Here, we will cover good practices for creating these Flow Graph containers and how they can be used to organize your scripting.

Host entities

For most projects, it's a good idea to store Flow Graphs on the **FlowgraphEntity** entities. This is to ensure that it's clear what the purpose of the entity is to you and others viewing the level; it can be easy to accidentally delete entire Flow Graphs if they are stored on unrelated entities such as triggers or characters. It also serves no function other than to host Flow Graphs, so it's a very lightweight entity and much cheaper than spawning other more featured entities in the world just to store scripting. Having them on their own bespoke entities and storing them in a safe place in the world keeps them separate and safe from everyday entity placement and deletion, while still preserving the ability to assign Flow Graphs to separate layers so as to allow multiuser editing of the level. To create a Flow Graph in this fashion, **FlowgraphEntities** can be found at **RollupBar** | **Objects Tab** | **Entity** | **FlowgraphEntity**. From here, simply press **Create** on the **FlowgraphEntity** entity's **Flow Graph** section, as shown in the following figure:

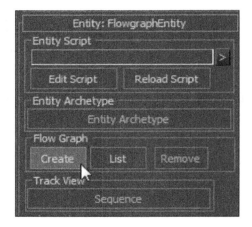

 As we have covered in the past, layer data is simply XML. Flow Graph is no different, and the source data for the Flow Graph we make can be found on the layer that the container object is assigned to. This can be useful if you want to perform mass find and replace operations on a Flow Graph script outside of the Editor. It's also invaluable if the flownode information in the layer goes out of sync with what is defined in the code if programmers rename things, as you can simply hand-edit the XML to amend the names to the correct updated version.

Splitting logic over multiple Flow Graphs

In larger productions with multiple playable areas, mission objectives, checkpoints, and other types of logic, you can easily become bogged down in one vast script that's difficult to navigate. This practice also stores all your Flow Graph data on one entity, which makes working with multiple users in the same level difficult. As such, it can often be useful to split different types of Flow Graph logic up into multiple containers for easier editing. It's a good idea to take the large sections of logic that can be easily consolidated and store them on separate entities, which can then be assigned to different layers if you need to support multiuser editing.

For example, in the fishing village level, we have multiple action bubbles that stretch across one large space. This is already delineated nicely and would be a good way to approach splitting logic. We will later have additional logic such as checkpoints and objectives that span all action bubbles in the scope. An example of how to work with containers that fit the setup of this level is shown in the following screenshot:

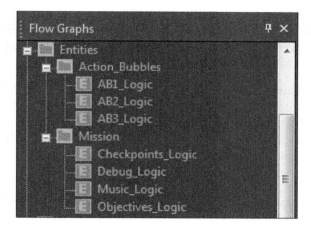

As you can see, this puts the **Action_Bubbles** specific scripting in its own logic containers with other logic types that affect the whole mission stored in their own mission category. This is by no means the only way to organize levels, and it is very much governed by personal preference. But this gives an indication of the kind of organization that can be achieved with a few extra named containers within your level. Anyone editing the level will now be able to find exactly where logic pertaining to certain sections is without having to search through a mass of scripting.

Using Game Tokens to create cleaner Flow Graphs

Before we start discussing how we lay out our Flow Graphs, we will first look at the concept of Game Tokens. Game Tokens store values in Flow Graph that can then be *modified or requested at any point within your scripting*. If you have ever dabbled in written scripting or programming, these are equivalent to variables and are an incredibly powerful concept when scripting within Sandbox. In every single player CRYENGINE game that has been shipped to date, Game Tokens have been the cornerstone of clean scripting. Let's dive in to make some in order to see how and where they will be useful to us.

Creating Game Tokens

Game Tokens live in an XML library created within **Database View**. While this requires a few extra steps to create them, this is a powerful feature as it allows not only multiple Flow Graphs to communicate with each other, but also multiple levels. So, you are able to do things such as branch scripting based on player choice in previous missions. Let's dive into setting them up!

1. To create a Game Token, go to **View | Open View Pane | Database View | Game Tokens**. Here, you will see a list of libraries in a dropdown list at the top of the view pane. By default, this will be **Level** (this is the Game Token library that exists local to your level only) and will be located at `GameSDK/*yourlevelname*/LevelData/gametokens.xml`.

If you want to create Game Tokens that can be referenced by multiple levels, you will need to create a new library by pressing the **Add Library** button. This will save the new library to `GameSDK/Libs/GameTokens/`, which can then be loaded into other levels with the **Load Library** button.

2. To create a new Game Token from the **Game Tokens** window, simply press **Add New Item** in the **Game Token Tasks** section, as shown in the following screenshot:

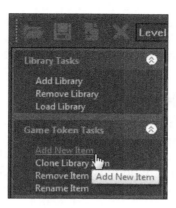

3. The resulting dialog box will then ask you to input **Group** and **Name**. Groups are essentially subfolders within the library and allow you to group Game Tokens together for better organization. For example, in the fishing village level outlined in the previous chapter, we have multiple action bubbles that make up the level. To organize our Game Tokens based on action bubbles (similar to our Flow Graph folders), we can take the AB acronym and use that as our group name. This will then allow us to easily find all the Game Tokens that are related to a specific action bubble. As an example, let's make a Game Token that represents the very first event we want to acknowledge with our example map: when the player starts the level. Following these naming practices, this could be named **AB1.Player_ Entered_Start_Trigger**, as shown in the following screenshot:

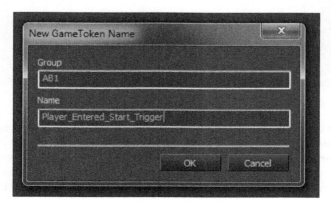

4. Once you have made the Game Token, you will be able to select it in **Database View** and modify a few available attributes. The **Type** references the type of data that it will store: for the preceding token, the default value of **Bool** (Boolean) is fine as the statement will always be either true or false. You can also specify **Value**, which is the default value the Game Token will start with when the game is run. Again, the default value of **False** is good here, as the player will not have entered the trigger when the game starts.

Using Game Tokens

Now that we have made a Game Token, we can return to Flow Graph and implement it in a simple setup. In Flow Graph, either press *Q* to bring up the quick search feature or right-click and then go to **Add Node | Mission | GameTokenSet**. The **Mission:GameTokenSet** flownode is used to set a Game Token's value to a new one. You can pick the Game Token you want to use by double-clicking the **Token** port and then clicking on the browse box to launch the **Game Token** browser, which will then display all the Game Tokens available for you to choose from. For our example of the player entering a trigger, we want to set the state of **AB1. Player_Entered_Start_Trigger** to **True** once the player has entered a trigger. To do this, we can simply hook up a simple ProximityTrigger to our **GameTokenSet** flownode by linking the **Enter** output of the ProximityTrigger to the **Set** input of the **GameTokenSet** node. Once this is done, set the **Value** to be **True**. This means the specified token will now be set to **True** when the player enters the trigger. An example setup for this is shown in the following screenshot:

The Game Token stored in the **Token** port on any **GameToken** flownode is simply a string that references the full Game Token name. This means it can easily be copied and pasted between Game Token flownodes for easier propagation of new tokens or names, which is faster than manually browsing for the token name on each flownode instance.

Now that we have set the token value, let's set up Flow Graph that can respond to this change:

1. First, create a **Mission:GameToken** flownode. This acts as a listener for Game Tokens changing, and is very useful in cases where you want to send events to other parts of your Flow Graph without stretching the links across your logic.

2. We again specify the name of the token, and then supply the value we wish to compare it to. In this case, to output when the value becomes **True**, simply enter true in the **CompareTo** port. When the token changes value as a result of the player walking into the trigger, the token value will be set, the Game Token listener will receive this information and will output from the **Equal** port when the value of the token and the value of the **CompareTo** ports match up.

3. From here, you can set up any scripting you like to trigger as a result. In the following screenshot, I have set up logic to print a debug message to the screen on this event, and enabled Flow Graph debugging to highlight the results (shown as the orange links):

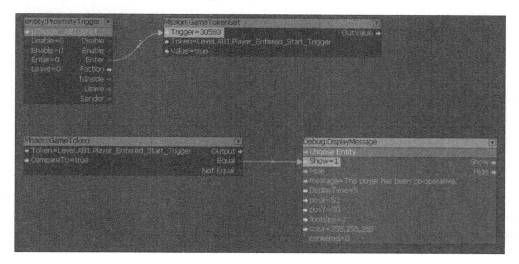

When you copy and paste Flow Graph (*Ctrl* + *Shift* +*V* to paste with links), you are actually copying the XML data itself. If you ever want to quickly send Flow Graph excerpts to another user, you can simply copy your selection and paste the result into an e-mail or other text file. The recipient is then able to directly paste this in on a completely different machine.

Graph Tokens

Along with Game Tokens, **Graph Tokens** are an additional type of Game Token that exist local to a specific Flow Graph. The information for these is saved within the Flow Graph container as opposed to an external XML library. These are useful in situations such as Flow Graphs within **prefabs** where you want to use Game Token style functionality to organize logic, but don't want to use global libraries which will affect all instances of the Flow Graph when modified. To create these, go to **Tools | Edit Graph Tokens** in the Flow Graph editor. They can then be found in the **Graph Tokens** group in the **Game Token** browser launched from any **GameToken** flownode, as shown in the following screenshot:

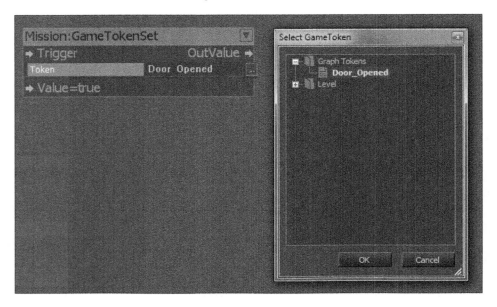

Using both Game Tokens and Graph Tokens, we should be fully equipped to cleanly send events and check conditions in both regular scripting and within contained prefabricated setups. Next, let's look at tidying up our mess!

Laying out Flow Graphs to aid readability

Now that we understand how to use Game Tokens to allow logic to be executed across Flow Graphs without drawing node links between all involved areas, we can look at how the actual Flow Graph script is organized in the editor. The primary tool for this task is the **comment box**.

Creating comment boxes

Comment boxes allow you to draw large boxes around portions of Flow Graph, letting you group together related logic so it's easily readable when zoomed out. To create a comment box, simply right-click and then go to **Add Comment | Add Comment Box**, as shown here:

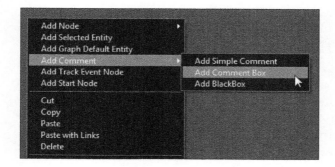

 A quick way to encapsulate a predefined portion of Flow Graph in a comment box is to select your desired nodes in Flow Graph by drawing a box around it, and then following the steps listed previously. This will automatically create a comment box that matches the size of your selected nodes.

This will present you with a box and some accompanying text. The text can be edited by double-clicking it, the size of the box can be modified by dragging the sides or corners, and the color and the **SortPriority** option can be edited in the **Inputs** section of Flow Graph when the box is selected. This section also offers the ability to disable **DisplayFilled** if you find the fill effect distracting, as well as the option to remove the box altogether with the **DisplayBox** parameter if you just want to display some large text without the box itself.

Using comment boxes

Now that we have comment boxes, we can use it to organize our graph. Our usage of this will change organically as we move on to actually scripting the work, as the types and quantities of scripting involved will change over time. For the fishing village level, I have elected to start with a simple split of logic: **player events** and **AI**. These tend to be two fairly consistent methods by which we script the level. **Player events** handles anything that the player does to progress the flow (for example. walk into a trigger, use an object, enter a vehicle, and so on) while the **AI** section handles all scripting that pertains to friendly or enemy AI.

Couple this with some extra boxes to show this against the level flow progression, and you can end up with something similar to the following layout, which represents the start of the fishing village level:

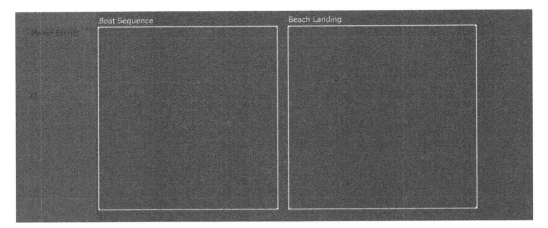

As you can see, this quickly provides a lot of our potential scripting with an organizational home, giving us a good basis to move forward.

If you find yourself unable to select or edit comment boxes, it's probably because there is another comment box overlapping it with a higher/equal **SortPriority**. Simply change the offending comment box to a lower **SortPriority**.

Next, we will move on to thinking about how we plan to construct our scripting, in order to make future iteration a quick process.

Thinking modularly to future-proof our work

The final aspect of working with Flow Graph that we are going to cover is **modularity**. This essentially means thinking about our scripting as a collection of individual elements that are able to operate somewhat autonomously, as opposed to one large script with lots of reliance upon itself. Working with modularity in mind ensures that as the level progresses and evolves through production, we are able to react comfortably to required scripting work, instead of spending hours picking apart a fragile script. As an example of how this specifically impacts our level logic, let's take a look at the very start of the level with the trigger and Game Token setup we outlined earlier.

Basic events

Let's regress to a hypothetical, apocalyptic world where we never set up the Game Token. We still need a way to tell our various scripting elements that the level has been started. Objectives, dialogue, music, AI scripting—all of these pieces need a message to say "It's go time, the player is here." We could do this by putting **Game:Start** nodes everywhere, but then every time you enter game mode in the editor, regardless of where you are, you will trigger the level start scripting. This makes it impossible to test the progression further down the line. We could solve this by putting a trigger in all of these places instead (part of our actual solution), but what if we want to change this event from being a trigger to the player spawning at a specific spawnpoint entity? We would then need to track down every instance of the trigger and replace it with a spawnpoint, which is a lot of hassle.

Instead, we have made this event a single Game Token. If we do want to change what triggers the event, we simply replace the node going into **GameTokenSet** from a **ProximityTrigger** to whatever is required. It's a small example, but this adds up throughout production and goes a long way towards making scripting content as painless as possible. Let's look at other ways we can take this principle and run with it.

Test-friendly scripting

Testing our work will end up being where we spend a lot of our time during level production. Is it fun? Does it work? Can I break it? What happens if I do this? However, in a 30-minute long scripted level, testing something that happens at the very end can slowly drive you to insanity if you need to play everything beforehand in order to reach the one section you want to try and break. Fortunately, thinking with modularity in mind means we can set up a few pieces of extra logic that allows us to test our content from half way through without compromising any of the scripting. Later on in this section, we will cover more explicit ways to easily set up functionality to skip through portions of level content. For now, let's come back to our example level. For the opening sequence, I want to have the player spawn on AI-driven boats that are speeding towards the initial confrontation. The basics required to get this to work would look something similar to what is shown in the following Flow Graph: our level start **GameToken** followed by some logic to enable the territory and wave of our driver AI (all of this logic being placed in the AI comment boxes we made earlier).

Once this is done, the driver is told to enter the vehicle and start driving along a path using **Vehicle:StickPath**.

This works perfectly fine on its own in isolation. However, let's say this driver character is required for an event later in the level. If we want to test this event, we need a way to get the driver character to the relevant point in the progression but still have the scripting for the initial sequence work on regular playthroughs. This means we need to decouple the AI activation (which will be required for testing the later content) from the boat sequence. We can do that by adding another Game Token event between the AI enabling and the boat scripting, so it looks something similar to the following screenshot. I have called this token **Level.AB1.Friendly_Wave_Activated**, again making sure it's part of the same **AB1** group.

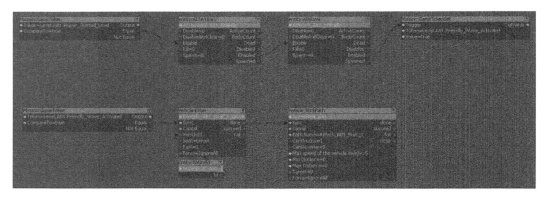

What this means is that we have a Game Token event that will be able to tell scripting later in the level that our driver AI is enabled. All we will then need to do in this section is add some extra checks to make sure the boat sequence is not initiated unless we are definitely playing from the start. With these few extra nodes, we can then jump to later events in the flow and have the driver AI work as expected in both cases. As a cleanliness bonus, we also have a Game Token event for the initial AI wave being enabled, which will be reusable elsewhere in this action bubble for scripting other AI.

Summary

In this chapter, we covered the main principles behind clean scripting work in Sandbox. We now know how to efficiently store our logic in the level and how to use Game Tokens to create Flow Graph scripting that is both easy to follow and flexible, as we continue to add and change content. Reinforcing this, we covered organizing this work cleanly and in a way that sets up our scripting for future iteration. Let's kick off the fun part: building the level!

In the next chapter we'll take a look at everything that goes into the actual setup of a scripted single player level, giving us the tools to create a huge variety of interesting and reactive content with which to populate our game world.

14
Scripting Gameplay Content

Now that we are acquainted with Flow Graphs and some of the principles that are useful for creating tidy and maintainable scripting, let's get to building things. When constructing AI-based gameplay setups in CRYENGINE, there are a few tools and techniques we can use that can help give us interesting, high-fidelity work. In this chapter, we will cover the following topics:

- Scripting the main level flow and events
- Setting up AI patrols and the supporting MNM navigation
- Using the Mannequin editor to create new AI animation fragments
- Adapting AI tasks based on player actions

Scripting the main level flow and events

We briefly covered organization of logic as part of the previous chapter, so let's put the theory into practice. We'll return to the example of starting the level with the player on a boat, driving towards the opening combat section. This relatively basic setup has lots of potential for us to add detail and interest to the events, elevating it to something that feels like a polished, exciting experience. Let's start with looking at blocking in support for the level events we are looking to build.

Event examples

As we touched on when looking at modularity, Game Tokens are absolutely the bee's knees, so get into the habit of making Game Tokens for every event that you expect to trigger *other* events with over the course of the level progression. This way, our logic is built as a sequence of modular parts and we will not fall into the trap of making a huge flow of dependencies that become a nightmare to pull apart later in development.

Back to our player cruising along in the boat; this sequence contains a few notable events that we can listen to and use as trigger conditions or branches for other events in the world. For example, when the boats reach the shore, we'll want something to trigger some reactions from the enemy AI. However, it's possible for the player to have fired their weapon before they reached the shore—maybe we want a different welcoming party if the enemies are already alerted? Let's set this up and see how it could play out.

Triggers

First, let's set up an event for when the player has reached the encampment. This is where we'll start triggering the more reactive scripting for the enemies inside. There are a few ways to detect this. We could listen for the player entering the perimeter of the encampment, or perhaps for the boats reaching their destination. Both have different applications, given that the player could potentially jump off the boat and swim to shore instead. Let's set up both to arm ourselves for any situation.

AreaTrigger

We'll start by listening for the player entering an area around the encampment. To do this, we can simply place a **Shape** around the desired perimeter by navigating to **RollupBar | Objects Tab | Area**. Once you're satisfied, spawn an AreaTrigger from **RollupBar | Objects Tab | Entity | Triggers**. From the **Shape** parameters, enable **Pick** mode and select **AreaTrigger** in the perspective view. This should now appear in the list of targeted entities on the shape, as shown in the following screenshot:

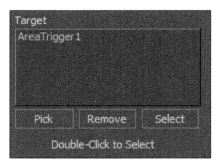

The trigger will now inherit the area of the shape we have placed. To use this trigger in Flow Graph, simply right-click in the Flow Graph and press **Add Selected Entity**. This is an ability that most entities in Sandbox support, and many have useful parameters and events that can be utilized.

We can now simply hook up the **Enter** port to setting the value of a new Game Token. I have opted to create **Level.AB1.Player_Reached_Encampment**, extending our existing **AB1** library.

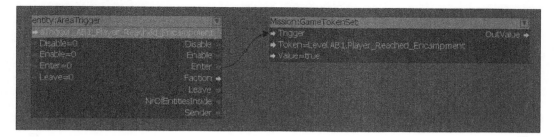

ProximityTrigger

The other primary trigger type used in Sandbox is the ProximityTrigger. This is essentially a box (as is visualized by the filled bounding box when selected), and makes up for its shape restrictions by having a few extra useful parameters. ProximityTriggers can listen for entities by name, which is useful when wanting to detect when specific objects other than the player. In our example, we'll use this feature to detect when the boat has reached a point on the shoreline. ProximityTriggers can be found in the same folder as AreaTriggers. However, unlike AreaTriggers, they listen for entities purely inside their bounding box (the size of which is defined via the **DimX**, **DimY**, and **DimZ** parameters) and as such require no shape setup to function.

 As ProximityTriggers are powered by a basic bounding box that is axis aligned for simpler calculations, they cannot be rotated. If you require a more complex shape for your setup, consider using AreaTriggers and filtering its outputs in Flow Graph if more precision is required.

Once we have one ProximityTrigger placed down, we can untick **PlayerOnly** to remove the player restrictions and then copy-and-paste the name of our chosen object into the **OnlySelectedEntity** parameter. We can then perform the same steps as we did for the AreaTrigger: adding the entity to Flow Graph and then linking up another Game Token that represents the event.

This is shown in the following screenshot:

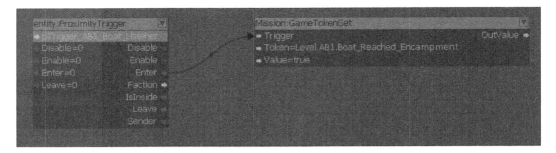

In both these trigger examples, I've left both nodes enabled via their entity parameters for testing purposes. However, staying this way would mean the triggers would still output when testing content further on in the level, which could wreak havoc with the scripting. A more optimal setup would be to have the node start disabled, with Game Tokens in Flow Graph triggering the **Enable** and **Disable** inputs on the entity's flownode when required.

Setting up an event listener

Next, let's find out if the player has fired a shot during the sequence. To do this, we need to use a few Flow Graph nodes. The primary node for this operation is **Weapon:Listener**, which outputs a few types of events that the player is able to perform with weapons. We'll be using **OnShoot**. However, the node requires a **WeaponClass**. So, before firing the **Enable** input on the listener node, we'll hook up an **Inventory:ItemSelected** node. This tells us what the player currently has selected. We can use the **ItemClass** output to feed into the **Enable** and **WeaponClass** inputs of the weapon listener, as this will both update the class we are listening to and then re-enable the node to listen to this new class. Adding a **Game:Start** node to this flow (linked to the **Active** and **Check** inputs to check the current item on start and enable the listener) gives us a working listener for the player firing their weapon.

This is shown in the following screenshot:

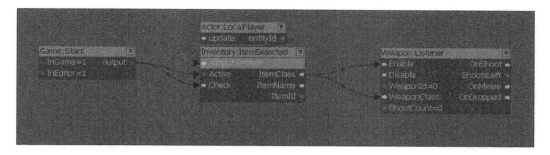

As explained with the triggers, having this work off **Game:Start** is useful for testing purposes, but we only want this to be enabled when it needs to be. Having it on **Game:Start** would mean testing content further on in the level would still trigger this listener. Thankfully, we still have the **Level.AB1.Player_Started_Level** Game Token that we made earlier. This can plug into the **Active** and **Check** inputs. We also need to make a Game Token for the event we're listening for. I've opted to add a **Level.AB1.Player_Fired_Weapon** token and trigger this to **true** from **OnShoot**. As well as firing our subsequent scripting, we can also use it to disable the listeners to clean up our active logic once the event has happened. This is shown in the following screenshot:

Apart from gunfire listeners, there are a few other player-specific listeners that you may find useful. The **Actor:Sensor** can output more general information about an actor, such as the player picking up a specific object, getting in a certain vehicle, or changing stance. Additionally, **Weapon:HitInfo** is handy for combat scripting as it outputs information about what the player has shot, allowing us to trigger events if the player has shot a certain object in the world or inflicted a specific amount of damage.

Working with events

Now that we have a little suite of Game Tokens that represent events in the opening section of the level, we can discuss how we're going to utilize them. If the player fires their weapon before the boat reaches the shore, I'm going to script a flare particle effect to fire into the sky, which causes a vehicle from a nearby enemy encampment to drive down to the shore and sit in wait for the player. However, if the player hasn't alerted the enemies when they reach the shore, I'll instead trigger an enemy running to fire a flare that the player is able to interrupt. If the enemy is successful, we'll call in the same vehicle but to a different location now that the player has already reached the encampment. We can iterate on this scenario over time, but this gives a good idea of the kind of branching logic that is made easily possible with Game Tokens. It helps us be more reactive to the player's actions, creating the sense of a believable functioning world instead of a rigid script that the player must follow.

Let's start by setting up the event logic. With our triggers and weapon listeners situated as part of our player events scripting, we can now add the resulting Game Token checks to our actual AI scripts. This can take the form of a few *when X and Y* statements, utilizing our newly made tokens. First off, let's look at the player prematurely alerting the encampment. When **Player_Fired_Weapon** triggers and **Player_Reached_Encampment** is **false**, we'll want to trigger our flare and any resulting reinforcements. We can perform this extra check with the **Mission:GameTokenCheck** flownode, resulting in the setup shown in the following screenshot:

To script the alternate chain of events, we can simply flip the Game Tokens and values around from the preceding screenshot. When **Player_Reached_Encampment** triggers and **Player_Fired_Weapon** is **false**, we want to trigger our player to run and try to fire the flare. This is shown in the following screenshot:

We now have a good grasp of how we can set up interesting script branches as part of the level progression, using Game Tokens to simplify the process. Next, we'll look at how to create the AI scripts and patrols that would be triggered as part of these events and how these are created in the latest iteration of CRYENGINE.

AI navigation and sequences

Scripting AI entities in CRYENGINE is something that has gone through many iterations during its lifetime. Initial versions of the engine supported games that had AI mechanics which were very hands-off from a scripting stand point. For the most part, AI existed to be interrupted from basic patrols and combat the player. The later incarnations have improved upon this by extending support for more controlled AI sequences while still offering the ability for the more simplistic patrol setups used in more open, player-driven games. We'll look at both types of setup here, but before we get AI doing our bidding, let's set up their navigation mesh so that they're able to find a path around the world.

Navigation mesh

Gone are the days of manual markup of navigation links, forbidden areas and boundaries. The latest CRYENGINE releases have a delightful piece of tech known as **multilayered navigation mesh** (**MNM**), which will automatically generate a navigation mesh for all navigable space within a given shape. This is incredibly powerful and allows us to spend our time on actual content generation instead of placement and maintenance of nodes and shapes. To create a new navigation area, go to **RollupBar | Objects Tab | AI | NavigationArea**. You can now simply draw out the shape as you would any other.

 Note that NavigationAreas have a fixed height for all their points. If you want to place one on a slope, simply make sure that the points start at the bottom and then allow a generous margin in the area's **Height** parameter.

Once we have the area placed, we need to specify which agent types we would like this area to be valid for. In the SDK, this consists of the **MediumSizedCharacters** and **VehicleMedium** options. As I'm going to require both human AI and vehicles to move around the level, I'm going to tick both boxes. Finally, to visualize the generation and resulting navmesh, simply navigate to **AI | Debug Agent Type | MediumSizedCharacters** (if this is one of the agent types you selected).

You should now see some debug rendering resembling the following screenshot:

Remember the Toolbox Macros from *Chapter 12, Initial Level Blockout and Setup*? This is another situation where they're useful. Instead of digging into the menus to find the button for the navigation debug rendering, you could enter the CVARs required into macros and have an on/off toggle button on your toolbar. The CVARs required are **ai_debugDrawNavigation = 3, ai_debugMNMAgentType MediumSizedCharacters**, and **ai_debugDraw = 1**.

Cover surfaces

The other major element of AI setup in CRYENGINE is cover. AI entities need to be able to know where they can take cover in the world. Again, this used to require the manual placement of **AIAnchor** entities at each individual cover spot – a time-consuming process. In the latest iteration of CRYENGINE, however, we have a new entity type called **CoverSurface**. This can be found at **RollupBar | Objects Tab | AI | CoverSurface**. This can be placed alongside objects that you want be used as cover in the world, and it will automatically generate cover spots along the edges of these objects.

When a **CoverSurface** is invalid, you will see a red helper appear on top of the object, as shown in the following screenshot:

However, when shifted into a position where there are objects that can support cover, the red helper will disappear and be replaced with the debug rendering shown in the following screenshot, indicating valid cover. This displays the cover system's knowledge of the surfaces available, with each of the small black dots along the white lines representing places AI would move to enter cover. The white lines are the path AI will take to move while inside cover (if they possess the ability to do so):

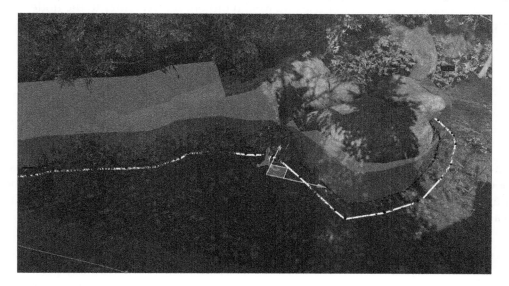

Parameters you may want to tweak away from the default values are **LimitLeft** and **LimitRight** on the cover surface entity parameters. This controls how far the cover surface will go to detect valid surfaces — the default of 2 meters often means you won't get long strips of cover as seen in the preceding screenshot.

Now that we have AI navigation and cover built into our level, let's take a look at scripting some AI!

AISequence

Scripting AI operations in CRYENGINE was also recently overhauled with the introduction of the AISequence flownodes. Previously, every action AI performed could be interrupted by external stimuli. Even though some individual nodes contained options to force the operation, it was inconsistent and messy. To solve this, AISequence nodes were introduced. An AISequence is essentially a wrapper for all other AI actions, and it applies a few parameters to everything within this wrapper. To start off, let's take a look at uninterruptible AISequence nodes.

Uninterruptible sequences

First things first, to start using AISequence, we need to put our AI in a sequence. To do this, spawn the **AISequence:Start** flownode. You will see two options here: **Interruptible** and **ResumeAfterInterruption**. For now, we're just concerned with **Interruptible**. Let's set this to **false** and assign our chosen AI entity to the node (triggering on **Game:Start** for testing purposes for now).

When we trigger **Start**, our assigned AI entity will perform the subsequent actions we choose without being kicked out of the commands by the player shooting at them or any other distraction. To demonstrate this, let's get our encampment enemy to run to a point and fire a flare.

Adding inventory

The flare firing animation that exists in the SDK doesn't involve selecting a flare gun, so we're going to have to improvise. If your chosen enemy archetype isn't of the pistol variant, we can use a Flow Graph to give him one so that shooting the flare looks roughly correct (even if the pistol isn't technically a flare gun). To do this, before placing the enemy in the AISequence, let's add a pistol to his inventory. Spawn a **Inventory:EquipPackAdd** flownode, assign the AI to the node, make sure **Add** is set to **true** (to add to rather than replace their inventory), and select the **AI_Pistol** equipment pack from the browser. This will add the pistol to the enemy's inventory alongside a rifle or shotgun and allow us to select it.

Animation events

Now that we've ensured the AI has a pistol in their inventory, let's equip it and get them to play the animation. **AISequence:WeaponDrawFromInventory** will allow us to force them to select the pistol first, so let's slot that in after **AISequence:Start**. Directly after this, we'll place the **AISequence:Animation** node. This is a powerful flownode, as not only does it allow us to select animation fragments, but we're able to encapsulate a move command in this action too. This means we won't need to place an **AISequence:Move** node to get them to run to the correct position (we'll cover these later as part of the interruptible sequences).

From the **Animation** port, we can open the Mannequin fragment browser. This displays a list of all animation fragments that are recommended for Flow Graph use, defined by the **IA** (idle action) and **SO** (smart object) prefix. Unfortunately, the pre-existing flare firing fragment doesn't have either of these prefixes, but it is still loadable by typing `fireFlare` manually into this space. Later, we'll look at generating our own fragments in Mannequin where this could be amended.

Finally, we need to define where the AI performs this animation and how they get there. The entity ID of a tagpoint (which can be generated from the **Entity:EntityID** node) can feed into here. Next, **Speed** and **Stance** dropdowns determine how the AI will traverse to the tagpoint we've placed. I've picked **Sprint** and **Combat** as these best fit the context, as shown in the following screenshot:

We now have a working animation! You'll notice no flare particle is triggered when the animation plays; we need to set one up. We'll cover adding this in the next section on Mannequin.

You'll also notice extra parameters on this animation node that are sometimes useful. **OneShot** and **LoopDuration** control whether looping animations can be selected and how long they play. **StartRadius** determines how far from the destination the AI needs to be before starting the animation, and **DirectionTolerance** is how exactly aligned with the destination rotation the AI need to be before playing the animation. These are useful to tweak if you need exact positioning.

Ending sequences

Now that we're done with the AISequence, we need to release our AI back into the wild. If we left the script in its current state, the enemy would stand there doing nothing while the player dances around attempting to kill them. To relinquish control, we simply need to append our sequence with the **AISequence:End** flownode.

This ends all actions inside the sequence and allows regular AI behavior to take control again.

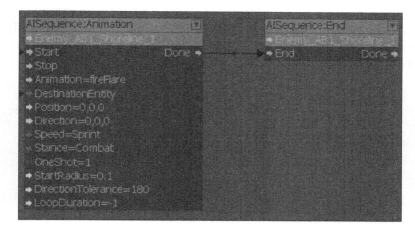

Now we know how to script more directed sequences of AI behavior, let's take a look at the more flexible patrols that are the cornerstone of Sandbox gameplay.

Interruptible sequences

Let's revisit the beginning of the sequences. We'll want to change the **Interruptible** port back to **true**. This will now allow whatever is encapsulated within the sequence to be stopped in favor of reacting to enemies. This also opens up usage of the **ResumeAfterInterruption** port. This controls whether the AI will go back to doing the AISequence it was in when it was interrupted. This is useful to keep ticked if you want the player to be able to interrupt patrols which are then able to return to occupying the space they were defending after losing track of threats. We'll leave this on its default value of **true** (unless you have different plans for your patrols), and move on to the patrol behavior itself.

AISequences only support a few non AISequence category nodes inside them. This is because if they are resumed after interruption, Flow Graph cannot guarantee a consistent result with many nonsequence nodes. If you ever see a signal going into **AISequence:Start** in the Flow Graph debugger and not coming out the other side, this is normally why. In this case, check your AISequence for nodes that may not be supported and make sure that these events are handled outside of the AISequence.

Looping movement

Traditional patrols are comprised of AI movements to a few positions in the world, with actions in-between to lend context and variety. **AISequence:Move** will be the core of this, with **AISequence:Animation** allowing some animated flavor between patrolling. Let's take a look at a simple three point patrol. A Flow Graph example is shown in the following screenshot:

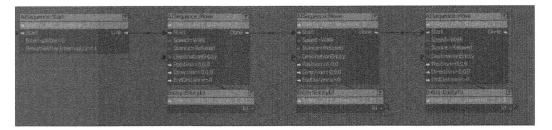

This will get our AI to walk to three points, but what happens when they end? We want them to repeat this action ad infinitum (unless they are interrupted of course). AISequence handily support the looping of actions inside them, so this is relatively straightforward to set up. We don't need to trigger the entire AISequence wrapper again. Using a few collapsed **Logic:Any** nodes, we can loop the last **Done** port back around to the first patrol node's **Start** input (shown in the following screenshot). Doing it this way gives us a more readable loop when zoomed out, and stops our links crossing over other nodes and looking messy.

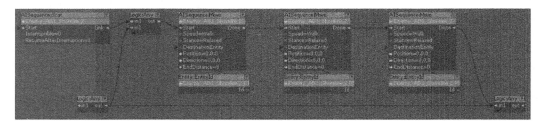

With this hooked up, our enemy will now reach the final move node, loop back around to the start, and repeat the sequence all over again. Let's look at making the interruption of this patrol a bit more seamless!

Bookmarking

Let's say we had a setup where we wanted AI to perform an animation only once as part of the patrol (firing a flare, for example). We could set this up as we did previously — an animation at the beginning of the sequence, which then continues onto a patrol. However, what if the player interrupts this and the AI resumes after the interruption? He'd fire that flare all over again. AISequence contains a way to combat this known as bookmarking. By inserting an **AISequence:Bookmark** node after the animation, when the AI resumes after interruption they will resume from the most recent bookmark instead of the **AISequence:Start** node. This branch would look similar to the following screenshot:

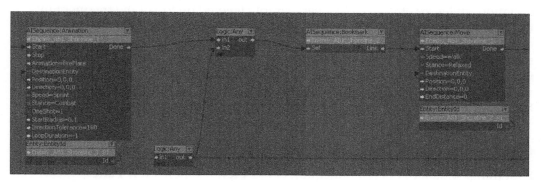

Here, you can see after the **fireFlare** animation, we enter the patrol loop, but not before an **AISequence:Bookmark** is triggered. This means that if the AI were to be interrupted by the player, they would resume from the bookmark, and never perform the animation again.

The **ResumeAfterInterruption** port also includes the enabling/disabling of an AIWave as "interruption." This means that if you disable an enemy wave when the player moves away as part of optimizing your level setup and then the player decides to revisit the area, you can simply re-enable the AIWave and AI will resume from the most recent **AISequence:Start** or **Bookmark** node.

Now we know how to set up both types of AI sequences in order to populate our level with interesting AI behavior, we can move onto adding more polish to our scripted animation events!

Using the Mannequin editor

Further continuing the theme of cumbersome-tools-made-better, let's take a look at animation in CRYENGINE. In the past, animation states were handled by a tool called Animation Graph. This is akin to Flow Graph but handled animations and transitions for all animated entities, and unfortunately reduced any transitions or variation in the animations to a spaghetti graph. Thankfully, we now have Mannequin! This is an animation system where the methods by which animation states are handled is all dealt with behind the scenes—all we need to take care of are the animations themselves. In Mannequin, an animation and its associated data is known as a fragment. Any extra detail that we might want to add (such as animation variation, styles, or effects) can be very simply layered on top of the fragment in the Mannequin editor. While complex and detailed results can be achieved with all manner of first and third person animation in Mannequin, for level design we're only really interested in basic fragments we want our NPCs to play as part of flavor and readability within level scripting. Before we look at generating some new fragments, we'll start off with looking at how we can add detail to an existing fragment— triggering a flare particle as part of our flare firing animation.

Getting familiar with the interface

First things first, let's open Mannequin! Go to **View** | **Open View Pane** | **Mannequin Editor**. This is initially quite a busy view pane so let's get our bearings on what's important to our work. You may want to drag and adjust the sizes of the windows to better see the information displayed. In the top left, we have the **Fragments** window. This lists all the fragments in the game that pertain to the currently loaded preview. Let's look at what this means for us when editing fragment entries.

The preview workflow

A preview is a complete list of fragments that pertains to a certain type of animation. For example, the default preview loaded is `sdk_playerpreview1p.xml`, which contains all the first person fragments used in the SDK. You can browse the list of fragments in this window to get an idea of what this means—everything from climbing ladders to sprinting is defined as a fragment. However, we're interested in the NPC animations. To change the currently loaded preview, go to **File** | **Load Preview Setup** and pick `sdk_humanpreview.xml`. This is the XML file that contains all the third person animations for human characters in the SDK. Once this is loaded, your fragment list should update to display a larger list of available fragments usable by AI.

This is shown in the following screenshot:

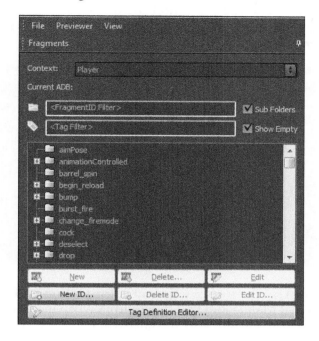

 If you don't want to perform this step every time you load Mannequin, you are able to change the default preview setup for the editor in the preferences we visited in *Chapter 12, Initial Level Blockout and Setup.* Go to **Tools** | **Preferences** | **Mannequin** | **General** and change the **Default Preview File** setting to the XML of your choice.

Working with fragments

Now we have the correct preview populating our fragment list, let's find our flare fragment. In the box with **<FragmentID Filter>** in it, type `flare` and press *Enter*. This will filter down the list, leaving you with the **fireFlare** fragment we used earlier. You'll see that the fragment is comprised of a tree. Expanding this tree one level brings us to the tag. A tag in mannequin is a method of choosing animations within a fragment based on a game condition. For example, in the player preview we were in earlier, the **begin_reload** fragment has two tags: one for **SDKRifle** and one for **SDKShotgun**. Depending on the weapon selected by the player, it applies a different tag and consequently picks a different animation.

This allows animators to group together animations of the same type that are required in different situations. For our **fireFlare** fragment, as there are no differing scenarios of this type, it simply has a **<default>** tag. This is shown in the following screenshot:

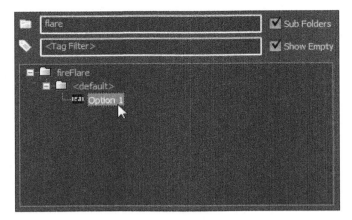

Inside this tag, we can see there's one fragment entry: **Option 1**. These are the possible variations that Mannequin will choose from when the fragment is chosen and the required tags are applied. We only have one variation within **fireFlare**, but other fragments in the human preview (for example, **IA_talkFunny**) offer extra entries to add variety to AI actions. To load this entry for further editing, double-click **Option 1**. Let's get to adding that flare!

Adding effects to fragments

After loading the fragment entry, the **Fragment Editor** window has now updated. This is the main window in the center of Mannequin and comprises of a preview window to view the animation and a list of all the available layers and details we can add.

The main piece of information currently visible here is the animation itself, shown in
AnimLayer under **FullBody3P**:

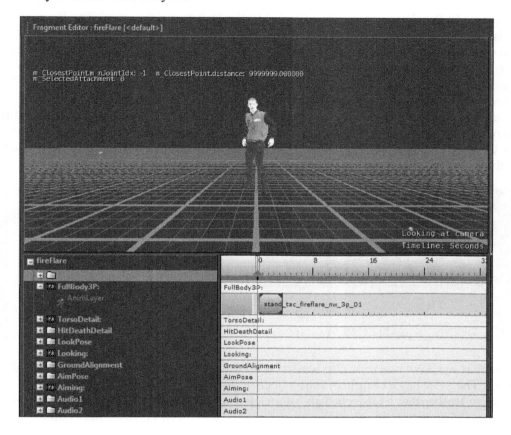

At the bottom of the **Fragment Editor** window, some buttons are
available that are useful for editing and previewing the fragment.
These include a play/pause toggle (along with a playspeed
dropdown) and a jump to start button. You are also able to zoom in
and out of the timeline with the mouse wheel, and scrub the timeline
by click-dragging the red timeline marker around the fragment. These
controls are similar to the Track View cinematics tool and should be
familiar if you've utilized this in the past.

Procedural layers

Here, we are able to add our particle effect to the animation fragment. To do this, we need to add **ProcLayer** (procedural layer) to the **FullBody3P** section. The **ProcLayer** runs parallel to **AnimLayer** and is where any extra layers of detail that fragments can contain are specified, from removing character collision to attaching props. For our purposes, we need to add a particle effect clip. To do this, double-click on the timeline within **ProcLayer**. This will spawn a blank proc clip for us to categorize. Select this clip and **Procedural Clip Properties** on the right-hand side of the **Fragment Editor** window will be populated with a list of parameters. All we need to do now is change the type of this clip from **None** to **ParticleEffect**. This is editable in the dropdown **Type** list. This should present us with a **ParticleEffect** proc clip visible in the **ProcLayer** alongside our animation, as shown in the following screenshot:

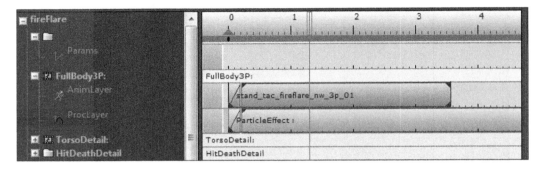

Now that we have our proc clip loaded with the correct type, we need to specify the effect. The SDK has a couple of flare effects in the particle libraries (searchable by going to **RollupBar | Objects Tab | Particle Entity**); I'm going to pick `explosions.flare.a`. To apply this, select the proc clip and paste your chosen effect name into the **Effect** parameter. If you now scrub through fragment, you should see the particle effect trigger! However, currently the effect fires from the base of the character in the wrong direction. We need to align the effect to the weapon of the enemy. Thankfully, the **ParticleEffect** proc clip already has support for this in its properties. In the **Reference Bone** parameter, enter `weapon_bone` and hit *Enter*. The `weapon_bone` is the generic bone name that character's weapons are attached too, and as such it is a good bet for any cases where we require effects or objects to be placed in a character's weapon position. Scrubbing through the fragment again, the effect will now fire from the weapon hand of the character.

If we ever need to find out bone names, there are a few ways to access this information within the editor. Hovering over the character in the Mannequin previewer will display the bone name. Alternatively, in **Character Editor** (we'll go into the details later), you can scroll down in the **Rollup** window on the right-hand side, expand **Debug Options**, and tick **ShowJointNames**. This will display the names of all bones over the character in the previewer.

With the particle attached, we can now ensure that the timing of the particle effect matches the animation. To do this, you can click-and-drag the proc clip around timeline—around 1.5 seconds seems to match the timings for this animation. With the effect timed correctly, we now have a fully functioning **fireFlare** fragment! Try testing out the setup we made earlier with this change. We should now have a far more polished looking event.

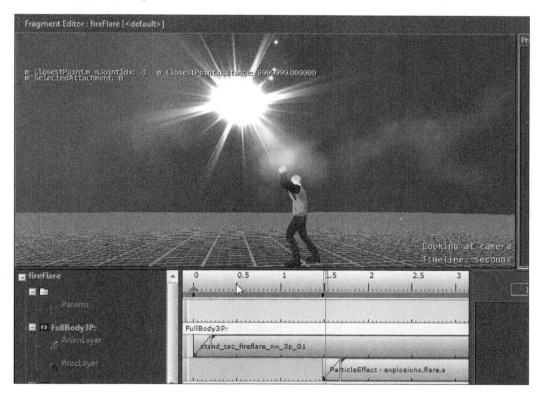

The previewer in Mannequin shares the same viewport controls as the perspective view in Sandbox. You can use this to zoom in and look around to gain a better view of the animation preview.

The final thing we need to do is save our changes to the Mannequin databases! To do this, go to **File** | **Save Changes**. When the list of changed files is displayed, press **Save**. Mannequin will then tell you that you're editing data from the .pak files. Click **Yes** to this prompt and your data will be saved to your project. The resulting changed database files will appear in GameSDK\Animations\Mannequin\ADB, and it should be distributed with your project if you package it for release.

Adding a new fragment

Now that we know how to add some effects feedback to existing fragments, let's look at making a new fragment to use as part of our scripting. This is useful to know if you have animators on your project and you want to get their assets in game quickly to hook up to your content. In our humble SDK project, we can effectively simulate this as there are a few animations that ship with the SDK that have no corresponding fragment. Now, we'll see how to browse the raw animation assets themselves, before adding them to a brand new Mannequin fragment.

The Character Editor window

Let's open the Character Editor. Apart from being used for editing characters and their attachments in the engine, this is a really handy way to browse the library of animation assets available and preview them in a viewport. To open the Character Editor, go to **View** | **Open View Pane** | **Character Editor**.

On some machines, the expense of rendering two scenes at once (that is, the main viewport and the viewports in the Character Editor or Mannequin Editor) can cause both to drop to a fairly sluggish frame rate. If you experience this, either close one of the other view panes you have on the screen or if you have it tabbed to other panes, simply select another tab. You can also open the Mannequin Editor or the Character Editors without a level loaded, which allows for better performance and minimal load times to edit content.

Similar to Mannequin, the Character Editor will initially look quite overwhelming. The primary aspects to focus on are the **Animations** window in the top-left corner and the **Preview** viewport in the middle. In the **Filter** option in the **Animations** window, we can search for search terms to narrow down the list of animations. An example of an animation that hasn't yet been turned into a Mannequin fragment is the **stand_tac_callreinforcements_nw_3p_01** animation. You can find this by entering `reinforcements` into the search filter:

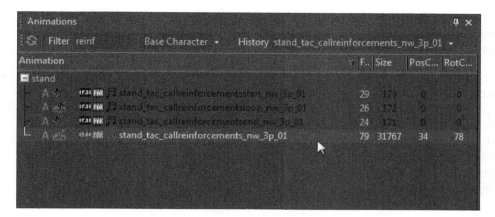

Selecting this animation will update the debug character in the Character Editor viewport so that they start to play the chosen animation. You can see this specific animation is a oneshot wave and might be useful as another trigger for enemy reinforcements further in our scripting. Let's turn this into a fragment! We need to make sure we don't forget this animation though; right-click on the animation and click **Copy**. This will copy the name to the clipboard for future reference in Mannequin. The animation can also be dragged and dropped into Mannequin manually to achieve the same result.

Creating fragment entries

With our animation located, let's get back to Mannequin and set up our fragment. Ensuring that we're still in the **sdk_humanpreview.xml** preview setup, take another look at the **Fragments** window in the top left of Mannequin. You'll see there are two rows of buttons: the top row controls creation and editing of fragment entries (the animation options we looked at earlier). The second row covers adding and editing of fragment IDs themselves: the top level fragment name. This is where we need to start. Press the **New ID** button on the second row of buttons to bring up the **New FragmentID Name** dialog.

Here, we need to add a name that conforms to the prefixes we discussed earlier. As this is an action, make sure you add **IA_** (interest action) as the prefix for the name you choose; otherwise, it won't appear in the fragment browser in the Flow Graph.

Once our fragment is named, we'll be presented with **Mannequin FragmentID Editor**. For the most part, we won't need to worry about these options. But it's useful to be aware of how they might be useful (and don't worry, these can be edited after creation). The main parameters to note are the **Scope** options. These control which elements of the character are controlled by the fragment. By default, all these boxes are ticked, which means that our fragment will take control of each ticked aspect of the character.

An example of where we might want to change this would be the character **LookAt** control. If we want to get an NPC to look at another entity in the world as part of a scripted sequence (using the **AI:LookAt** Flow Graph node), it would not be possible with the current settings. This is because the **LookPose** and **Looking** scopes are controlled by the fragment. If we were to want to control this via Flow Graph, these would need to be unticked, freeing up the look scopes for scripted control. With scopes covered, press **OK** at the bottom of the dialog box to continue adding our **callReinforcements** animation!

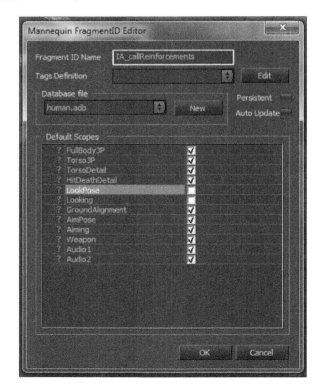

We now have a fragment ID created in our **Fragments** window, but it has no entries! With our new fragment selected, press the **New** button on the first row of buttons to add an entry. This will automatically add itself under the **<default>** tag, which is the desired behavior as our fragment will be tag-agnostic for the moment. This has now created a blank fragment in the Fragment Editor.

Adding the AnimLayer

This is where our animation from earlier comes in. Right-click on the **FullBody3P** track in the editor and go to **Add Track | AnimLayer**. As we did previously with our effect on **ProcLayer**, double-click on **AnimLayer** to add a new clip. This will create our new **Anim Clip**, with some red **None** markup to signify the lack of animation. Now, all we need to do is select the clip, go to the **Anim Clip Properties**, and paste in our animation name by double-clicking the **Animation** parameter.

The **Animation** parameter has a helpful browser that will allow you to search for animations—simply click on the browse icon in the parameter entry section. It lacks the previewer found in the Character Editor but can be a quick way to find animation candidates by name within Mannequin.

With our animation finally loaded into a fragment, we should now have a fragment setup that displays a valid animation name on the AnimLayer. Clicking on Play will now play our reinforcements wave animation!

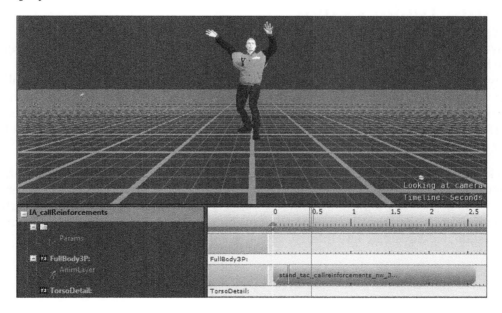

Once we save our changes, all we need to do now is load our fragment in an **AISequence:Animation** node in Flow Graph. This can be done by repeating the steps outlined earlier. This time, our new fragment should appear in the fragment dialog.

Now that we're up to speed on how to generate and use animated content in CRYENGINE, let's take a look at some of the more complex scripting methods in the editor (and perhaps try and sneak in our new fragment).

Adapting AI tasks based on player actions

A powerful aspect of scripting across all game engines is the ability to create simple and flexible ways in which the game can respond to player actions. Within Sandbox and Flow Graph, we are able to cater to a huge amount of possible scenarios and then design reactions for them into the level scripting. These kinds of setups make the game feel like a real world with believable boundaries that can be pushed. Think of the narrator in Bastion or assassinating targets in Dishonored—the designers authored outcomes for the most unlikely of player paths, and as a result players feel validated and immersed in the world. In this chapter, we'll look at a simple example in our boat sequence where we can add dynamic responses to player action.

Game Token states

Let's take our boat sequence. The player is sitting on the back of a boat speeding towards the shoreline. However, what if the player decides to go for a swim? Does the boat just ride off into the sunset? Does it stop and wait? Does it follow the player? Creating logic to handle this might sound complex, but we can cater for all these scenarios by simply assigning a *state* to the boat's appropriate response in the scene. Then, based on the value of the state, we can get our boat and its occupants to perform different responses. This will serve as a far more interesting replacement to our single move-along-path command.

To kick off this setup, we need to create a Game Token that stores this state. So far, we've only used Game Tokens to send events and create simple Boolean true/false checks to branch our logic. However, the Game Token system is a lot more powerful than this, and can store all value types—anything from vectors to integers. For our boat state, we can create any number of token values to represent its state.

To do this, let's go back to our Game Token library in **Database View** and add a new Game Token. This time, however, we'll select **String** as the token type in the **Selected Token** parameters. This will allow us to name the various states of the boat in a readable fashion so that our logic is as transparent as possible. I've added a token called **AB1.Boat_Approach_Task** for my setup.

> Although strings are the best value type for Flow Graph readability, as you're essentially able to read them as though it's English, if you're feeling optimal, a more efficient way to handle multiple states of a Game Token is to use integers that represent the state. Comparing integers is a cheaper operation to perform than comparing strings; if it's something that's going to be checked at very high update rates, it could be worth transitioning to them instead.

Now that we have a token that represents the current task of the boat, we need to decide on all the tasks we want to support, and the conditions by which we want each to trigger. These don't need to be saved to a file anywhere. These will simply be the values we enter into the **Value** input of **Mission:GameTokenSet** when setting the approach task Game Token. For my setup, I'm going to opt for the following tasks and rules:

- **move_to_encampment**: This will be triggered when the player is on the boat, staying within the confines of the sequence. I'll also set this off when the player is close to the encampment, as at a certain distance there's little point in the boat waiting around for the player.

- **wait**: This will be triggered when the player has jumped ship but is close by. This will give the player opportunity to climb back on board.

- **follow**: This will be triggered when the player is a certain distance from the boat. The boat will try and get as close as possible to the player, then trigger the **wait** task.

Now that we have some task values outlined, let's look at the logic that will trigger them and how this can support repeated activation of each state.

State control

Let's start with the default **move_to_encampment** state (this is default, as this is how the player spawns in the world). This is a simple state to start with: we just want this to activate when the player is on the boat. However, I don't want them to be fixed in a seat—I want the player to have the freedom to move around and use the existing movement controls while the physics system still carries them along in the boat. This means that we can't use functionalities such as **Vehicle:Passenger** or **Actor:Sensor** to detect whether the player is explicitly seated, and we will have to improvise! What we can do is create an AreaShape encompassing the deck of the boat and parent it to the boat by using the **Link Object** tool (found to the right of **Undo/Redo** buttons).

 When linking objects to either vehicles or characters, you'll be given an extra popup list when releasing the mouse button. This gives you a list of the parts (for vehicles) and bones (for characters). This will allow you to parent objects to smaller moving parts of these object types for more specific linking requirements.

With an **AreaTrigger** picked as the target entity in its **Shape Parameters**, adding **AreaTrigger** to the Flow Graph will now allow us to listen for the player being on the boat. As this is going to factor in a lot of our state logic, adding this as a Game Token will be helpful because we don't need to copy the same trigger setup to each condition. I've created **Level.AB1.Player_On_Boat** for this purpose, setting the value in the **Player Events** section. As this is the only condition required, we can just use the output of this Game Token to set **Boat_Approach_Task** to **move_to_encampment**—both elements of the setup are shown in the following screenshot:

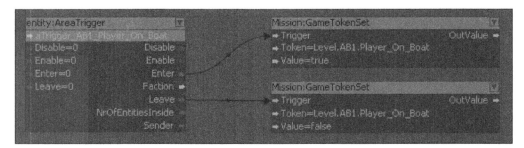

I've also added a similarly set up Game Token that forces this state when the player has reached a certain distance from the shore (outlined by an **AreaTrigger**), so the boat doesn't get stuck at sea if the player runs ahead.

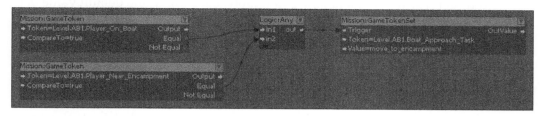

Next we have the **wait** state. We can actually achieve this with the Game Tokens we have already have created. We want this to be triggered when the player has left the boat. However, we want this to be blocked if they've reached the encampment already. By shifting around the statements from the **move_to_ encampment** trigger, we can use the following setup to give us our **wait** task. Using **Mission:GameTokenCheck**, we can verify that we still want the boat to wait before triggering the **wait** task.

The final state is the **follow** task. We want this to trigger when the player is a certain distance from the boat. We could do this by parenting another trigger to the boat that encompasses our desired distance, but let's experiment with another way to perform this task: range checks. We can measure this by using the **Entity:EntitiesInRange** flownode, which evaluates whether two given entities are within a specified range. As this node requires that we manually input trigger for it to output, we'll need to trigger this input repeatedly in order to make it check constantly. To do this, we can use the **Time:Timer** flownode. Although initially this node looks confusing, it will allow us to repeatedly fire signals from the **Out** output into our **Trigger** input. Let's quickly run through an explanation of the inputs in order of usage:

- **Paused**: This a Boolean input controlling whether the timer is ticking. By default, this is 0 (it's unpaused, that is, active). If we want it to start disabled, we can simply make **Paused** true. When we later want to enable the timer, we can use **Math:BooleanTo** to convert our inputs cleanly.

- **Min/Max**: The **Timer** node will tick upwards (limited to integers) from the **Min** to the **Max** value. For example, setting the **Min** to 0 and **Max** to 3 would output 0, 1, 2, 3, 0, 1, 2, 3, and so on. As we don't care about the value of the output (only the frequency), we can safely leave this at the default value of 0 for both parameters.

- **Period**: This is how often the **Timer** node ticks between the **Min** and **Max** values. This is essentially our update rate: how often the node will output into our **EntitiesInRange** checks. A faster update will yield a more up-to-date range check reading, at the expense of some more computational time.

With a **Timer** node set up with sensible settings feeding into the **EntitiesInRange** node (and a new **AB1.Player_Outside_Boat_Wait_Range** Game Token representing the outcome), we now have a Game Token we can use to evaluate when this should be triggered.

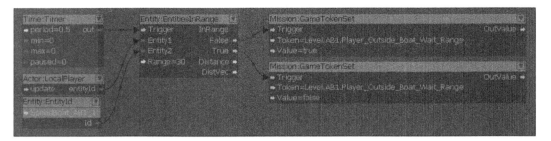

Now, all that we need to do is mirror the **wait** task control, but replace the initial event for the player leaving the boat with an event for the player having left the wait range. This is shown in the following screenshot, and so we completed our final task's control logic:

We now have a working state machine that's ready to control our boats behavior! Jump in the game a few times and watch the states update with the Flow Graph debugger enabled as you test the boundaries of the system. After we make sure everything's working, let's set up the scripting of these states.

Another way to debug Game Token states that present their updates in an easier-to-digest fashion is using the console variable `gt_show = 1`. This will print the most recently updated Game Tokens in the top left of the screen. Use `gt_addToDebugList <Token Name>` to force a specific token to stay active on this debug view, for example, `gt_addToDebugList AB1.Player_Outside_Boat_Wait_Range`.

Task scripting

Now that we've got functional states, let's dive into scripting our first task: **move_to_encampment**. As discussed in the previous chapter, the flownode we're using here (and what we'll be using for other vehicle movement tasks) is **Vehicle:StickPath**. This is a vehicle movement flownode that requires no navigation mesh to function. The vehicle will simply move along the specified **AIPath** with various behavioral differences based on the parameter values supplied. For our simple **move_to_encampment** state, we want the boat to move along the path until it stops. All we need to do is supply the **Path Name** value and enter a suitable speed in the **Max speed field of the vehicle (m/s)** port. This can then be triggered as a result of our boat task being **move_to_encampment**! Using **Mission:GameToken**, we can evaluate the current task against this value, allowing us to only trigger the right **StickPath** command when our desired task is active. Combine that with our checks established in the previous chapter to make sure we're playing from the start and not from a skipped point further in the level, and we have a setup that looks as shown in the following screenshot:

Next up, we have the **wait** task. This is simple to set up for the boat as we want it to do nothing for the duration of the task. We can essentially reuse what we've just made for the **move_to_encampment** task, but leave **Path Name** blank. This will cause the boat to cancel its existing **StickPath** command in favor of the new one, but then stop due to the null path supplied.

This Flow Graph is shown in the following screenshot:

 Vehicle:StickPath makes it easy to cancel existing tasks and start new ones, as other instances of the node being used will cancel existing commands. However, with other types of tasks that involve a flownode that isn't so developed, you may need to think about cancelling tasks manually in order to ensure clean transitions.

Another way in which we can help the player during the **wait** task is by adding a small feature that allows the player to beam themselves back on to the boat when they're close by. There's no good existing mechanic for the player to climb or jump out of the water in the SDK build at the time of writing, so this will aid playability. To do this, we can use the same technique we used to check that the player is on the boat: we check whether the player is inside a parented AreaShape. In this case, we want it to encompass the bounds we deem suitable for climbing aboard the boat. Once we have this implemented with an associated Game Token, we can use a combination of **Input:Action**, **HUD:DisplayMessage** and **Entity:BeamEntity** to give the player a prompt to climb aboard the boat, then execute this command if pressed. A working setup of this mechanic is shown in the following screenshot. To trigger it off, I used **Logic:AND** and a combination of the **On_Boat** and **Near_Boat** Game Tokens to trigger this at the correct time.

We'll look at the **AND** node and its application soon.

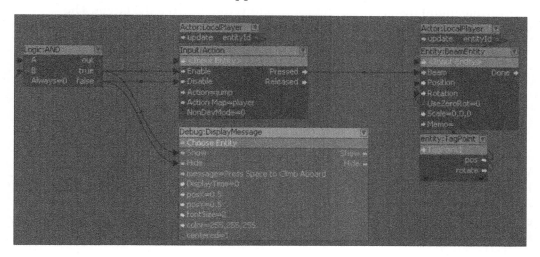

Input:Action utilizes action and actionmap names from `GameSDK/Libs/Config/defaultProfile.xml` (which you'll need to extract from `GameData.pak` found in `GameSDK`). Using this node is preferred to **Debug:InputKey**, as it will support inputs from both keyboard and gamepad, and it will function even if the user sets up custom button mappings.

The final task to script up is our **follow** task. This is similar to our **move_to_encampment** task, except this time we're going to utilize some other features of the **Vehicle:StickPath** flownode to get the boat to follow the player instead of moving continuously along the path in one direction. To do this, we simply need to link up the player's **entityID** to the **Target** port. This can be ascertained using **Actor:LocalPlayer**. From here, we have a few parameters we'll want to be aware of:

- **Continuous**: Setting this to **true** will mean that if the player updates their position after the boat has arrived at the closest location, the boat will start moving again to get closer. This defaults to **true**, which we'll probably want to keep.

- **CanReverse**: Defaulting to **false**, this allows the vehicle to turn around and move backwards along the path to track the target. As the boats in the SDK build have a very large turning circle, unless you have a very large body of water, its beneficial to keep this disabled and just leave the boat ahead of the player if they decide to turn back.

- **Min Distance/Max Distance**: These values control the minimum and maximum distances the vehicle is allowed to be from the target. The difference between these values will control the amount of space the player has to move around in before the boat starts moving again.

 A lesser known feature of **Vehicle:StickPath** is that it also supports dynamic speed inputs. By entering new values into the speed port while **StickPath** is operational, we can dynamically control the speed of the vehicle. This can be useful for scripting more advanced chase/follow behavior.

With this configured, we should now have a fully functioning mini-behavior for our boat that ably responds to the player testing the boundaries of the setup! From here, it's very straightforward to add more tasks, modify existing ones, or remove them entirely. The modular way in which the tasks of the boat are set up makes this a very simple process. Next, let's look at some more advanced logic in a pursuit to improve our **follow** task.

Advanced conditional logic

Now, we have our **follow** task that adequately follows the player. You may have already noticed a limitation of this if you've set it up and tested the system. The boat is great at following you if you're moving along the direction of the path, but what if the player moves perpendicularly away from the boat? It can't do anything except sit idle hoping you return. Ideally, the boat would be able to navigate towards the player's position, but as boats have no navigation mesh support set up in the SDK, let's look at a way to fix this within the limitations of the systems that we *can* use.

Multiple area triggers

One way to achieve this goal is to have multiple paths that cover the swimmable space in our opening area. We are then able to seamlessly get the boat to transition between the paths closest to the player's position, all by just adding a few extra values to our boat tasks.

The first step involved here is to create extra paths and corresponding AreaTriggers that we can then use to trigger our new tasks. Here, we just need to add as many paths as we feel is optimal—not too many to bloat the logic, but not too few to make the boat feel too unwieldy in its path changing.

This will vary based on the size of the area. Here's a partial screenshot of my setup:

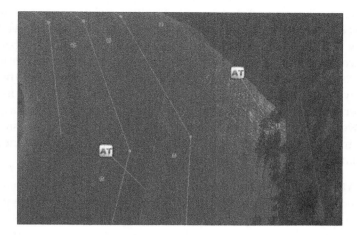

 When aligning AreaShapes to each other, it can be useful to enable the grid as you edit/create points. As points from separate shapes exist on the same grid, you're can precisely align the boundaries of shapes to make the borders seamless.

With our AreaShapes and AreaTriggers laid down, all we need to do now is revisit our state control logic and add some extra tasks based on these new triggers. As always, our first step is to add new Game Tokens that represent these triggers. As the player's current closest path could be one of many, this is another chance for us to use Game Token states. I've created a **Level.AB1.Players_Closest_Path** token that can then take multiple values. An example of how this would be set up for two of the triggers is shown in the following screenshot:

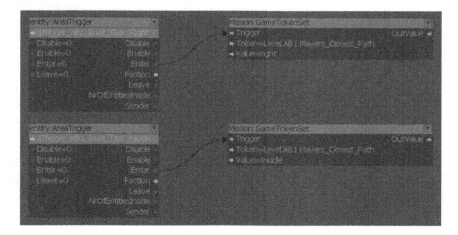

AND gates

With our new Game Token and its associated values, we now need to add this Game Token to our state control logic for the boat tasks. Right now, we have a singular **follow** task. Let's change this. As I now have three paths instead of one in my setup, I've converted my **follow** task into **follow_left**, **follow_middle**, and **follow_right**. As you'll recall from the previous implementation, **follow** was implemented by simply triggering the new task when the player had left the **wait** range. However, now we also need to choose from the various paths available. Here's where we need add some extra logic for each task that makes sure both conditions are true before triggering. Let's look at our available logic nodes and pick the one that best suits this application:

- **Logic:All**: This node outputs when all of the linked inputs have been triggered (with any value input). This is useful in cases where you want an event to trigger once any number of existing oneshot events have occurred. For example, once the player has killed some enemies *and* used a switch, trigger some reinforcements:

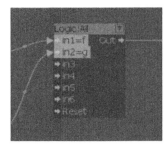

- **Logic:AND**: This node outputs true when both inputs A and B are true (or 1). This is useful when you want two conditions to be true, but these conditions are able to change state. For example, if the player is in a trigger *and* has a certain weapon selected (two changeable states), trigger some reinforcements:

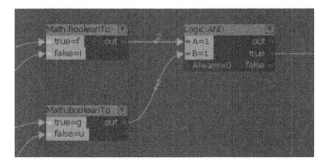

In our case, the player is able to enter and leave the wait range, *and* they are able to enter and leave a path's associated AreaTrigger. As such, we want to use **Logic:AND** in this setup.

 As the **Logic:AND** node takes Boolean (true/false) input only, any inputs that don't start life in this format need to be converted to a Boolean value. To do this (as demonstrated with the **EntitiesInRange** node earlier), we can use the **Math:BooleanTo** nodes to translate our events cleanly. This is shown in the previous example.

Armed with this knowledge, we can now ensure that the preceding conditions are set up to work neatly with our existing Game Tokens. An example of this setup is shown in the following screenshot, which is split into two images for ease of depiction.

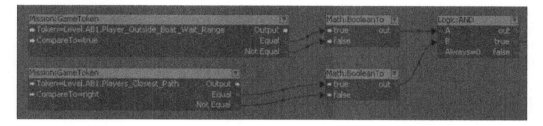

Finally, this allows us to create the resulting task scripting that is triggered from this new setup:

This is identical to our previous **follow** behavior, except that we now have multiple **follow** tasks that respect the player's position in the world:

Implementing objectives and checkpoints

Given the scale and complexity of many modern games, or simply the desire to directly guide the player through an experience, mission objectives is a common way to inform the player of what they need to do in order to progress with the events of the level. The SDK's implementation of objectives gives us a bare bones implementation of mission objectives to work with; let's dive into them and add an objective to our fishing village assault.

Defining the objective information

The first step to implement our objectives is to define their names and descriptions outside Sandbox. These are then loaded by the game when we activate our mission objectives. To do this, simply navigate to the LevelData folder in your level folder, where you'll find Objectives.xml. This is a simple XML file that contains a name, description, and **MissionID** for each objective. The following snippet is an example of a setup that I've created for the fishing village level; only one objective is listed for simplicity, but more can be made by simply duplicating the MissionID line and changing the attributes to suit our needs:

```
<Root>
  <FishingVillage>
    <Clear_Encampment Name="Clear The Shore Encampment"
Description="Terrorists have taken a small fishing village - reclaim
it." />
  </FishingVillage>
</Root>
```

Here are a few customizable parameters:

- The level name (shown in the example as `<FishingVillage>`) does not need to be the actual name of your level. This is just the folder name that the objective will appear under when we browse it in the Editor.

- The MissionID (shown in the example as `Clear_Encampment`) won't be exposed to the player and is just used to identify the objective for you when you browse the Editor.

- The `Name` attribute is what appears to the player as the primary name of the objective when the notification is displayed.

- The `Description` attribute is what appears to the player under the name, which offers more information about the task.

As well as the file within the `LevelData` folder, we are also able to define objectives with one file global to all levels. This file is called `Objectives_new.xml`, and this can be found in `GameData.pak` under the `Libs/UI` directory. Remember that you'll need to extract the file to that path external to the `.pak` file, if you want to use it. This is an older way of defining objectives, but it is still relevant if you want to keep all the objectives contained in one file instead of across levels.

With our objectives now filled out, we can return to the Editor and get our new mission setup implemented.

Using the MissionObjective entities

Now, we have a name and description defined for our objective. Let's place it and activate it as part of our level flow. To start off, we first need to give it a physical manifestation somewhere in the world—this requires placing a **MissionObjective** entity in our level. These can be found by navigating to **Rollup Bar | Objects Tab | Entity | Others | MissionObjective**, and they should be placed where you want the objective marker to appear on the minimap. Once you've placed the entity, here's where our MissionID from the XML setup comes into play. In the **MissionID** parameter, click on the browse icon, and you'll be presented with a hierarchy, displaying all the available objectives.

The **Clear_Encampment** objective created in the previous section is shown in the following screenshot, with its accompanying name loaded in the description box:

An additional parameter on the **MissionObjective** entity is the **TrackedEntityName** option. If the name of an object is entered as this parameter, the game will track the root of that object instead of using the marker position when displaying the marker on the radar. This can be useful if your objective is a moving object, such as an AI entity or a vehicle.

Activating the objective

With our objective placed and ready for action, all that remains to start in order to test our setup is to trigger the objective in Flow Graph. This is done by simply right-clicking on your Flow Graph of choice and hitting **Add Selected Entity**, while the **MissionObjective** entity is selected. We are then given a suite of objective inputs that represent the various ways in which we can present the player with updates to their current objectives. To activate the objective, we can simply trigger **Activate**, and to complete the objective, the **Completed** input needs to be triggered.

An example of this is shown in the following screenshot:

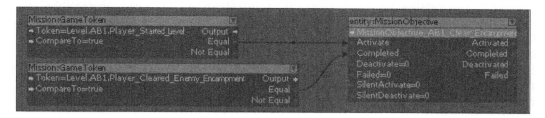

In the SDK build, at the time of writing, the feedback that the objective has been activated includes the text summary that was provided in the Objectives.xml, as well as a red dot on the minimap, as shown in the following screenshot. Use these features to verify that your setup has worked as expected.

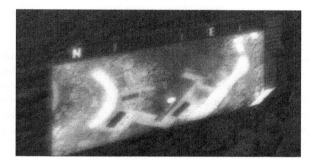

Organizing the objective logic

We now know how to activate objectives — let's think of a suitable Flow Graph workflow for our objective triggering. If you've seen the screenshot of a Flow Graph container structure in the previous chapter, then this scripting would live in the **Objectives_Logic** container under the **Mission** category. This in itself isn't vitally important, but it is important to maintain a separation of the objectives from the rest of the scripting. With the setup shown here, although functional, it starts to fall apart if we want to change the conditions that trigger the objective. What if we want to activate the objective once the level starts *and* the player has seen the encampment? Or if we want to complete it after the player has killed all the enemies *and* explored the interior spaces? We can complicate the objective triggering logic, but it would be cleaner just to have one token per event.

By creating an objective library of Game Tokens and keeping the objectives all in one place, you can easily alter the objective flow and track down what's triggering certain events, without scouring the Flow Graph for all the events contributing toward an objective state. So far, I've created the **Objective_Player_Clear_Encampment_Active** and **Objective_Player_Clear_Encampment_Completed** Game Tokens and added these to the setup, as shown in the following screenshot. These tokens are then triggered by the relevant combination of events elsewhere in the level flow, keeping the objective scripting simple and clean.

Try not to trigger the level events *from* the objective outputs. If you end up changing your objective ordering or removing objectives from the level, you'll end up with a totally broken flow that needs reordering to preserve the functionality you had before. Keeping the objectives separate from the level flow and modular as described here will help you proof your setup from any iteration that takes place in future. Use the regular event tokens, as discussed in the next chapter.

Now we have the objective set up in place, let's make sure that the player is able to play with our absurdly challenging setup, without throwing his monitor out of the window in frustration.

Adding checkpoints

A simple extra feature that we can add to our mission flow is a checkpoint (or save game). This will save the state of all the entities and Flow Graph scripts, allowing the game to restore its state if the player dies or chooses to manually load a previous save. The setup required to achieve this is simple; the **Game:SaveGame** flownode handles all the level-side controls of checkpointing in CRYENGINE.

This flownode is shown in the following screenshot. Let's take a look at the functionality it offers:

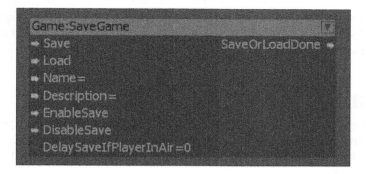

The following are the functions that are available:

- **Save** and **Load**: These are self-explanatory and will save/load **SaveGame** of a specified name when triggered.

- **Name** and **Description**: If your menu UI supports it, this will be what is displayed in the load checkpoint menu. The name is also printed on the game.log file on saving, which means that you're able to track the checkpoints in the log when testing in a pure game mode.

- **EnableSave** and **DisableSave**: This allows us to control whether the player is able to use any quicksave functionality present in the game.

- **DelaySaveIfPlayerInAir**: This is a useful parameter if your level has lots of verticality, and you're unsure about the player's position when saving. This will stop save/death loops caused by a bad checkpoint when the player is about to take a critical damage.

A useful functionality hidden in the **Name** port tooltip is that, as well as loading explicit save games by names, we're also able to load the previous saved game's state. This can be useful in cases where the player has manually saved its own checkpoint, or if we have multiple checkpoints that could have been saved after each other. To do this, we can simply enter $LAST in the **Name** port when triggering **Load**.

We now have a scripted sequence that not only responds to player actions, but is able to adapt its behavior based on player position. We also used this example to discuss more on how the various logic functionalities in CRYENGINE can be used to create a flexible and interesting game world that offers believable responses. Equipped with this toolbox of scripting techniques, we should be able to create almost any level system that tickles our fancy.

Summary

We now have a level flow that takes the player through a variety of experiences and offers them room to breathe if they experiment with the setup. We also looked at higher fidelity components of level scripting with detailed animated events that trigger based on player progress.

With the basics of AI scripting covered, let's look at polishing our work with the extra supporting systems that help lead the player through the game and improve the general gameplay experience.

15
Maintaining Our Work

Now that we have got a better understanding of scripting level events, we should be able to script up any level ideas our imagination throws at us. However, if our level turns into a 30-minute epic and we need to tweak the timing of a sequence 25 minutes in, testing can soon become a huge headache. Having already covered logic modularity in our progress so far, let's take a look at the ways in which we can exploit that to make testing a simple, manageable process. We will cover the following topics:

- Skipping through the level flow
- Advancing the states of other level elements
- Debugging pure game issues

Skipping through the level flow

Before we get to the actual events and entity progressions that make up our level design, first let's look at how we want to trigger these skip events so that they are quick and accessible for us as developers, but immune to people playing the level via the regular flow. To achieve this, we'll set up some triggers at various locations in the world that fire off some skipping logic when used. These locations are generally in "safe" areas in the world, so as to allow us to test the content that follows. For example, the transition space between action bubbles before entering a large combat arena. However, to use these, we need to be able to get to these locations precisely and easily. There are a few ways for us to quickly jump around the world in CRYENGINE. Let's take a look at how these can be set up.

Spawnpoint entities

Spawnpoint entities are not just used as spawn locations for multiplayer game modes—they can also be used to move through the level in a single player development environment too. By simply pressing *F2*, you can jump sequentially to every spawnpoint entity in the level. These are processed alphanumerically, that is, the order is determined by the entity names of the spawnpoints. This will work in pure game mode too, allowing us to skip content even when running from the launcher. Spawnpoints can be found at **RollupBar | Objects Tab | Entity | Others | Spawnpoint**, and any number of them can be placed in the level.

Remember that spawnpoints are also how the game determines where to start the player when they load into the level in a single player session. If you decide to place extra spawnpoints to facilitate skipping content, make sure that only one has the `InitialSpawn` flag ticked in its entity parameters. The player will be placed here when the level is finished loading.

The tags system

Another system that offers a lot of versatility within Sandbox is the tags system. The premise is straightforward: press *Ctrl* and a function key (for example, *F4*), and a tag position is saved. Press *Shift* and the same function key, and the player is moved to that tag position. This works in both edit mode and game mode, which means the system can also be used to preserve exact positions for screenshots or quick locations to jump around whilst editing the level. The reliance on function keys does mean the quantity of tags is limited to your number of keys. However, if you have relatively few skip locations within the level, then the tags system can be invaluable for debug skipping in editor and in-game.

Tags information is not saved in layers or into editor settings; it is saved into a `tags.txt` file within `GameSDK/Levels/yourlevelfolder`. This will save the list of camera positions and rotations in plain text, allowing you to back up or send versions of tags to other people, or even carry camera positions across levels.

There's no right or wrong system to pick here—we can even have both set up at once to complement each other. Spawnpoints allow quick and unlimited sequential progression, while tags offer extra functionality in the editor and more precise selection. With a few debug locations set up with either system, we can now move on to having moving to these areas progress the required level content.

Advancing the state of other level elements

Now we have some places in the level flow we know we want to skip to, let's look at one of the ways this kind of system would be set up. One way to simply implement this system would be to have a single Game Token that enables any and all debug triggers that we place in the level. This allows us to enable the debug functionality via any condition we choose. When this token is true, we'll enable ProximityTriggers at every debug location (which can be jumped to either by a spawnpoint or a tag). When the player enters one of these triggers, we know that the debug functionality has been enabled. As a result, we can then trigger the various skipping logics required by each location. As we've already set up all of our gameplay systems with modularity in mind, it should be straightforward for us to retro-fit this concept into our level flow without unnecessary headaches. Let's dive in to setting up these debug triggers and their sister Game Token!

Debug location triggers

The first thing we need to do is place our ProximityTriggers. These should encapsulate the spawnpoint and/or tag locations that are placed around that debug point. As soon as either method is used to teleport the player, the trigger will instantly output. These should also have **Enabled** set to **false** by default on their entity parameters. We want to make sure that if the player progresses through the level as part of a regular playthrough, they don't accidentally trigger off our debug logic.

We do, however, want to make sure that the triggers are active when our debug functionality is enabled. The easiest and most common use case for this will be testing our content in the editor. In this case, what we want is for every trigger to be enabled for a short amount of time when game mode is entered. That way, jumping to a debug location and then pressing *Ctrl + G* to drop in to game will mean that regardless of which location we're at, the level progression will skip accordingly. Let's start implementing this by getting the state of the debug Game Token to follow those rules.

An example of this is shown in the following screenshot, where **Time:Delay** is used to allow the debug mode to be active for 2 seconds when entering the game and then it is disabled:

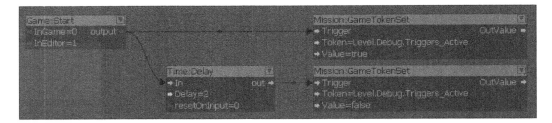

 This is a good use case for modifying the **InGame** flag on the **Game:Start** node. Although it's unlikely that players would be able to make it to our debug triggers in the level before the timeout, unticking **InGame** (as shown in the previous screenshot) means that this will never fire at all when in pure game mode, preventing false positives.

We need to enable the ProximityTriggers via our Game Token. This is shown in the following screenshot:

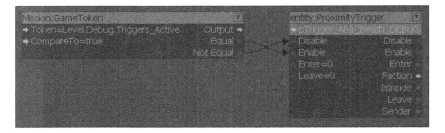

From here, we are able to hook up any relevant logic that advances the level flow! In the previous example, I have a debug location placed at the beach where the encampment assault occurs. This allows testing the content further on from this without having to play the opening boat attack sequence. In this example, useful events that could be placed here include updating the active mission objective and forcibly killing all the AI within the encampment to simulate the successful attack. However, what if the accompanying NPCs from the boat sequence are integral to the next objective? We need to make sure they're with the player and not at the start of the level. Let's look at how we can achieve this.

Advancing complex AI sequences

One of the complicating factors of directed scripting-driven experiences are often the very complex and intricate AI sequence setups that are involved. These can be long and involve many different phases and branches, depending on how far through the level the AI accompanies the player. From the beginning of our level production, we've sought to make sure that the AI setup has been constructed with modularity in mind. Here is where we are able to take advantage of that.

To start with, we need a way for our debug skipping to communicate with our AI scripting. To do this, we can make an extra token representing the skip location that we've used. When we hook this up to our debug ProximityTrigger, this can be used to add extra gates and listeners to our AI scripting to massage the flow of events towards our intended level state at the point we've skipped to. In the following screenshot, you can see my example setup for this: one token can be used with a unique state name per debug location, which is then hooked up to the debug ProximityTrigger.

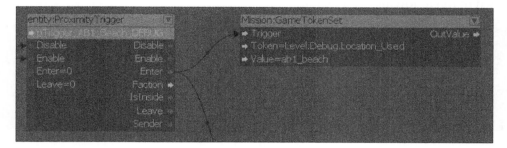

Now, we just need to insert this into our AI script. In *Chapter 14*, *Scripting Gameplay Content*, we looked at splitting up our AI activation from their sequence scripting to help prepare for any future changes. We are now in the future! We want to make it so that when using this debug location, the AI are enabled but do not proceed straight to their boat tasks. Instead, we'll skip ahead to our post-beach part of the level flow.

Let's start with the activation. We want the AI wave to be enabled not only on level start, but also when we hit our **ab1_beach** debug location. This is easily appended to our setup from *Chapter 14, Scripting Gameplay Content*, as shown in the following screenshot:

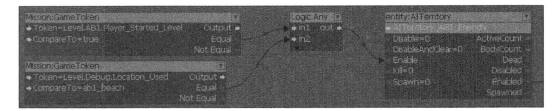

However, the boat scripting is still linked to **Wave_Activated** Game Token. This isn't quite what we want—when our **ab1_beach** debug location is used, the AI will still try and enter and drive the boats. To solve this, we can simply add a check to this scripting that ensures no debug location is active before it is executed. This is also shown in the following screenshot:

There's a reason we're not explicitly checking against **ab1_beach** here. If we checked against every location being used before allowing the scripting to continue, there's potential for a huge number of token check nodes required: one for each location. Instead, simply checking that the current location is false (that is, the debugging hasn't been used) is a more painless and future-proof method of validating that the playthrough is not being skipped.

With this set up, we can simply add a listener for the **ab1_beach** value being true to our subsequent scripting after the beach assault, allowing it to trigger from both debug skipping and regular playthrough. An example of this is shown in the following screenshot, with additional beam commands added to make sure the AI are in the correct position before continuing with the level flow:

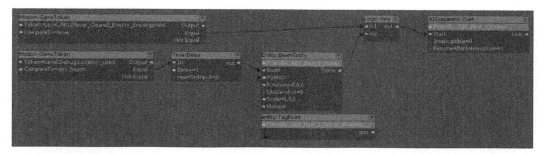

> Although not 100 percent necessary, the **Time:Delay** node used here is just to give the game enough time to spawn the AI entity before we beam them away from the initial setup. Without it, there's a potential to try and execute the operations too early before the AI is fully prepared in the world.

We now have a fully-featured debug setup, facilitating a catch-up of important level elements when we skip through to certain points in the level. Utilizing our modular focus, we were able to easily implement this alongside existing scripting instead of ripping out large chunks of work. Let's see how we can improve this system so that we're able to catch up scripting in the middle of a playthrough, instead of only on entering game mode!

Extending support to mid-playthrough updates

By simply enabling our debug token with some additional input checks, we're able to allow the triggers to fire when we use either the spawnpoint or tag systems in the middle of a play session. The following screenshot shows a Flow Graph that achieves this goal when the player uses the tag system. When both keys required to access the location are pressed, the debug token is enabled. This means when the player arrives at the chosen tag, the **Triggers_Active** token will be true (as the buttons will be held down), allowing the debug skip functionality to play out identically to our on-start behavior.

The same behavior can be set up using the spawnpoint system by having a single **Debug:InputKey** node listening for *F2*.

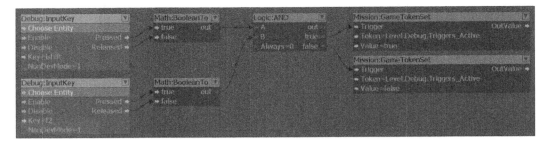

 Remember to tick **NonDevMode** in the **Debug:InputKey** properties if you intend to use this functionality in pure game mode. This allows the flownode to function when outside of the editor.

With our skipping functionality set up, we now have a versatile way to test our content quickly that is easy to both use and implement. Finally, let's look at some useful tools that can help debug common setup issues that could present during production.

Debugging setup issues

As the saying goes, *nothing is certain but death and taxes (and bugs)*. Due to the complexities of modern level design, there are many ways that setup issues can present themselves and cause hours of hair-pulling frustration in an attempt to deconstruct the problem. In this section, we'll briefly run through some useful tools available to level designers in Sandbox and what kind of problems they can solve.

Game Token debugging

As you'll be aware if you've got this far, Game Tokens are a vital aspect of level scripting in Sandbox. In situations with lots of moving parts or frequently updating values, it can be useful to better visualize the states of Game Tokens during gameplay.

There are a few CVARs that allow us to do this:

- **gt_show = 1**: This enables the Game Token debugger, which will display a list of the Game Tokens in the top-left corner of the screen in order of the most recent changes made.

- **gt_addToDebugList TokenName** and **gt_removeFromDebugList**: When **gt_show** is true, this command will add the specified token(s) above the updating list, making it easier to see updates for important tokens.

AI debugging

AI entities are another complex system that can fail operations for a few reasons, such as pathfinding problems, behavior interruption, and so on. Here are a few AI-related CVARs that will help pin down the root of problems:

- **ai_debugDraw = 1**: This displays a basic set of information above each AI entity (including active vehicles). This includes some basic stats as well as their current target and behavior. These are useful to check if AI are running off and doing things that you don't expect them to be doing.

- **ai_drawPathFollower = 1**: This draws the path for every AI entity currently following paths. This is also useful in cases where AI are moving to unexpected locations—knowing their endpoints can be useful in highlighting what they are moving towards.

Summary

With debugging under our belt, we have finished the final chapter on singleplayer level creation. We looked at all the aspects of the level design process in CRYENGINE from editor best practices to in-depth scripting, and we have kept our work stable and maintainable with a focus on modular construction to aid the debugging of our work. Coupled with a grounding in advanced tools such as Mannequin and the AI system, we are ready to continue developing and iterating singleplayer content as far as our crazy level ideas can take us.

Index

A

Thank you for buying
CRYENGINE Game Development Blueprints

About Packt Publishing

Packt, pronounced 'packed', published its first book, *Mastering phpMyAdmin for Effective MySQL Management*, in April 2004, and subsequently continued to specialize in publishing highly focused books on specific technologies and solutions.

Our books and publications share the experiences of your fellow IT professionals in adapting and customizing today's systems, applications, and frameworks. Our solution-based books give you the knowledge and power to customize the software and technologies you're using to get the job done. Packt books are more specific and less general than the IT books you have seen in the past. Our unique business model allows us to bring you more focused information, giving you more of what you need to know, and less of what you don't.

Packt is a modern yet unique publishing company that focuses on producing quality, cutting-edge books for communities of developers, administrators, and newbies alike. For more information, please visit our website at www.packtpub.com.

Writing for Packt

We welcome all inquiries from people who are interested in authoring. Book proposals should be sent to author@packtpub.com. If your book idea is still at an early stage and you would like to discuss it first before writing a formal book proposal, then please contact us; one of our commissioning editors will get in touch with you.

We're not just looking for published authors; if you have strong technical skills but no writing experience, our experienced editors can help you develop a writing career, or simply get some additional reward for your expertise.

Mastering CryENGINE

ISBN: 978-1-78355-025-8   Paperback: 278 pages

Use CryENGINE at a professional level and master
the engine's advanced features to build AAA
quality games

1. Explore the CryENGINE production
    methods used by industry professionals.

2. Master the advanced features of
    CryENGINE, such as facial animation
    and the input system.

3. A Comprehensive guide with
    interesting, practical examples
    and step-by-step instructions.

CryENGINE 3 Game Development: Beginner's Guide

ISBN: 978-1-84969-200-7   Paperback: 354 pages

Discover how to use the CryENGINE 3 free SDK,
the next-generation, real-time development tool

1. Begin developing your own games of any
    scale by learning to harness the power of the
    Award Winning CryENGINE 3 game engine.

2. Build your game worlds in real-time with
    CryENGINE 3 Sandbox as we share insights
    into some of the tools and features useable
    right out of the box.

3. Harness your imagination by learning how to
    create customized content for use within your
    own custom games through the detailed asset
    creation examples within the book.

Please check **www.PacktPub.com** for information on our titles

CryENGINE 3 Cookbook

ISBN: 978-1-84969-106-2   Paperback: 324 pages

Over 90 recipes written by Crytek developers for creating third-generation real-time games

1. Begin developing your AAA game or simulation by harnessing the power of the award winning CryENGINE3.

2. Create entire game worlds using the powerful CryENGINE 3 Sandbox.

3. Create your very own customized content for use within the CryENGINE3 with the multiple creation recipes in this book.

CryENGINE Game Programming with C++, C#, and Lua

ISBN: 978-1-84969-590-9   Paperback: 276 pages

Get to grips with the essential tools for developing games with the awesome and powerful CryENGINE

1. Dive into the various CryENGINE subsystems to quickly learn how to master the engine.

2. Create your very own game using C++, C#, or Lua in CryENGINE.

3. Understand the structure and design of the engine.

Please check **www.PacktPub.com** for information on our titles

Lightning Source UK Ltd.
Milton Keynes UK
UKOW05f1442290416

273240UK00001B/50/P